French Intellectual Nobility

SUNY Series in the Sociology of Culture
Charles R. Simpson, editor

FRENCH INTELLECTUAL NOBILITY

Institutional and Symbolic Transformations in the Post-Sartrian Era

by
Niilo Kauppi

State University of New York Press

Published by
State University of New York Press, Albany

For information, address the State University of New York Press,
State University Plaza, Albany, NY 12246

Production by Christine Lynch
Marketing by Bernadette LaManna

Library of Congress Cataloging-in-Publication Data

Kauppi, Niilo.
    French intellectual nobility : institutional and symbolic
transformations in the post-Sartrian era / by Niilo Kauppi.
        p.   cm. — (SUNY series in the sociology of culture)
    Includes bibliographical references and index.
    ISBN 0-7914-3143-6 (HC : alk. paper). — ISBN 0-7914-3144-4 (pbk.
    alk. paper)
    1. France—Intellectual life—20th century.   2. Philosophy,
French—20th century.   3. French literature—20th century.
I. Title.   II. Series.
B2421.K38   1996
194—dc20   96-3771
                                                               CIP

10 9 8 7 6 5 4 3 2 1

To Anne

Contents

List of Figures and Illustrations

Acknowledgments

Grants from the Fulbright commission, the Academy of Finland, and the Finnish Cultural Foundation (EKA-Fellowship) enabled me start this work at Indiana University in 1991. Initially a project concerned with the social mechanisms regulating the exportation of French theory to the United States starting from the 1960s, the work turned into a more general exploration of the local social and historical context of French theory ("isms" such as "structuralism" and "post-structuralism"). My warmest thanks to Richard Bauman and Thomas A. Sebeok for having me as a Research Associate at the Research Center for Language and Semiotic Studies (1991–95). I am also grateful to my supportive employer, the Council for Cultural and Social Research of the Academy of Finland, for having provided a grant to help publish this work. Anne Epstein contributed critical remarks at various stages. Without her support this book could never have been written. Nely Keinänen helped with the style and gave many constructive comments, Edward Epstein assisted with the figures, and Ira J. Cohen, Yvette Rollins, and Evan P. Young encouraged me to continue despite momentary lapses into despair.

The whole text was critically commented on by Priscilla Parkhurst Ferguson, Herbert Kalthoff, Ilpo Koskinen, Jean-Philippe Mathy, Juri Mykkänen, Edward Schaffer, Jean Umiker-Sebeok, and three anonymous reviewers. Pierre Bourdieu, Paul DiMaggio, Visa Heinonen, and Loïc J. D. Wacquant were kind enough to comment on chapter 2 of part II. I wish to thank them all for their time. I owe many thanks, as well, to Christine Worden and Christine Lynch at SUNY Press for guiding me through the editing process. All errors are of course the sole responsibility of the author. An earlier version of a section of chapter 8 of part III has been published in Pertti Ahonen (ed.), *Tracing the Semiotic Boundaries of Politics* (Berlin and New York: Mouton de Gruyter, 1993). I would like to thank Mouton de Gruyter (a division of Walter de Gruyter & Co.) for the permission to produce a slightly modified version of that text here. I would also like to thank Pekka Vuori, Ford France, Éditions Gallimard, Éditions du Seuil, and Columbia

University Press for permissions to reprint visual material. All translations from French to English are mine unless otherwise indicated.

Bloomington, October 1995

Introduction

> One needs, in order to write well, habits as
> well as ideas; and though the ideas may be
> born in solitude, the forms taken by these
> ideas, the images one uses to render them
> understandable, almost always belong to the
> memories of one's upbringing and of the
> society in which one has lived.
>
> Madame de Staël-Holstein, *De la littérature*
> *considérée dans ses rapports avec les*
> *institutions sociales*
>
> Why is authority sometimes accepted, and
> sometimes rejected? Why do revolutions
> always end with the restoration of order?
>
> Vincent Descombes, *Modern French*
> *Philosophy*

Beginning in the 1950s and 1960s, when Sartrian dominance was on the decline, a new generation of thinkers, composed of the social-and human-scientific intelligentsia[1] and of avant-garde writers representing the *Nouveau Roman*, rose into positions of power in the French intellectual field. This succession was concomitant with a redefinition in the relationship between state-created and market-created intellectuals.[2] The former, mainly academics and writers, were reproduced through Republican education in elite schools such as the Écoles Normales Supérieures, since their establishment at the end of the eighteenth century the breeding ground of the intellectual elite.[3] Market-created intellectuals, on the other hand, came into being with the expansion of, and qualitative changes in the cultural market, the audience, the press, and publishing. After World War II, the intellectual audience started to include more and more

1

students in humanities; the cultural press and the publishing business specialized. Numerous state-created intellectuals began to find employment in the expanding cultural industry. For the first time, there began to exist a market large enough for constant opposition to the academic and literary establishment. In the 1950s and 1960s, new ideas, promoted by avant-garde publishers, found support in the cultural media and an audience in the university students.

The conversion of young scholars and writers from the traditional humanities and from psychological literature to the developing human and social sciences and avant-garde literature was simultaneous with the conversion of terms, schemas, and ideas. A scientific style ("structuralism") was developed by this second generation of postwar intellectuals,[4] and it spread to a growing audience for whom the new and dangerous was also necessarily antibourgeois. Literary scholars, such as Gérard Genette, moved from traditional literary history to literary theory; linguists, such as A. J. Greimas, from the history of linguistics or lexicology to linguistic theory and semiology; and philosophers, such as Michel Foucault, to history. Terms and schemas developed in the human and social sciences were increasingly used in internal philosophical debates by such philosophers as Jacques Derrida, Jean Hyppolite, Maurice Merleau-Ponty, and their followers. For many intellectuals trained in philosophy, the dominant discipline in the traditional humanities, disciplines like anthropology, linguistics, psychoanalysis, semiology, and sociology, presented an alternative, scientific worldview in contrast with philosophy's largely literary culture, as well as a basis for internal critique of philosophy. For instance, Pierre Bourdieu's cultural sociology provided sociologists with an alternative both to Anglo-American technical and moral dominance, and to German critical philosophy;[5] whereas for historians, literary researchers, and philosophers, Bourdieu's sociology presented instruments for a modern, sophisticated analysis of the social world.

Change was gradual and uneven, varying according to the sector of the intellectual field. It was thus not mechanical, and its tempo is very difficult to assess and describe. In the French university field, there was a long-standing tradition of philosophers converting to other approaches. Émile Durkheim, Claude Lévi-Strauss, Marcel Mauss, Michel Foucault, and Pierre Bourdieu had all studied philosophy. At the turn of the twentieth century, numerous philosophers converted to historical studies.[6] At that time, the history of philosophy became the leading specialty. Both Sartre and Lévi-Strauss, who represented two distinct and competing intellectual generations starting from the 1950s, had a philosophical background in common. Philosophy was still the royal road. His philosophical training led Foucault to teach philosophy, while he wrote about medicine, prisons, and sexuality.[7] It was no accident that Foucault understood by human sciences not political economy, biology, or philology, which were professionalized and developed disciplines in France, but anthropology, psychology, sociology, and literary studies.[8]

In terms of ideas, the magnet which attracted the new generation was structural linguistics.[9] Institutionally, the social and human sciences expanded considerably in marginal institutions such as in the Sixth Section of the École Pratique des Hautes Études,[10] the center being the university system. The attraction of the human and social sciences and of the intermediate space between university and literary fields[11] modified the functioning of the intellectual field. However, these forces were molded by scholars and writers having different social characteristics and occupying different positions in various subfields. The complex unity of these intellectuals was in their discordance, in the differences between Foucault, Derrida, Lévi-Strauss, and the others. It was no accident that the human and social scientific intelligentsia was the closest socially to the expanding group of cultural journalists and publishers, many of whom had gone to the same elite schools. Also, numerous human and social scientists became editors themselves. Consequently, these new intellectuals were the ones who could most easily become cultural celebrities. Because of the complicity between radical ideas, the new cultural industries and the young audience, intellectual fame was a type of capital the value whose increased drastically during this time compared to both academic and literary recognition.[12]

In the 1950s, it was unacceptable for an intellectual to publish an article in *France-Soir* (an evening paper like the *New York Post*). By the 1960s, publishing academic works through commercial publishing houses was no longer unusual. Publishers and journalists began to challenge older, elitist definitions of intellectual nobility by promoting a kind of cultural democracy.[13] In the 1970s, noted philosophers Gilles Deleuze and Michel Foucault could be seen advertising men's underwear. Advertisements for *Diamantissimo* mail-order jewelry in the 1980s featured Julia Kristeva and Philippe Sollers. The relationship of intellectuals to publicity had changed completely in twenty years, and this change was linked to specific structural and morphological transformations. A chronicle, interview or article published in a cultural weekly brought more money and wider recognition. It did not require a time-consuming investment in form, as in the case of an academic work.[14] In short, the mass media created new models for French intellectuals.[15] This new configuration stressed the crucial connection between certain parts of academe, the *literati*, and journalists and publishers, a link which has subsequently been missing since the disappearance in the early 1980s of some of the most famous members of the second postwar intellectual generation (Roland Barthes, Michel Foucault, A. J. Greimas, Jacques Lacan).

The focus of this study will be the sociohistorical conditions for the production of theory in the French intellectual field in the post-Sartrian era, roughly since the end of the 1950s. Rather than being a critique of ideas, an intellectual history, or a theoretical study of "isms," all of which abound on this topic,[16] this book aims to present a historical and structural analysis of the institutional and symbolic mold in which French ideas and intellectuals are shaped.[17] In it, I will examine several strategic areas—sociology, semiology, and avant-garde literature (*Nouveau Roman*, *Tel Quel*)—in order to analyze changes in the local institutional and symbolic constraints imposed on what I shall term the "intellectual nobility," a group composed of individuals occupying the highest positions in the intellectual field. In other words, how has this nobility reinvented itself since the 1950s? From this specific study, I will move, in the epilogue, to the development of a sociohistorical model of the French intellectual field that will highlight the originality of this field in relation to other national intellectual fields, among others the U.S. intellectual field.[18]

There are two limitations on this kind of work. First, it is humanly impossible to make a *grand tour* of all the ideas developed in France in the 1950s and 1960s.[19] Therefore I will choose a few strategic areas, from which I will project more general traits of local rationales and of the logic of symbolic power. Second, all the complex structural interactions between subareas of the intellectual field cannot possibly be taken into account. Thus, my ambitions will be largely fulfilled by the construction of a simplified, "ideal-typical" model, in the Weberian sense of the term.

My standpoint is that of a Finnish social scientist, who has been educated in French-speaking schools from kindergarten to university, and who completed a doctoral dissertation under the guidance of Pierre Bourdieu.[20] The present study has required me to distance myself somewhat from Bourdieu's sociology and to move into the margins of French and "English-speaking" traditions in the social sciences and humanities. This has enabled me to take steps toward a critical examination of my own approach. My perspective on the French intellectual field is oblique, combining familiarity with distance. Because of too much familiarity, French intellectuals may be prevented from examining in a disinterested manner their own activities, whereas a lack of familiarity that easily turns into worship or indifference hinders foreign observers from creating a focused image of French cultural life. It is important to note, however, that I do not intend this work to be a presentation or theoretical critique of Bourdieu's *oeuvre*.[21] Rather, I will examine the creation context of Bourdieu's theory, showing its historical and social embeddedness in a specific status culture (part II). In this way, some of the strengths and weaknesses of his approach may be brought to light without, however, falling into the fallacy of theoreticism, and without disregarding the social creation context and the interests behind the ideas. I believe that the greatest homage that can be paid to a given method is to attempt to understand it critically in its own environment, to turn it partially upon itself, and to build upon it.

The specific inspirations for this study are Bourdieu's works on the French university and literary fields;[22] Foucault's study on the constitution of the human sciences;[23] and Elias's work on the history of manners and culture.[24] Bourdieu's works demonstrated how specific social constraints directed intellectual work and artistic innovation. Foucault clarified the discursive rules that enabled the creation of the human sciences. For his part, Elias's works provided a basis for a better understanding of the various aspects of French high culture. However, taken alone, each of these approaches is in many respects unsatisfactory. Although Bourdieu has, in his theoretical works, propagated a dynamic examination of the intellectual field, his empirical work lacks a historical perspective. Even in one of the latest collections of his studies translated into English,[25] temporal changes and comparative analysis are minimized. In addition, it is not clear if the figures and schemas developed in *The Field of Cultural Production* represent a theoretical model or if they merely formalize and simplify a specific case. This kind of confusion renders comparative research difficult. I hope to clarify in my work the sociohistorical conditions which contribute to this kind of confusion, and develop further the historical and comparative dimensions of field theory. By distinguishing state-created elites from market-created elites I wish to underline another dimension that has been downplayed in Bourdieu's works on French culture: the state.[26] Bourdieu's studies on culture frequently create the impression that France is a stateless society, although it is clear to everyone that French intellectuals are, in many ways and especially in contrast to American intellectuals, for instance, creations of the monarchist and Republican state.

Michel Foucault's otherwise very inspiring analysis[27] of the constitution of the discourses of the human sciences[28] does not account sufficiently for the institutional basis which allows the constitution of new approaches. Furthermore, in accordance with the interests of his time, Foucault reduces the constraints on intellectual creation to discursive ones, to codes or epistemes, in my view without sufficiently emphasizing the social constraints created and reproduced by the thinkers themselves. The missing link is precisely the habitus, already discussed by Durkheim, Norbert Elias, and Erwin Panofsky, and developed above all by Bourdieu.[29] The obvious danger is that an overt emphasis on texts or individual actions[30] will push to the background major explanatory factors, such as the structure of the literary or academic field of a particular time. Finally, Elias[31] does not press enough for a social-scientific assessment of culture, specifically, in its complex relations with economics, which was a crucial connection in the 1960s.

The obstacles to a sophisticated sociohistorical analysis of symbolic goods are several. The first is found in sociological tradition. In contrast to Talcott Parsons, who asserts that culture has to do with ideas and values and little else,[32] I will argue that specific symbolic goods have to be examined in relation to material conditions and as part of complex social processes. The second obstacle is Herbert Spencer's "great man theory of History,"[33] which argues that individuals, such as Foucault or Lacan, create culture. In accordance with this theory, historians of French literature constantly bring individuals to the fore,[34] forgetting that institutions shape opportunities and that some of these are actualized in individual symbolic works (Fernand Braudel's *structure, conjoncture, événement*). Education and society more broadly mold intellectual habits and styles, which are the core of thought and are not simple forms as opposed to substance. When this education changes, certain customs, instincts, and habits[35]—or a certain relatively durable social habitus, to use Elias's term[36]—change with it. Subjectivity and agency are socially constructed on the basis of cultural taste reproduced by educational and cultural institutions like schools, universities, publishing houses, and reviews, as well as by individuals.

With structured modifications in education, cultural ideals, and values, as well as changes in the economic processes underlying culture,[37] styles, habit-patterns, and the collective strategies applied by social groups are modified. The point of view adopted in this work is that the life of an individual in an environment is above all a question of accommodation and reaction to "the pattern and standards traditionally handed down in his community,"[38] which s/he modifies by his/her own activity, and against the background of which this activity acquires its specific meaning.

The third obstacle to a sophisticated sociohistorical account of intellectual creation is the theoretical inclination of much research on French ideas.[39] In my opinion, many critics systematically distort the works and present effortless generalizations—parade theories such as "structuralism" or "functionalism"—that circulate among intellectuals and prevent students and scholars from delving deeper into the complexities of cultural phenomena. Through the universalization and individualization of cultural artefacts, ideas are detached from local struggles and contradictions and from the collective sociopsychological mechanisms behind intellectual creation. Once the point of view behind them is erased, ideas can be bent to further any interest.

The problem in the current mode of circulation of ideas is precisely the disqualification as unimportant of the social and historical contextuality of intellectual works and canons. Accordingly, the local is frequently confused with the universal,[40] whereas, in order to find real universality, ideas should be examined in the context of their creation and reception.[41] Indeed, universality is a question of degree: every individual combines universal and local features of various levels of generality. I believe it is urgent, in current cultural studies, to promote a point of view which places the creation of ideas in context, thereby highlighting their originality without rendering them either too exotic or too familiar.

The present study of the transformation of the social and historical mechanisms which produced the French intellectual nobility will be organized in the following way. Part I examines the dominant French intellectual habitus historically starting from the 1950s and sketches in an "ideal-typical" way the social conventions regulating intellectual invention in this context. This collective habitus is not easily definable. It is composed of a combination of relatively stable and changing elements. However, its use enables us to perceive fundamental similarities between individuals as different as Roland Barthes and Michel Foucault. The main idea in part I is that this French intellectual habitus changed radically beginning in the 1950s, with Lévi-Straussian anthropology becoming the example for the human- and social-scientific intelligentsia. By symbolically killing Sartre, these new aristocrats of culture created a common bond despite their differences.

The modifications in the human and social sciences and in literature are studied in parts II and III. Part II examines through two case studies the ways by which institutional and symbolic transformations were reflected both in the new disciplines and in individual works. Structural constructivism and semiology are seen as subareas which had to define their positions in relation to French literary culture as well as with respect to competing disciplines,[42] making possible a structured metamorphosis. Bourdieu successfully redefined his sociological project by combining Durkheimian sociology with recent developments in anthropology, linguistics, and art history, among other areas. Bourdieu's use of economics is examined as a means to surpass the most developed social science and present a more fundamental approach. In the case of semiology, I argue that its social identity as a broad intellectual approach which attracted a heterogeneous group of followers is perhaps the main reason for its partial integration into the academic system in the beginning of the 1970s. Both structural constructivism and semiology are examined here from the inside, by tracing the more general traits of symbolic production and discursive rules—especially those of philosophical style and scientific culture—imposed on them in this context. In the last chapter of part II, the similarities between philosophical and scientific styles and the impact of Republican education on intellectual work are analyzed.

Part III examines through two case studies the development of literary conventions—the rise of an objective literature—after the breakthrough of the *Nouveau Roman* in the late 1950s. The *Nouveau Roman* was the invention of

"Vos papiers s'il vous plait".
Le flic a tapé sur la vitre, le silence est tel dans une Scorpio que je n'aurai pas entendu sa voix, pas plus que le bruit de la circulation. Vitres affleurantes... J'avais mis une cassette de Mozart, le vingt sixième concerto pour piano: une vraie salle de concert.
"Vous êtes l'écrivain? l'auteur de Femmes?"
"Oui".   Philippe Sollers
                              Ecrivain

Reproduit avec l'aimable autorisation de Globe.

"Your papers, please! The cop knocked on the window. It's so quiet in a Scorpio that I would no more have heard his voice than the sound of the traffic. Soundproof windows...I had just put on a Mozart cassette, the 26th concerto for piano. A real concert hall. 'You're the writer? The author of *Women*? Yes.'"
Philippe Sollers. Writer. Reproduced with the authorization of *Globe*.

"Si j'avais à noter la Scorpio 4 × 4, je dirais 18/20. J'espère que les journalistes spécialisés me suivront".
(Ford Scorpio, Voiture de l'année 1986, bien vu Guy Laroche!)

                    Guy Laroche
                 Créateur de mode

Reproduit avec l'aimable autorisation du Figaro Magazine.

"If I had to rate the Scorpio 4x4, I would give it 18 out of 20. I hope the specialized journalists will agree with me! (Ford Scorpio, car of the year 1986. Well said, Guy Laroche)
Guy Laroche. Fashion designer. Reproduced with the permission of *Figaro Magazine*.

The formerly iconoclastic writer Philippe Sollers in an advertisement for Ford Scorpio, portrayed as legitimate representative of French culture along with Jean-Paul Lepelley (President of Hermès Perfumes), Guy Laroche (Fashion designer), and Gaston Lenôtre (caterer). Ford prospectus, 1987. Reproduced with the authorization of Ford France.

Illustration 1. Icons of French cultural nobility.

"Cette voiture m'a beaucoup plu. Elle est extraordinairement bien pensée, bien finie, conçue pour ceux qui comme moi, aiment conduire".

Jean-Paul Lepelley
Président d'Hermès Parfum

Reproduit avec l'aimable autorisation de l'Express.

"I like this car a lot. It is extraordinarily well-designed, and well-finished, conceived for those who , like me, love to drive."
Jean-Paul Lepelley. President of Hermès Perfumes. Reproduced with the authorization of *L'Express*.

"J'ai tout particulièrement apprécié la sureté que procure le système de freinage anti-blocage ABS qui équipe en série toutes les Scorpio. Un pas en avant considérable en matière de sécurité".

Gaston Lenôtre
Traiteur

Reproduit avec l'aimable autorisation de Gault-Millau.

"I expecially appreciate the safety provided by the ABS anti-lock braking system, standard on all Scorpios. A considerable step forward in security."
Gaston Lenôtre. Caterer. Reproduced with the permission of *Gault-Mihault*.

literary publishers and journalists. Its success was supported by numerous struggles in the literary field of the moment, especially by resistance to Sartre—a philosopher and thus an intruder—and by more specific sociological processes such as the creation of new literary prizes and their affinities with other avant-gardes. The second generation of the *Nouveau Roman*, whose main representatives were grouped around the review *Tel Quel*, profited from the visibility of the *Nouveau Roman* and produced works in the same style. But changes in the market for ideas led to a transformation of interests: general intellectual discourse and theoretical essayism quickly replaced literary concerns in the Telquelians' works. Consequently, in literary history, the second generation of the *Nouveau Roman* has remained in the shadow of the first generation and has provided the first generation with a group of legitimizers and followers.[43]

Finally, in the epilogue, I will develop a more theoretical model of the structuration of the French intellectual field based on the previous chapters. This processual model synthesizes the structural metamorphosis that, starting from the 1950s, caused changes in the definition of intellectual nobility and local intellectual canons. In my view, observers have not stressed sufficiently the dynamic structural aspects of French cultural tradition.

Part I

The French Intellectual Habitus and Literary Culture

> There are no deaths in philosophy.
>
> Etienne Gilson

Beginning in the 1950s, the collective social habitus of the French intellectual underwent radical changes. Whereas from World War II onward Sartre, a philosopher, had represented the total intellectual and the first generation of postwar Parisian intellectuals, in the 1950s Lévi-Strauss, an anthropologist, embodied a more specific kind of total intellectual and was the leading figure of the second generation of postwar Parisian intellectuals.[1] With this polysemic and often contradictory symbolic displacement of emphasis from the classical humanities to the human and social sciences, the structure of the social conventions relative to cultural inventions was modified and new, hybrid intellectual products were created.

How was the dominant French intellectual habitus transformed since the 1950s? In order to shed light upon this and the symbolic revolution that took place in the 1960s ("structuralism" and "poststructuralism"), it is appropriate to examine both in relation to local cultural forms and traditions[2] and to the structural constraints imposed on intellectual innovation in this context.[3]

11

CHAPTER 1

The *Ancien Régime*: French Literary Culture

Didier Eribon: Is there a book you would
have liked to write or that you regret you
didn't write?

Claude Lévi-Strauss: I'm very sorry that I
haven't written a literary work.

Conversations with Claude Lévi Strauss

Traditionally, the man or woman of letters (*philosophe* or *littérateur*) has been the model for all French intellectuals.[1] In most other national intellectual fields, for instance in Germany[2] or the United States, the model was the specialist or academic.[3] In opposition to Latin humanism, scientific culture developed with the Reformation mainly in Germany, England, and other European countries. In Germany a dual structure can be isolated in the intellectual field, consisting of two socially and geographically separated parts, the university and literary poles, and occasionally some parts of the artistic field. In France on the other hand, for centuries these two poles were united both geographically and socially in the politico-administrative center, Paris. From the 1960s on, a clearer triadic structure emerged in the French intellectual field, consisting of the university, media, and literary poles. As such, these poles have existed since the eighteenth century and the typically Gallic trait of impersonal and abstract thought has been dated back at least to the sixteenth century and Jesuit pedagogical techniques.[4] The French Revolution emphasized French culture's cosmopolitanism, which opposed the national particularism of Protestant countries. For the intellectuals in France at the end of the eighteenth century, the media became a sphere of political intervention, distinct from the arenas of professional politics. The essay became the medium. The role of the *savant* was traditionally dominated by the role of the *philosophe* or *littérateur*, the representative of Latin humanism and literary culture. This domination took multiple forms and could be noticed after

13

the Second World War even in the education of linguists. According to an eyewitness, "Everything that appeared precise, meticulous, *scientific* was rejected."[5]

A profound structural transformation took place in the 1960s. Instead of two subcategories of intellectual capital, literary and academic, there began to exist three subcategories of intellectual capital: academic, literary, and journalistic.[6] The exchange rate for journalistic capital rose drastically in the 1960s, thus enabling, via its acquisition, the opening of new channels of social ascension and the updating of the French intellectual habitus: social and human scientific dilettantism, coupled with political and ethical radicalism, cast in the form of theoretical essays, became the order of the day. In the 1960s, some areas in the academic system, namely all the new sciences of the text, became areas of high social mobility as a result of their structural relations with the expanding media. This structural change enabled the symbolic revolutions under way to achieve their fullest scope—the importance of which is not sufficiently emphasized in studies of French cultural history.

Despite such deep changes, in the postwar period a specific kind of literary culture still determined the social conventions regulating symbolic goods. By definition, the man or woman of letters as a social role was a philosophical-literary type and his or her training—in literature, philosophy, and, beginning at the end of the nineteenth century, the human or social sciences—emphasized abstract reasoning and a concern with ends such as morality, for instance, not means. The valued style required the use of imposing proportions. Moral problems were not posed as national ones, as in other countries, but as problems affecting the whole of humanity. Some men or women of letters were also close to political power, under the aegis of which polite society had developed for centuries; their ambitions could not be separated from their political stances, something which became very clear in times of political turmoil and rapid social change, for instance, the 1890s and the 1960s. Literary criteria and the abstract individualism they conveyed were reproduced by informal and formal cultural learning, which favored dealing with ideas in a general way, in terms understandable to a large, learned audience. A classical education shaped certain tendencies: a concern for style, for surprising turns in the text, for play with concepts, and for so-called universal values—in short, for verbal and literary skills. Consider Georges Steiner's description of Lévi-Strauss's style:

> A page of Lévi-Strauss is unmistakable (the two opening sentences of *Tristes Tropiques* have passed into the mythology of French language). The prose of Lévi-Strauss is a very special instrument, and one that many are trying to imitate. It has an austere, dry detachment, at times reminiscent of La Bruyère and Gide. It uses a careful alternance of long sentences, usually organized in ascending rhythm, and of abrupt Latinate phrases. While seeming to observe

the conventions of neutral, learned presentation, it allows for brusque personal interventions and asides.[7]

The aim of this prose was to find in man what was the most abstract and general. This ambition was a distinctive trait of French literary culture and moral temperament.[8] Because of the valorization of this generalized critique of values, some academics, like the anthropologist Lévi-Strauss, could, by being experts on "primitive" human societies, easily fulfill the minimal requirements of the prized intellectual role. This role produced two opposing and hierarchical terms like writer and academic, sophisticated and pedantic, imaginative and dry, and so on.

The man or woman of letters was a generalist, dealing with general problems, who processed information by generalizing, by taking local or particular problems or themes as universal ones at an abstract, often moral level (the *moraliste*).[9] The canonized form of intervention was nontechnical language, accessible to the cultivated public, coupled with an extremist rhetoric and a universal message. For a long time, writing novels and essays was the only way to show one's talent. However, beginning in the 1950s, as the general schooling level rose and the composition of the reading public changed, even more technical terms entered the vocabulary, which led to the emergence of philosophers straddling two cultures: trained in philosophy, many were autodidacts in the human and social sciences. Like philosophers of previous generations, they switched from philosophy to other approaches, until the 1950s to literature, as in the case of Sartre.

The human and social scientists were forced to create their education for themselves. This situation of urgency can be seen clearly in the debates in the 1960s compared to those in the 1930s. Proof of this fundamental change can also be seen in the ascension of sociologists like Pierre Bourdieu and Alain Touraine into positions of intellectual prominence. In contrast to the interpretations of some observers, who have approached the problem of modernity mainly from the point of view of a sociology of science,[10] I will argue here that the complex relationships between radicality and Joseph Ben-David's third public, the laymen, is the crucial element for an understanding of intellectual and academic activity in the French context.

The updating of a dominant habitus depended on the structures of the field as a whole: it made sense in relation to the totality of practices in this entity. However, because of the habitus's flexibility and context-sensitivity, the habitus also left space for individual variations and improvisations. Because of the flexibility of the base, individuals could suddenly find common ground and knowledge based on a frame of reference unknown to those from another context. This unity was manifest in the discussions between Lévi-Strauss and the journalist Didier Eribon[11] concerning the anthropologist's youth.

Claude Lévi-Strauss: I believe, heaven forgive me, that at time I began composing an opera. I got no further than the prelude.
Didier Eribon: That's pure Rousseau.
Claude Lévi-Strauss: Except that Rousseau would do it and I couldn't.[12]

This dialogue, apart from demonstrating a shared social fund of knowledge, expresses common taste and cultural memory, which are reproduced informally via inherited cultural competence and formally via scholarly culture. To put the example in perspective, it could be said that Rousseau's or Lévi-Strauss's musical ambitions were as meaningless to a foreigner as baseball scores were to a Frenchman: they were part of local taste. To a member of the cultivated French public, Lévi-Strauss's comment was a clear sign of cultural competence.[13] It was considered legitimate to desire artistic or literary success.[14] This local taste was a system of constraints and incentives relative to cultural creation and consumption that differed from the conventions prevalent in contexts where the model to follow was a specialist. An observer of French intellectual life, David Pace, expressed it thus: "despite Lévi-Strauss's repeated identification with the ideal of the *savant* he remains in many ways a *philosophe*."[15] This contradiction was the main trait of French intellectual culture during the period studied here. In both roles, symbolic goods were placed in order of importance and their consumption modalities were relatively strictly controlled both implicitly and diffusely. The logic of the *philosophe* cannot be understood by examining it from the point of view of the logic of the *savant*, and vice versa.

The French intellectual habitus was made up of elements which were constantly reorganized and might not show direct relations to previous manifestations: the relationship was conceptually loose and vague ("family"), but still recognizable.[16] This historical continuity took the form of a dotted line. For instance there was a definite iconic relationship between the eighteenth-century men of letters like Voltaire and Diderot and the early twentieth-century intellectual as a member of the social group the intellectuals. This continuity could be detected by tracing the whole historical continuum, from the eighteenth century, to the Dreyfus affair and beyond, taking into account the social formation of mass-media mandarins.[17] Each time the habitus was realized, elements of past realizations and the requirements of the present—the values which must be fulfilled in order for the habitus to be legitimate and to work— were combined with the intellectuals' activities. There was thus a process of parallel connection of diverse structures which is called invention; updating was a continuing manifestation of social invention. The social pool of knowledge and taste changed in a structured manner as a result of modifications in the social structure, notably in the intellectual field, and in the intellectuals' dispositions. For example, starting from the mid-nineteenth century, romanticism and psychologism gave way to realism, personal letters to collective petitions, and cynicism and elitism to Republicanism or popular elitism. In the 1950s, general philosophical discourse gave way to more technical language drawn from the evolving human and social sciences. Thus, in this market for ideas, a structural imperative stood out: the necessity of creation of new positions according to certain conventions in relation to previous positions which were sedimented at different levels and constituted a tradition.

The complexity of local intellectual creations was often due to a constant, because internalized, problematic relationship with tradition and transmitted ideals, and to continued attempts to present new combinations which became, for the most versatile social groups of the moment, "as obligatory as the wearing of clothes."[18] For instance, a novel combination in the 1960s was to use terms from structural linguistics and also certain, at that time, esoteric terms from philosophy in order to analyze French classics like Rousseau in the case of Derrida and Lévi-Strauss, Racine or Michelet in Barthes's case. In the eyes of many philosophers, German phenomenology was a way to supersede Sartre. A thinker could also choose more avant-gardist authors like de Sade, Lautréamont, Mallarmé, and Freud, who had already been present in the Surrealist repertoire between the wars. This combining of new concepts with old objects[19] had a good chance of succeeding in this local market, because the resulting work referred simultaneously to the national cultural heritage and to novelty.[20]

REORGANIZATION OF THE SOCIAL CONVENTIONS

The transformation of the structure of the social conventions as the habitus acquired more and more elements from the evolving human and social sciences, was simultaneous with modifications in the French academic system: the rapid growth in the number of both university students and teachers, and the institutionalization of many disciplines such as sociology and linguistics.[21] A separate degree in sociology was created in 1958. In the 1960s, the number of students in letters tripled from 7,000 in 1960 to 20,000 in 1969.[22] Both of these factors—the increase in the intellectual population and the founding of new chairs in higher education[23]—contributed to important changes in the structure of the market of symbolic goods and in the models of intellectual modernity.

In the academic system, the combined effect of these factors meant that some young academics could get tenured positions without having to wait for older professors to retire. New ideas and the influx of money necessary for the establishment of new posts were synchronized. Some sectors were more dynamic than others. There was both a material and symbolic decline in certain specific subareas tied to the classical humanities, for instance, Romance philology, the history of the French language, and lexicology. Some linguists, such as Greimas or Barthes, converted from lexicology to expanding fields like structural linguistics. Certain types of knowledge which had previously been considered more or less worthless, such as certain areas of mathematics, languages like Russian, or areas like East European linguistics, could become invaluable and enable previously unforeseen social ascension.[24] Some linguists became *bricoleurs*, which led both to relative chaos and innovation, for instance, in philosophical semantics. Many became—and this is no accident—fervent supporters of interdisciplinary studies. Intellectual novelty was thus simultaneous with wide-ranging institutional reorganization. The growth in the number of students in the human and social sciences, and the new disciplines that were detaching themselves from the guardianship of philosophy, also enhanced the need to invent radical ideas which could be incorporated into the expanding curriculum. The transformations underway also opened new doors of opportunity for publishers. As the novelty of the administrative profile of the university posts created in the 1960s demanded improvisation, an individual could (or had to) be at the same time dangerous and tenured. It was no accident that most of the inventors of successful neologisms (or rather, derivations and metaphors) like grammatology and archeology were philosophers. They were the ones who had so much initial symbolic credit that a risky move was what was expected from them.

It is difficult for an outsider to imagine the overwhelming predominance of philosophy, the dominant discipline in the traditional French humanities,[25] and of philosophers in French cultural discourse and in the social habitus of the French intellectual. According to local beliefs, degrees in philosophy were not taken (*prendre*) by the student like other degrees in mathematics, political science or law. They were given (*donner*), as if by providence, pointing to the quasi-ontological difference between those who had not succeeded in taking philosophy as their main subject and those to whom this privilege had been granted. If an individual had not taken philosophy as a major, it had to be because s/he had tried but failed. The writer Alain Robbe-Grillet expressed the valuation of philosophy, common to both philosophers, who were the included, and the others, who were seen as the excluded. "I received the grade 'good' in mathematics, but I was never 'given' the baccalaureate in philosophy. I failed twice in a row."[26]

The importance of the aspirations of the new, young consumers increased, as did of the role of the cultural press as an instance which gave form to the multiple events in an expanding field of cultural production. A larger-than-ever social demand for radical ideas developed: for publishers, it became symbolically and economically profitable to diffuse ideas which had circulated only in small avant-gardist circles during the interwar period.[27] Thus, for some intellectuals it became possible to popularize, or to contribute to the creation of a certain intellectual popular elitism—something which had not existed on such a scale before—and simultaneously to accumulate intellectual fame, a resource which could be reconverted into academic power.[28] Concomitantly, the rhythm of production of the goods accelerated. Publications and instruction in the human and social sciences increased.[29] Barthes's statement about his book, *Système de la mode* (1967), corroborates this general transformation of the circulation of symbolic goods: "In those years, intellectual history moved very fast, an unfinished manuscript quickly became anachronistic and I even hesitated to publish it."[30]

This general change also modified the social conventions relative to the forms intellectual intervention should take. Sartre, who had been trained as a philosopher and who was in a dominant position in the French intellectual field after World War II, had enlarged the repertoire of legitimate intellectual media interventions to include the theater and also journalism. In the 1930s, this repertoire already included protoscientific products, or theoretical essays, but the intellectual field was dominated by philosophic-literary discourse. This discourse had its own public, reviews, and publishing houses. The development of this new variant, the human and social scientist, was interrupted by the war; however, in the 1950s the relationship between the types represented by Sartre and Lévi-Strauss started to change gradually, concomitantly with the morphological modifications in the structure of the intellectual field mentioned above. The development of this new variant led gradually, at an unequal tempo, to changes in the structure of the discursive rules. Freudianism and anthropologism had already become fashionable in the 1930s. But in the 1950s and 1960s these currents, along with the fields of history (e.g., the *Annales* school), linguistics, and semiology would become the symbolically dominant perspectives.[31] By producing theoretical essays and becoming cultural celebrities, the intellectuals engaged in these areas gave backing to, and in fact, often indirectly supported the founding of new academic disciplines.

Even the scientific dimension can be found in earlier manifestations of the habitus: in Balzac's or Zola's nonacademic sociology, for instance.[32] There has thus been a constant interaction between the current scientific achievements and the concerns of the man or woman of letters. In semiotic terms, there has existed a sophisticated mechanism which transcoded scientific texts to the language of literature, and it can be argued that there has also existed a sophisticated, but much less publicized, mechanism for the incorporation of literary and philosophical techniques into scientific works. This combination of science and literature was especially clear in the semiliterary and semiscientific *Tristes Tropiques* (1955), Lévi-Strauss's travel diary, which became a literary best-seller and a standard anthropology textbook.

Claude Lévi-Strauss: Did you know that the Académie Goncourt—the book came out just before prizes were awarded that year—published a notice saying they regretted being unable to give the award to *Tristes Tropiques* because it wasn't a novel.[33]

An American anthropologist has described the book as a combination of "autobiography, traveler's tale, philosophical treatise, ethnographic report, colonial history, and prophetic myth."[34] But even this novel work had its antecedents, works like André Gide's *Voyage au Congo*. The hybrid character of Lévi-Strauss's book should not hide the fact that, in the French field of ethnography, Lévi-Strauss's use of the Anglo-Saxon term "anthropology" was simultaneous with a distancing from the museum and studies relative to technologies, the traditional context and object of ethnography, and an association with the large intellectual audience and with theoretical discourse.[35]

At a conceptual level, there was a dialectical relationship between the collective habitus and the individuals: the habitus influenced social actions and their criteria, and social actions shaped the habitus. In reality, there was a quasi-corporate relationship between the habitus and the individuals: the two were inseparable. It was very difficult for intellectuals to distance themselves from their own symbolic conventions, because the condition for the effectiveness of cultural capital as a social force is precisely that it was personalized as gifts and talent. Only in extreme cases, such as Althusser's, could this illusion be unmasked.[36] Because of the dialectical, quasi-corporate, and collective relationship between habitus and individuals, being a cultural hero was, in reality, as much the choice of others as it is one's own: it was a social construction, which was a culturally created and reproduced, loose, and largely implicit, pattern of both theoretical and practical knowledge.[37]

The blending of literary and scientific values was institutionalized in such academic settings as the École Pratique des Hautes Études, which had close relations with the traditionally large nonspecialist public that was a central feature of the French intellectual field.[38] This allowed interaction between marginal sections that were usually composed of young academics and writers. These marginal sections formed an area of innovation. The existence of this social space can be traced to the creation of the school and beyond.[39] Close relations between the poles and a unifying dominant intellectual habitus—the man or woman of letters—created a unique structural dynamic for the invention of unforeseen symbolic and institutional combinations. This unity and even affinity with distant disciplinary representatives was expressed by Robbe-Grillet. "Among the great intellectuals the first ones to be seriously interested in us were the philosophers. Hyppolite gave a class on *La Jalousie* at the École Normale Supérieure and Merleau-Ponty gave a few classes on Claude Simon at Collège de France."[40] The literary works that interested Robbe-Grillet and the authors that shared common values with him were either other writers or philosophers.

These marginal sections of the university system were close to the increasingly influential cultural press, which expanded considerably, especially in the 1960s. Because of the rapid evolution of this sphere, which was an intermediate area between the producers and the consumers on the one hand and the academic and literary networks on the other hand, the traditional order in cultural careers could be reversed in the 1970s. From then on, even journalists, the gatekeepers to cultural celebrity, could become university professors.[41] This dynamic was also the condition for the establishment of new sciences and models beginning in the 1950s. If the value hierarchies were inverted, so were the temporal orders according to which diverse social resources could be accumulated. For the pretenders, the means to become part of the local intellectual nobility changed. Alternative channels of social ascension which took advantage of this intermediate sector were created.

Social proximity and density, due to geographical concentration and the common training of cultural creators, were another feature of this local market. The Écoles Normales Supérieures had traditionally been the common training ground for the local cultural elite.[42] A conventional education stressed classical languages like Greek and Latin, French literature, rhetoric, and philosophy: these subjects constituted the central portion of specific educational credentials. The effects of this formation took multiple forms. Theoretical, deductive, *a priori* reasoning was favored over practical, experimental, and empirical thought.[43] Philosophical training stressed analysis of texts and a search for systematicity in philosophical works (e.g., Spinoza's system). This very strong and uniform scholarly basis was the background against which all subsequent intellectual endeavors developed in this sociocultural environment could be evaluated. In contrast to this institutional and intellectual background, the specificity of the foreground, individual works, would become apparent. Often, once outside of the walls of the École Normale Supérieure, the young intellectual abandoned all scholarly models—the philosophical system, the mode of exposition, the style of writing. After a violent rejection there was, later, a return to a compromise position between scholarly and avant-garde models.

Numerous elements could be seen in the later works of a thinker which pointed to a *normalien*-habitus, to a specific, basic intellectual training: extreme presumption, pedantic concern with style, hatred of verbal improvisation, frequent Latin or Greek citations, a conceptual way of thinking, use of French classics, excessive abstraction, and so forth. As a counterreaction to this, an intellectual could, like many representatives of the human and social-scientific intelligentsia did in the 1960s, romanticize scientific method by developing quantitative history, deductive models, and statistics methods, for instance, and place excessive confidence in it.[44] Against this educational background scientization—a partial detachment from this background as a reaction to it—

acquired its full meaning. The highly competitive environment in the schools (*lycées*, Écoles Normales Supérieures), based on examinations, created tensions not only between the individuals but also between ideas. Personal dislikes mingled with intellectual taste. It was not strange to hate Sartrian philosophy in the 1960s: everyone had to be either "for" and "against" concepts, which were the property of groups. The followers of Sartre—an intellectual totem—would use certain concepts and schemas, different from those of the followers of Lévi-Strauss, for instance. Robbe-Grillet's comment on some of his friends' attitudes toward Sartre exemplify this: "Moreover, I believe that Duras and Simon really hate Sartre."[45]

Let us explore more closely through a few examples the implicit, fragile, and changing habitus which has regulated cultural excellence in this market for ideas. Before Lévi-Strauss, it was impossible to imagine a known French intellectual doing fieldwork and interviewing indigenous people. For one thing, neither physical labor nor listening to peoples' accounts of events were part of cultured taste or shared cognitive disposition. An event, and all the instruments relative to its analysis, was something vulgar and thus not valuable enough. Events were at the bottom of the hierarchy of intellectual objects. In this respect, some affinity can be detected with the ideals of courtly or literary society where manners or form, not actions or studious work, decided an individual's reputation.[46] However, it was possible to talk about the university as an idea, as Edmund Husserl had done, and thus be radical symbolically. It was legitimate to talk about mental disorders in a distant manner—that is, combining psychoanalysis, history, the social sciences with general philosophical discourse, as Foucault would do. Lévi-Strauss, and the social-scientific intellectual type he represented, was thus something new. But his anthropology also contained something distinctively French in its overly optimistic scientism. It was legitimate, in this context, to analyze empirical issues only if they were linked, in methodological, epistemological, or other theoretical works, to universal issues by abstract dichotomies: normal and pathological, or primitive and modern, for instance. Objects of knowledge were constructed in this way.

This social fund of knowledge and the dominant *normalien*-habitus, tied to the national cultural heritage transmitted by family, also favored dramatic, theatrical, and poetic effects. Consider the introduction to Michel Foucault's *Folie et déraison* (1961). The author had a poetic gift: even scholars like Georges Canguilhem, a member of Foucault's doctoral jury, thought so. The opening sentence to his *Birth of the Clinic* was revealing: "This book is about space, about language, and about death; it is about the act of seeing, the gaze."[47] No wonder science became a sort of conceptualized literature, and vice versa. For the young readership of the 1950s and 1960s in search of models and idols, only this type of discourse had collective meaning. It fit the categories of perception. On the other hand, the criteria of excellence were not fulfilled if the work consisted of graphs and tables and made no clear connections to very abstract levels of analysis: this would not be socially or psychologically rewarding. Even reorganization of the elements of the conventions did not lead to this.

The definition of the prized intellectual followed literary criteria closely due to a long-standing and homogeneous literary culture, despite the impact of scientization. This influence can clearly be seen in the French social sciences, which have not, for a variety of reasons linked to the persistence of literary criteria, detached themselves from literary culture and its imperatives. The works of sociologists of culture—such as Bourdieu's—are still compared to Sartre's works on Flaubert or on literature, which constitute the category of reference in this area and which condition the expectations of the large public. The persistence of this standard is one of the main obstacles to a thorough professionalization of the human-science pole of the social sciences. But this should not be taken as an essentially restrictive position, as these conditions enable the sociology of culture and related disciplines to have a substantial and durable cultural impact.

A highly selective and competitive environment favored originality, but with certain restrictions. The quest for symbolic distinction, esteem, and admiration took place at an abstract and euphemistic level, and was guided by the informal constraints on language and interesting topics implicit in the conventions. Moreover, a certain type of behavior was expected by others: it was considered normal to be brilliant in a specified, local manner. The recoining of words borrowed from valorized disciplines like the natural sciences and linguistics, for example, was the most visible transcoding mechanism of scientific texts.[48]

CHAPTER 2

The *Nouveau Régime*: The Weight of Past Deeds

> Lévi-Strauss hasn't written novels, and no
> one knows the poems of Foucault. Each
> occupies his compartment, and it is
> devilishly difficult to get one of them to
> come out to take a bit of air. The specialist is
> in power!
>
> Gilles Lapouge

In order to challenge the Sartrian total intellectual,[1] the goals of the new intellectual generation had to fulfill certain intrinsic requirements. This was especially true in disciplines in the arts and letters that did not prepare for professions and to whose intellectual identity the transmission of cultural heritage was primordial. They had to conform to the inherited conventions of French intellectual legitimacy, an imperative frequently overlooked by outside observers. As Vincent Descombes has put it, "the great undertaking of each generation is to settle the debts handed down by the preceding one. *The sins of the father are visited upon the sons.*"[2]

The emotional need of the aristocracy of culture to be part of the legacy was reflected in the ambitions attached to certain venerated institutions that embodied this tradition. Lévi-Strauss's description of his own aspirations with respect to the Collège de France is revealing:

> I was seized with a sudden desire. Nowhere else, I thought, would I rather spend my days than in the spacious, silent, and secret rooms, which still retained the aura of a mid-nineteenth-century library or laboratory. That was how I saw the Collège de France I aspired to enter: the workplace of Claude Bernard, Ernest Renan.[3]

It was precisely science and objectivity which enabled the question of one's relationship with the past to be settled for the second postwar generation.

Lévi-Strauss challenged Sartre with the authority of science, which had made a business out of finding inevitabilities in human life. The movie director Jean-Luc Godard criticized precisely this tendency in the thinking of the most visible intellectuals of the moment.

> It [a text by Pasolini on film] is beautiful, like Foucault's text on Velasquez. But I fail to see its *necessity*. Other things could be equally true. If I do not like Foucault, it is because he says: "At this period of time people thought so and so, and starting from this date, people thought that" . . . why not, but can one be so sure? It is precisely for this reason that we are doing movies, in order to prevent a future Foucault from affirming things like that with such a presumption. Sartre does not escape this reproach either.[4]

This imperative of finding necessities, "structures," at whatever price was according to Godard coupled with another requirement, an alienation from real life. Barthes's work *Système de la mode* (1967) exemplified this faith, this habit of rationalizing: "All this makes me think about Barthes's book on fashion. It is unreadable for one simple reason. Because Barthes reads a phenomenon which has to be seen and felt because it is *worn*, thus *experienced*."[5] Science, and more precisely, linguistics, inspired the stars of the 1960s: Barthes, Derrida, and Foucault. In this sense, they were Lévi-Strauss's followers. Meanwhile, science permitted the esteemed role of the intellectual to be reproduced. The idealized myth of the human-and social-scientific intelligentsia is a self-perception which organizes the behavioral strategies of individuals.[6] Scientific discourse enabled the requirements of the dual model of cultural dynamics to be fulfilled via an aggressive and even arbitrary redefinition of intellectual activity and its value hierarchies.

The fulfillment of the internal demands of this French cultural heritage authorized the new generation to oust Sartre and his solutions to the problems between intellectual and political commitment, and to reinvent the man or woman of letters. In the 1960s, Sartre's philosophy became too humanistic; that is, it did not permit the radicalization necessary for scientization. His philosophy was considered too loose and not rigid enough. Sartre's discourse was seen as lagging behind modernity in its vocabulary: identification followed a dual model of culture. Lévi-Strauss was idolized while Sartre was ridiculed.

As the continual updating of the collective habitus was both a subjective and objective necessity for legitimate symbolic creation because the challenge of past achievements had to be met, intellectual bulimia[7] was a structural feature of the intellectual field. Bulimia was a sign of a high level of dynamism. This characteristic stemmed from the by now very well-known structural features of the French intellectual field, which enabled structured change: first, a high level of interaction between the two poles of the field, the academic and the literary;

second, centralization within a relatively restricted geographical area, Paris; third, relatively high and dense population; fourth, rapid circulation of models and ideas, which is related to highly developed differentiation and to reciprocal emulation and transcoding mechanisms; fifth, relatively homogeneous intellectual formation of individuals and a social fund of knowledge tied to literary culture and the Écoles Normales Supérieures;[8] and sixth, a common ideal, the man or woman of letters, challenged constantly by numerous subcodes. In practice, bulimia was transformed into eclectism, the combination of everything that could be found at a certain moment in time and corresponded to the conventions and to the restrictions relative to the individuals' positions.[9]

However, in the 1960s, this dominant habitus evolved as internal channels of social ascension relative to both the literary and university fields began to be challenged by the expansion of an intermediary sector. The media and cultural journalism made possible accumulation of economic income and cultural fame with less investment, and, in fact, dislocated the dynamics of the intellectual field, breaking the previous regularities.

It is only in a context such as the French intellectual field that Foucault's work could be considered that of a specialist. This can be explained by the fact that, paradoxically, both the specialist in the human and social sciences and intellectual fame as a legitimate social resource developed hand in hand. For this reason, it is misleading to analyze the human and social sciences as if they were natural sciences and by isolating one pole of the social sciences from the intellectual field as a whole.[10] To label this period, as Debray has, as the age of media, also creates as misleading picture.

The internal division of the field, which is both a symbolic and institutional space, reflects a more general structural tension: that between a declining literary culture embodied by the man or woman of letters—representing a relatively low-codified field of social activity, literature—and a more highly codified one, science and the ascending scientific culture. The symbiosis of these two partly contradictory dimensions—that is, the interplay of the *littérateur* and the *savant* as intellectual types—combined with the expansion in volume of the whole intellectual field, made possible, in the 1950s, the radical detachment of young intellectuals from the dominant models. It resulted in the creation of new models which fulfilled the internal requirements of legitimacy. Young intellectuals such as Derrida and Foucault combined the traditional institutional signs of the legitimate intellectual[11] and the marginal academic. They were able to take advantage of the higher value of cultural celebrity as a social resource. As a French journalist and writer observed, "Ideas are now on the market."[12]

It is in this sociohistorical context, with relation to the structural tensions created by the dynamic between the *littérateur* and the *savant,* that the birth of new variations in the French intellectual habitus—the simultaneous rise of movements such as "structuralism" and "poststructuralism" and of groups such as the human- and social-scientific intelligentsia—must be analyzed. With the subsequent decline of philosophical and literary culture in school programs, a gradual modification in the cultural dynamics in the 1980s in favor of audio-visual culture and media-culture has taken place. The symbolic dominance of human and social scientific discourse in the 1960s has not been reproduced since because, among other factors, of the absence of teaching at the pre-university level, the strength of literary culture and the changes in the interests of the young public, notably the rise of an audiovisual culture.[13] A side industry of cultural video films sprang up as the following advertisement for Scherzo publishers indicates. The photographs of some of the great thinkers, Edmond Jabès, Claude Lévi-Strauss, Pierre Bourdieu, and Jacques Derrida, accompanied the advertisement.[14]

> You know their works . . . now discover the men! Presented by *La Sept*, "Contemporary Profiles" presents, on film, these enlightened minds of our time. They respond to the testimony and interpellations of those whose lives or work they have influenced. From their responses, rich, profound, and often surprising portraits emerge through which the man behind the author and thinker is revealed. A live presence, documentary evidence that cannot be found on television: A new means to create for yourself a living archive. At last, video cassettes that you have every reason to include in your library. "Intelligence and television are not necessarily incompatible." These films, rich in content, finally show your VCR its true vocation: that of intelligent tool, the source of live, current documentation, not to be found elsewhere. These video cassettes are very simply presented, suitable for the library of today's "gentleman." You may order these directly by mail at a special "publisher's price," very reasonable for material of this quality, currently available only at Scherzo Publishers.

INTERGENERATIONAL SYMBOLIC TRANSMISSION

> Mystery is not one of the possibilities of reality. Mystery is what is necessary for reality to exist.
>
> Magritte

Sartre and Lévi-Strauss were the main representatives of the two intellectual generations in the 1960s. These generations were engaged in numerous symbolic struggles starting from the 1950s.[15] Precisely because they had different gods, the representatives of "structuralism" and "poststructuralism" were considered legitimate successors to Sartrian philosophy. If they had shared

Sartrian philosophy's precepts, the structuralists and poststructuralists would have been only followers. Very important social and psychological incentives prompted the second postwar generation of intellectuals to perceive itself in terms of filiation and rebellion against the previous dominant worldview represented by Sartre. As such, this membership in an intellectual generation implied an act of faith. This perception of one's own role as an intellectual enabled structured change and compliance to an order of succession and to certain rules relative to symbolic domination. These rules of symbolic domination were related to the fact that the dominant habitus had been defined by men who had a certain formal and informal education. Not surprisingly, questions of ethnicity, gender, and religion were absent. According to the rules, surpassing the previous generation could be done only in relatively specific ways. As techniques do not exist in the humanities and philosophy in the same way as they exist in more specialized areas, and as the members of the new generation were brought up in the classical humanities, the only way to succeed Sartre in the 1950s and 1960s was to propagate a fresh, new start: science, that is, something universal and disinterested, and the role of the *savant* that went with it. More general restrictions on succession were imposed by the very nature of legitimate symbolic domination.

Symbolic domination means domination by and through symbols. Domination is the likelihood of being obeyed, following Weber's definition. Symbolic violence is mediated and made possible by symbolic credit: the amount of the "given." The "given" has as much to do with values, trust, respect, and reputation, which are often results of a lifetime of work, as with organizational structures[16] and socioeconomic classes. The "given" is that which is self-evident, tacitly agreed upon—for instance, the canons of a discipline or of a subculture, the sudden value given to Saussure in the 1950s and 1960s, or the reputation of intellectuals like Lévi-Strauss. The "given" also has to do with the valorization of certain institutions like the Écoles Normales Supérieures, the alumni of which are objects of added value, certain noble traditions like philosophy in the classical humanities or structural linguistics for the social and human sciences, or of certain authors and their works (classics): in short, with a gerontocratic order.

In opposition to practices that are constitutive of strongly codified and structured social worlds, the functioning of the French intellectual field with its unregistered trademarks and numerous quali-signs (such as "philosopher") is guaranteed by institutionalized charisma. This charisma is the superior quality of intellectual excellence, the specific social resource relative to this world. This personal quality manifests itself by extraordinary and undefinable deeds. It is the opposite of everything which is codified and explicated directly in manuals or indirectly in the reconstruction of canons such as those of the history of philosophy or sociological methods, for instance. These codified criteria, which are transmitted from one generation to another explicitly and unequivocally, are

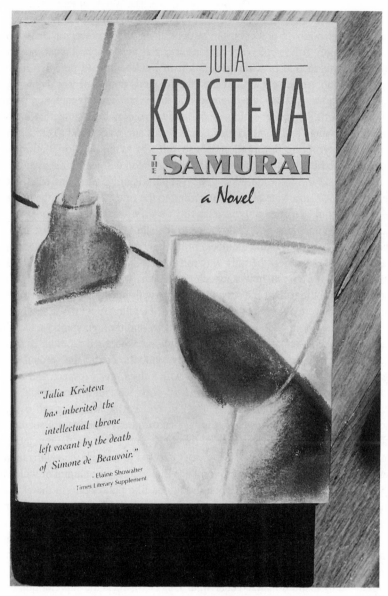

Julia Kristeva becomes the new Simone de Beauvoir. Cover from the *Samurai* by Julia Kristeva. Copyright 1992 Columbia University Press. Reprinted with permission of the publisher.

Illustration 2. An example of creation of intellectual succession, whereby superficial similarity between two individuals becomes a manifestation of common essence (e.g., literary genius).

always considered as inferior, because accessible to everybody, to the personal and unique features of the creation of ideas. In this sense, there is a sharp contrast between these criteria of excellence and those relative to specialized disciplines, which emphasize mastery of specific techniques. From the point of view of intergenerational transmission of cultural values, tradition and innovation, and the future patterns of innovation, the problem is how to transmit and protect the value of this charisma, that is, to reproduce in time the essence of intellectual activity, creation, which is by definition unique and singular. Following Max Weber,[17] charisma is transmitted through routinization, by the integration of acts and qualities considered as extra-ordinary into the world of everyday.

But rarity exists only in relation to other acts, qualities or miraculous works. In the French intellectual world, rarity can have to do with having been the student or follower of a hero, and thus an attachment to a patronymic or eponymous hero symbolizing intellectual modernity like Claude Lévi-Strauss, with having published in a prestigious review like *Critique*, or with having defended a thesis at a very young age in a valorized institution. All these acts are apt to function as accumulators of symbolic credit and contribute to the determination of the individuals' pedigrees. One general criteria is precocity, tied to temporal structures, that is, to the rhythms of production and consecration. To the individual who has these qualities or who is behind certain acts, rarity thus means becoming the object of transfer of credit, trust, or respect that is the object of social and psychological investments on the part of others. Lévi-Strauss is an excellent example of this in the 1950s and 1960s. Rarity involves accumulating exterior signs of superiority, to be, for diverse reasons, designated by the index, to stand out. In this context, precocity is often coupled with a pretentious style. Consider Derrida's over one hundred page introduction to Husserl's *Origin of Geometry*. This kind of inflated introduction to a master's work still is, in the French intellectual field, a socially accepted way of showing one's talents. In other contexts, where philosophical and literary culture do not have the same status, modesty and sensitivity toward modesty are *de rigueur* for a beginner.

But to separate individual and social would mean to go back to individual methodologism or sociologism and to psychologize charisma, a frequent criticism addressed to Weber.[18] In contrast, symbolic credit and intellectual capital enable us to look at charisma as a social phenomenon. The solution to the transfer of creative power is the social construction of certain extraordinary acts and qualities which are partially and negatively codified. Most often, the qualities collectively invented have their *raison d'être* in nothing else but the numerous interests that are attached to the existence of these so-called qualities. Reproduction occurs by the transmission of the belief in the existence of certain qualities to individuals (the elect), whose interest in believing in this existence is structural. In the 1960s, these qualities could be rigorous, systematic, and scientific. But these qualities have to be indefinable, thus accessible to everybody. In this way, they can be effectively transmitted.

The dominant academics and writers, one of the social groups representing symbolic gerontocracy, traditions, and the weight of history, are one of the privileged specialized groups in this function of intergenerational transmission not only of values but also of ambitions. Indeed, Sartre's intellectual achievements could be reversed in the French intellectual field of the 1950s and 1960s only by an equally panoramic and fundamental endeavor, such as the structuralist project with its canons—language and structure instead of subject and freedom—and prophets—Lévi-Strauss, instead of Sartre, being their figurehead. The originality of these movements has thus mostly to do with the whole system of symbolic and material transmission of the French intellectual field. The dominant intellectuals are the transferrers of symbolic power who present youth, privileged social stratum of transfers of credit, under the aegis of the old. The problem is that nobody really knows *what* they transmit. In fact, it seems that what they transmit is, from the point of view of creation, altogether secondary. The transmitted can be advice, invitations to publish, personal relations, that is, various social services. But the role of dominant intellectuals as guarantors is crucial for access to dominant positions. In opposition to a shoemaker, whose power (can this term even be used?) derives from a practical function, the power of the dominant individuals seems to derive mostly from the fact that nobody really knows what they do. They seem to be rather the symbol of something important which surpasses the comprehension of laymen. They are the flesh and blood representatives of timelessness, the future marble busts of the corridors.

For professionals of the symbolic, the common will be reproduced by more or less general standards and criteria: what stays outside this transmission is worthy of being called charisma, something abstract which stirs the imagination. The function of numerous academic and literary rituals is mostly to impress through forms and maintain the illusion of an undefinable excellence, legitimate because universal. Symbolic artefacts such as gifts or charisma are socially created and start to have, from the beginning, a life of their own and effects on the actions of individuals. Distance guarantees the effect of magic.

But this illusion is effective because of the bias of the multiple material and symbolic interests of individuals implicated in this illusion. Their interests, like those of the politicians and pollsters in defining public opinion, is to reproduce and reinforce this constitutive illusion. This magical power has to be kept up by multiple processes, the principal of which is to promote and keep up this subjective, intuitive, inexplicable, in a word, magical,[19] relationship to the valued social resource. Paradoxically, this subjectification, as a specific social operator, is the surest means—because it imposes itself in silence and imposes silence (tacit acceptance)—to reproduce this intellectual excellence, as the criteria of this excellence will stay in a definitive position of extraterritoriality.

Ambitions are transmitted through education, but the outcomes can only be individual works. The ways in which the signs of excellence and the rules of accessibility to the works fulfilling the criteria of excellence are combined are context-bound. For the intellectual, the problem is always how to show and affirm the existence of these qualities without falling into vulgarity, thus transgressing the fragile rules of worthiness. The signs of this intellectual excellence are created most often by the struggles for recognition of diverse groups, anxious to promote others in order to promote themselves. In the French intellectual field, this complicity united a heterogeneous group of intellectuals that formed a new generation in the 1960s. This recognition has as its function the creation of an illusion of the extraordinary and of extreme complexity. It is an illusion to which all the individuals in the field are attached, even the most virulent denunciators whose strategy[20] is to reveal the actions of the others (for instance, their opportunism or conformism), thus creating the illusion of doing something different than the others. Recognition follows specific rules of etiquette, which are rarely violated.

A critique of French academic and literary rituals will not "bite" in the present cycle of transmission, as it would be integrated in this cycle, and would in the last instance only reinforce the illusion in which symbolic work is grounded in this context. However, it is possible to produce, from a distance, cumulative and critical information about the processes that uphold the specific interests, even if the social scientist remains, following Weber's image, an observer who intervenes *post festum*, after the bottles have been emptied and the lights put out. However, this critical point of view requires abandoning specialized sociological discourse like the sociology of science by examining cultural creation in a larger context, the French intellectual field.

In the next part I will examine some aspects of the academic avant-garde in the 1960s in the context of the larger intellectual field. What were the effects of the structural changes on the formation of this area of the intellectual field? How did the expansion of the social and human sciences renew French intellectual canons?

Part II

The Rise of Structural Constructivism and Semiology: The Academic Avant-Garde

First fact, first clue. I never left the École.

Louis Althusser

The specific tensions of the human and social sciences in the 1960s have to do with their position in relation to other disciplines in the academic community and the social conventions conditioning intellectual activity. In the case of sociology, the concerns of its practitioners have to be calibrated into the tripartite structure of the French social sciences, which consists of the following poles: the literary and human science pole—which is intellectually the most visible one during this period—the economic pole, and the politico-administrative pole, which was represented by institutions such as the École Nationale d'Administration (E.N.A.) and the Institut d'Études Politiques (I.E.P.).[1] Intellectually, the social sciences developed mainly in relation to the human sciences and against philosophy.

In the 1950s, linguistics became the scientific model for the human and social sciences. Semiology emerged as high-tech linguistics. It would remain dominant until the end of the 1970s. Human and social scientists started to critique systematically the applicability of the linguistic model only in the 1990s.[2] Since Durkheim, the French social sciences had defined themselves in

35

relation to philosophy, the dominant discipline in the traditional humanities.[3] Philosophy was the basis of an intellectual education. This philosophical education explains the violent opposition and frequent uses of philosophy by members of new intellectual groups. Philosophy's hegemony was contested by intellectuals having a double culture, trained in philosophy and often using philosophical schemas but frequently autodidacts in the human and social sciences. For many philosophers, the social sciences were refuge disciplines where they could avoid the overcrowded philosophical field. But these philosophers could not rid themselves of their philosophical habit-patterns and ambitions, which are not questions of simple choice. These are not disposed of by an act of will. The antiphilosophical social philosophies developed in the 1960s by social scientists were constrained by symbolic and institutional divisions. In some types of sociology, this philosophical heritage has led to an overt sociologization, often in conjunction with a leftist political profile, where everything has been reduced to the social.[4] In this way, sociology has become a metaphysics.

In chapters 3 and 4, I will examine Bourdieu's sociology as an example of the synchronization between material, symbolic, and institutional changes in the French intellectual field. Bourdieu endeavored to integrate into his approach innovations in such areas as linguistics and economics, which were considered the leading social sciences in the 1960s. By combining principles from Saussure's semiology and Lévi-Strauss's anthropology into the study of French society, Bourdieu developed a variation of structural sociology. By seeking to incorporate economics into a larger examination of social values, he attempted to dethrone economics and present sociology as the leading social science. Both these strategies have to be evaluated in relation to the transformations in the intellectual field, which crystallized in individual intellectual projects in the form of various textual strategies. More precisely, these textual strategies included definitions of concepts, the conception of the project as a scientific one that would literally create a science of society, and the use of explicit and implicit references to competing authors such as Sartre, Lévi-Strauss, and Foucault. The key to understanding the originality of Bourdieu's sociology is, first, to examine its pretensions in relation to the characteristics of the French intellectual field, and, second, to analyze sociology with its own methods, thus contributing to a sociology of sociological production, including a sociology of various forms of sociological discourse.

If Bourdieu's sociology follows the precepts of Durkheimian sociology, it also broadens it by appealing successfully to the growing intellectual audience. Partly because of his training, and partly because of the social conventions conditioning intellectual work, Bourdieu combined in his studies the same dimensions as other members of his generation. He created a sophisticated, theoretical science, which, combined with political radicalism, aimed at overcoming philosophy and competing disciplines like history. This new science was conceived in a mixture of academic and nonacademic format, the content of which consisted of radical ideas digestible by a large and young intellectual audience. To a certain extent, in order to be successful Bourdieu's sociology had to fulfill the requirements handed down by tradition: theoreticism and Romanticism.

In the chapters on structural constructivism, I will concentrate on the complex interaction of inherited cultural forms and original ideas in the theory itself, whereas in the chapter on semiology and semiotics I will emphasize the institutional constraints on the formation of those disciplines. In chapter 6, I will discuss the main contradictions of this generation's scientific style, a style that sought to wed tradition and novelty.

CHAPTER 3

Scientific Practice and Epistemological *A priori*: Durkheim, Mauss, Lévi-Strauss, Bourdieu

> Can the anthropologist, using a method
> analogous *in form* (if not in content) to the
> method used in structural linguistics,
> achieve the same kind of progress in his
> own science as that which has taken place in
> linguistics?
>
> Claude Lévi-Strauss, *Structural
> Anthropology*

After the Durkheimian school, the ethnology practiced between the wars, and Lévi-Strauss's anthropology, one of the most visible schools in the French social sciences has been without doubt structural constructivism.[1] This approach was developed mainly by Pierre Bourdieu.[2] The institutional seat of this approach, as of the majority of the radical academic productions in this context, has been the Sixth Section of the École Pratique des Hautes Études in Paris[3] and more specifically, the Centre de sociologie européenne created by Raymond Aron and directed from 1968 on by Bourdieu.[4]

The main epistemological work is *The Craft of Sociology*,[5] written by Pierre Bourdieu, Jean-Claude Chamboredon, and Jean-Claude Passeron, in which the basic principles of the school of thought are presented. These principles are reflected in all of Bourdieu's work and *The Craft of Sociology* can be considered a great scientific declaration, resembling Trubetskoy's declaration on phonology forty years earlier, in which Bourdieu and his colleagues link the principles of structural constructivism to other sociological, philosophical, and historical traditions. By the beginning of the 1970s, this intellectual project enabled Bourdieusian sociology to claim for itself the status of an attractive, theoretically sophisticated approach. Its popularity had demanded the development of new methods such as statistics and interviews, new topics of research like culture and

39

education, and theoretical sophistication with new concepts such as "habitus" and "strategy."

In its search for more objective knowledge on social processes, structural constructivism has followed the old Durkheimian motto that sociology has to unravel the partly unconscious and hidden mechanisms and laws behind social phenomena. Truth is not found once and for all. The effects of the invisible hand of the Enlightenment can thus be seen as a type of rationalism and a striving to overcome the purely phenomenal and empirical level of observation. According to this way of thinking, preconceptions are research *a priori* which guide the research process without the researcher knowing it. If the researcher does not realize this, the result might be that some aspects of the research objects will be represented as self-evident, under the sign of common and immediate or spontaneous knowledge. By avoiding any immediate or spontaneous knowledge of the social, one can simultaneously avoid latent political and moral ethnocentrism. Thus, two levels are separated: spontaneous and unproblematic common knowledge, and scientific knowledge. In scientific knowledge itself, levels of self-consciousness can be isolated. In order to understand this clear-cut division, one has to calibrate these principles to structural constructivism's ethnological background, sociology's ambitions in relation to philosophy and history, and the characteristics of French philosophy of science.[6] The status of the researcher as a Romantic hero, who liberates him/herself from the chains of preconceptions and illusions, enables Bourdieu to demand larger legitimacy for his project. Like Plato, he would lead the way out from the cave of shadows.

In relation to the object of research, the researcher must be able to work from a distance in order to produce scientifically objective knowledge. Following Bachelard, science advances by putting concepts and phenomena into brackets. The ethnological emphasis of structural constructivism is most clear in this aspect. Bourdieu began his academic career—after passing the *agrégration* in philosophy at the École Normale Supérieure of the rue d'Ulm in Paris—as an anthropologist in Kabylia in Algeria at the end of the 1950s. He developed his anthropological approach further after shifting his research interests from Kabylia to France. This development differentiates Bourdieu clearly from Lévi-Strauss, whose research assistant Bourdieu had been. Lévi-Strauss had restricted the validity of his method to "cold" and "ahistorical" societies. The adaptation of the ethnological method from relatively less-developed societies to the analysis of "developed" societies led to a seemingly trivial, but perhaps crucial shift: the researcher did not have to travel to the *tristes tropiques* to reveal the regularities governing social processes. This is because, according to another Durkheimian motto which illustrates Durkheim's "armchair sociology," if an experiment is well done and proven correct, it can be considered as universally valid.[7] Without doubt this was a practical principle for an essentially philosophical and anti-empirist type of sociology. No control mechanisms for the projection of individual examples to general principles existed. Contrary to Lévi-Strauss, Bourdieu began in the beginning of the 1960s to study more complex interaction systems, which led to theoretical improvements and to the adoption of different intellectual ideals inspired by Marxism and the student radicalism of the 1960s, for instance.

Although sharing with Lévi-Strauss the principle of the distant gaze,[8] the "primitive" community was reduced/enlarged in Bourdieu's work into the concept of "field" at the end of the 1960s, especially in relation to research in Weberian sociology and French intellectual and literary life. It was through analysis of the religious and artistic worlds that Bourdieu developed the concept of "field."[9] Following Durkheim, social events have to be viewed from the outside as things (*choses*).[10] These have to be explained through deep causes that might escape the actors themselves.[11] Compared to these Durkheimian principles, structural constructivism argues more straightforwardly that the unconscious is the *sine qua non* of science. The impact of psychoanalysis is evident here. This is clear is the following statement by Bourdieu and his associates:

> By contrast, the principle of non-consciousness requires one to construct the system of objective relations in which individuals are located, which are expressed more adequately in the economy or morphology of groups than in the subjects' opinions and declared intentions.[12]

The concern to avoid the spiderweb of subjectivism led Bourdieu and his associates to argue that unconscious structures form a more or less objective ground against which the subjectivities of the research objects as the internalization of certain objective structures can be evaluated. Science was the means by which the sociologist found legitimacy. The term "habitus" was not developed in the 1960s, but its creation flows, retrospectively at least, directly from this dialectical process between the subjectivities of both subject and object of research and their objective qualities. Bourdieu also developed the notion of strategy in the context of his research in Kabylia, in order to distance himself from Lévi-Strauss's structures. Following Sartre, the goal was to bring the subject back into the focus of social-scientific research. For Bourdieu, however, strategy is not the result of a totally conscious or a totally unconscious activity: it combines these two dimensions.

Thus, the unconscious is formed, following a "Kantianism without a transcendental subject,"[13] in accordance with formal, eternal and universal structural laws. Here, we are closer to Kant's classifying and combining unconscious than to Freud's unconscious. Lévi-Strauss elegantly describes the role and character of the unconscious: "The unconscious . . . is always empty—or, more accurately, it is as alien to mental images as is the stomach to the foods which pass through it."[14] Social life stems from the unconscious, but it is itself but a pure structure.[15]

Social structures are thus not reducible to social relations, as Radcliffe-Brown and Raymond Aron have argued. Structures are rather the result of the construction of the researcher,[16] and are part of the superstructure, to use a Marxist term.

Structural constructivism argues that every field is a more or less autonomous interaction system which has its own socio-logic. The term "field" is Bourdieu's answer to criticisms of contextual analysis. Only the individual positioned at the edge or margins of the field in question can produce, because of her/his position, relatively objective knowledge of the field. The basic requirement for objectivity is thus that the researcher isn't like a fish in the water. But how can one understand, if one is at a distance? Will concepts solve the problem of objectivity? What about values and the discrepancy in the *Weltanschauung* of the subject and object? These questions have to be answered in specific cases and made explicit in relation to empirical material.

Distance in its conceptual, temporal, and spatial sense is the prerequisite of science; thus, structural constructivism is closely tied to the Durkheimian tradition, according to which three principles of sociological method are valid:

> First, it [sociological method] is entirely independent of philosophy. . . . In the second place, our method is objective. It is dominated entirely by the idea that social facts are things and must be treated as such. . . . If we consider social facts as things, we consider them as social things.[17]

The idea of conceptual distance connects structural constructivism to French traditions in epistemology and philosophy of science, to such names as Bachelard, Canguilhem, Cavaillès, and Duhem. For structural constructivism, however, epistemology means the sociological research on science, or sociology of sociology, not philosophy of science or philosophy of the social sciences. Sociology has to examine itself through the instruments provided by sociology. This new definition of epistemology can be explained as a reaction to philosophical dominance in France and to the requirement of internal explication of Durkheimian sociology. The basic idea is that conceptual elaboration is the only way to achieve objective knowledge of reality and the social. Conceptual elaboration, following the Kantian tradition, removes *de facto* numerous differences between the social and physical sciences. Structural constructivism aims at hypothetic-deductive model building through continuous operations of objectification. This does not mean formalism, but the application in research practices of certain schemas which have been empirically verified, and which will be dialectically connected to further data-gathering. Thus, in principle, structural constructivism maintains that a status of science for the social sciences is possible, following Durkheim and Elias.[18]

Closely tied to the idea of conceptual elaboration is that of an epistemological break, borrowed from Bachelard.[19] The problem of knowledge has to be formulated in terms of obstacles to scientific knowledge. These obstacles are interpreted as being interior to the development process of science. The problem will not be solved by appealing to processes exterior to the formation of knowledge. Structural constructivism has inflated this interior to include all social processes and has made out of this principle one of the basic requirements of social-scientific research. The reason for this is that, as Bachelard notes, reality does not give itself in its totality at once, but knowledge about reality is a light that throws shadows in some places. As total knowledge is not possible, it is seen as legitimate to turn epistemological problems into social problems. With this break, it is possible to distance oneself from common sense, thus enabling a more objective perspective. The break is not, however, momentary and final, which would permit by a stroke the shift from error to certainty. It does not guarantee once and for all the dominance of a theory and its concepts, as some scholars, such as the French structural Marxists like Althusser, who had been Bachelard's student, have argued. The break demands a qualitative change, but its effectiveness will depend on the concepts.[20] This schema of thought leads to an idea of a scientific hierarchy, but it is unclear how one could evaluate the quality of research methods and the power of the instruments of objectification of the social. Rather than argue for a definitive break, like Althusser did, structural constructivism is in practice closer to the Weberian principle, according to which science is becoming a science, an endless stream of conceptual elaboration. This conceptual aspect is also close to Elias's view:

> The complexity of many modern sociological theories is due not to the complexity of the field of investigation which they seek to elucidate, but to the kind of concepts employed. These may be concepts which either have proved their worth in other (usually physical) sciences, or are treated as self-evident in everyday usage, but which are not at all appropriate to the investigation of specifically social functional nexuses.[21]

More generally, instruments such as concepts, theories, and statistical instruments by which social phenomena are categorized and perceived are tied to two factors: the perception grid of the researcher (or his glasses, following Kant), and the previous usages of these instruments. In the second case, the instruments will tend, by being used, to bring forth the traces and effects of their previous usages. Given these constraints, the first step of the sociologist is the critical sociological analysis of his research instruments. This evaluation is not a ritual, something that could be carried out before the research, once and for all, but something recurrent. The Kantian things-in-themselves have to be taken into the research process, and the research is not restricted to phenomena, or to the presenting itself and the being known. *A priori* have to be concreted and sociologized.

The relationship with the instruments of analysis is accompanied by the active incorporation of the research subject into the research process. The subject is part of perception, or following Merleau-Ponty, the research process is part of the research object. The subject of research has to objectify itself endlessly, without being able to suppress itself as the subject of the research. The research process is a continuous objectification of the subject, which leads to an endless chain of objects and subjects.

Structural constructivism as a scientific enterprise rests on the separation of scientific knowledge from phenomenal knowledge. The second is an obstacle to scientific culture. In Durkheimian sociology, this separation is seen as being concordant with the Cartesian tradition of systematic doubt. The critique of all preconceptions is as such the premise of scientific method.[22] But such critique would ring hollow, if it were simply carried out by the researcher before beginning the research process, at one stroke. The object of scientific research is always this real or essential reality and simpler infrastructure, which is the opposite of "particular events" and history's "superficial manifestations."[23] Raymond Aron, the single most visible importer of German sociology and social philosophy to France, states:

> At the risk of shocking sociologists, I should be inclined to say that it is their job to render social or historical content more intelligible than it was in the experience of those who lived it. All sociology is a reconstruction that aspires to confer intelligibility on human existences which, like all human existences, are confused and obscure.[24]

Because of the imperative that sociology be a reconstruction according to specific rules, the research does not always do justice to the personal experiences of its objects and more generally to the fact that for individuals choices are difficult, that they hesitate, change their minds—that is, that they are, to use Sartre's term, in a situation. However, the subjectivities of the research objects, their dreams, feelings, intuitions, and so on are of primary importance for the research, both as erroneous information and objective or correct information, but only after a certain phase of the objectification process has been passed, when the break with intuitive vision has been effected.[25] The structures of the entity under study have to be connected to personal backgrounds, experiences, and formations. In this case, the subjectivities of the research objects will be taken into account and integrated into the research by a hermeneutic turn.

It would thus be totally misleading to decide before the research on certain precise relationships between categories such as the objective and the subjective. These relationships are shifting and have to be evaluated over and over again. Such a decision would hinder more than help the research itself. But because the subjectivities of the objects and the objectivities of the subjects have to be taken into account one has to notice also the subjectivity of the researcher him or herself. Thus, the practice of the research itself enables a researcher to surpass the simplistic subjectivism/objectivism dichotomy and to reach by the interaction of subjectivism and objectivism a so-called praxeological knowledge.[26]

In structural constructivism, the sociology of sociology is conceived as the sociology of the sociologist and in a single research study the effects of a habitus on the research process. This sociology of sociology is an inseparable part of the critique of the perception categories, which leads to a socio-analysis by the researcher of his or her position as the research subject. Epistemological introspection is as such nothing more than a requirement for intellectual honesty and openness. As such it is a criteria of intellectual excellence, following the Enlightenment's ideals. Playing with an open hand does not free the researcher from more sophisticated psychological or psychoanalytical analysis, the only criteria being that these self-analyses can be incorporated into a social-scientific framework.[27]

Structural constructivism's insistence inevitably restricts research options, but there is a good reason for this. Bourdieu's approach follows the precepts of French sociological tradition. Durkheim's central aim was to produce an autonomous science of the social[28] and with this in mind the following principles were created: (1) that an entity is always more than the sum of its parts; that is, the principle of holism;[29] and (2) that phenomena on a level have to be explained by phenomena of the same level, the so-called argument of the same level. Durkheim's aim was to prevent the reduction of the social to other phenomena and particularly to academic disciplines such as philosophy and psychology.[30] According to the principle of holism, a phenomena such as the moral code cannot be fully explained by geographical, historical, or psychological factors. The moral code is above all a sociological problem. The second principle leads to the guideline according to which social phenomena have to be explained by other social phenomena, or that the social has to be explained by the social.[31] For an outside observer, the problem is obvious: what are the limits of social analysis?

The researcher's self-critique also leads to openness in research practices, the use of a research diary, so that the mistakes could be included in this historical process. But, as in the case of the break, this auto-analysis is not a momentary event, a kind of ritual, which could be done only before the research itself. Durkheim realized the difficulty of this break:

> The frequent interference of sentiment makes this emancipation from lay ideas particularly difficult in sociology. Indeed, our political and religious beliefs and our moral standards carry with them an emotional tone that is not characteristic of our attitude toward physical objects; consequently, this emotional character infects our manner of conceiving and explaining them.[32]

In practice, the researcher evaluates his/her position in relation to his/her research practices and the objects, and thus the unfolding of the research as the construction of certain social phenomena is simultaneously the researcher's process of auto-analysis. The two are inseparable from one another. The researcher finds him/herself in an environment, in which s/he and the objects of research change constantly and orientation is possible only because of the relative permanence of certain signs and of the habitus of the researcher. One could say that structural constructivism, by trying to combine structures and the unconscious, also finds its ideal—with the exception of in Ernst Cassirer's analysis and Durkheimian sociology—in structural linguistics and more precisely in the phonological method developed by Jakobson and Trubetskoy. According to Lévi-Strauss, erroneously citing Trubetskoy,[33] its program consists of four points:

> First, structural linguistics shifts from the study of *conscious* linguistic phenomena to study their *unconscious* infrastructure; second, it does not treat *terms* as independent entities, taking instead as its basis of analysis the *relations* between terms; Third, it introduces the concept of *system* . . . finally, structural linguistics aims at discovering general laws, either by induction "or . . . by logical deduction, which would give them an absolute character."[34]

Bourdieu's structural constructivism thus follows in many important respects Durkheim's principles of holism and explanation of the social by the social. However, Bourdieu combines to Durkheimian traditions epistemological principles borrowed from Bachelard as well as structural principles that were developed by thinkers such as Saussure, Trubetskoy, and Lévi-Strauss. Many of these principles were shared by intellectuals such as Althusser and Foucault.

STRUCTURES AS GUARANTEES OF SCIENTIFICITY

As in Lévi-Strauss' anthropology, structures are in Bourdieu's sociology logical entities and the result of the construction of the researcher. This premise keeps Bourdieu close to Lévi-Strauss. Structural constructivism is based, following Durkheim and structural anthropology, on an idealism which follows the example given by the phonological or kinship system. Structures manifest themselves as symbolic forms, as the positive and empirical basis of Kantian *a priorism*.[35] Compared to its predecessors, the novelty of structural constructivism was to develop further the problem of homological relations between different levels of analysis, and especially between social structures and mental structures. The connection was crucial for a sociology of culture, combining familiar topics like French literary traditions, for instance, with new, scientific methods. Following structural constructivism's generalizing approach and the tendency to search for invariants, the determination of concepts has to be maximized. For instance, the conceptual pair priest/prophet, drawn from Weberian sociology of religion, can be examined in other contexts, for instance, in the intellectual field in the conceptual pair professor/writer. The determinations will be maximized in the research through the analysis of all spheres of social activity following this division. Dry or imaginative intellectual styles, steady and predictable or irregular lifestyles, the consumption of traditional dishes or exotic foods, drinking red wine or beer and whisky, driving a Volvo or a Chevrolet, and so on, can be analyzed in relation to other divisions. Homologies or analogies are the logic of invention in structural constructivism. By this Spinozism some spheres of social activity are examined through other spheres of social activity: a cumulative relationship between them can be created, for instance, by realizing that analogies do not work in some cases. The question the researcher has to ask him/herself is: "But is it really so different from that?" But homologies can also be looked for between social and mental structures. This relationship is specified by Bourdieu in his text on Weberian sociology of religion, in which the theory of the field was initially developed:

> Religion contributes to the (dissimulated) imposition of the principles which structure perception and thought of the world and particularly of the social world to the degree that religion imposes a system of practices and representations whose structure, objectively founded on a principle of political division, presents itself as the natural-supernatural structure of the cosmos.[36]

A religion directly legitimizes a political order. But the relation between the two is not symmetrical.[37] The critique of certain symbolic forms like language, religion, or art as such is not effective without the political critique of a conception of reality. Symbolic forms directly back power structures, but are not powerful enough to undermine a social order. Furthermore, the isolation of symbolic forms from the social order *de facto* legitimizes this social order, which is identified as everything natural and in accordance with common sense. Symbolic forms are legitimized by referring to their essence, that is, to their supernatural quality. Analogically, but aimed in the opposite direction, the belief in the revolutionary nature of some symbolic forms, which can be labeled as the myth of the avant-garde, as such backs central elements of the dominant ideology.

"Structure" has a specific meaning in structural constructivism. The concept of "structure" has two main definitions, though hundreds of theoretical ones exist. According to these definitions, *grosso modo*, a structure is a formal system of interaction, or a relational system where the elements are in a differential relationship to one another and where a change in one element reorganizes the system.[38] Following the second, more sociological definition, a structure is a set of conventional ways of doing things. Despite its clear advantages, the second definition is, from a field-theoretical point of view, too narrow. First, it emphasizes a more substantial approach than the first one, in which the relations are not in same central position. Second, it neglects the scientific ideal, the construction of a model, like the one which consists of homological relations between different entities. "Scientific" was thought of as equivalent to "natural scientific": deductive models were the ideal. Binary logic was adopted following the example of information theory and cybernetics.

A structure thus forms the simpler infrastructure, by which structural constructivism tries to explain reality. A field is made of a structure, a system of differences, in which an element gets its meaning from its relations with the other elements, and without which it would not have any meaning. The relative value of an element—a social resource of some sort, for instance—stems from its relations system. A structure also forms an unconscious, moving system, which "directs" the actions and is ultimately tied to the body. In the unconscious, subjectivities and objectivities are combined. Unconscious processes and the individuals' practical logic are the primordial research objects of structural constructivism. The rationalist tendency of the approach is satisfied with the unconscious. The subjectivities have to be returned by the unconscious and its symbolic processes to the objectivities of the subject of research. This way, the argument of semi-exteriority or shifting otherness is legitimized. Mauss commented in the same vein when defining magic as a social phenomena:

> We shall have to provide this definition for ourselves, since we cannot be content to accept facts as "magical" simply because they have been so called by the actors themselves or observers. The points of view of such people are subjective, hence not necessarily scientific.[39]

With the continuous interaction of subject and object other antinomies are surpassed, such as that between physical/psychical and more fundamentally the division social/psychological. The general is in the small detail—this is the leitmotif of social scientific research. Structural constructivism's radical monism tries to overcome conceptual divisions, which are interpreted as hindering research more than helping it, by scientifically solving them. This idea is tied to Mauss's and Lévi-Strauss's total social fact.[40] Mauss writes:

> In reality in our science, sociology, we rarely, or even ever, find, except in pure literature or science, man divided in faculties. We are also faced with his body and mentality as a whole and suddenly. Basically, body, soul and society are mixed. These are not anymore special facts of that or that part of a mentality which interest us, but rather facts of a very complex order, of the most complex imaginable order. I propose to call these phenomena of *totality*, in which not only the group, but also all individuals in their moral, social, mental, and above all, bodily or material integrity take part.[41]

Durkheim's, Mauss's, and Bourdieu's sociology tries to surpass divisions which are considered artificial and simplistic and examine social phenomena as totalities, where "everything is mixed" and to understand restrictions on this view from a sociological point of view.[42] For instance, when reconstructing events one cannot decide beforehand what processes and strategies are unconscious, preconscious, or conscious. The strategies are examined in relation to the structures and positions and after this their level of consciousness is decided by the sociologist. The role of sociology in a context, in a field, is dependent on the social division of intellectual labor as a whole, and thus this structure "directs" the objective possibilities offered.

Another idea borrowed by Bourdieu from Bachelard is that of epistemological vigilance. The usage of concepts and techniques in research practices are systematically scrutinized and their limits and conditions analyzed.[43] The result of this activity is reinvested in scientific work, leading to a reflexive sociology. In other words the professionalism of the researcher works on a quasi-prereflexive—nearly bodily—level and the principle of epistemological rigor is supposed to control and direct the research practices of the researcher. Analogically with the requirement to subject research practices to strict scrutiny, the first task of the social sciences is a sociological analysis of its conditions of existence. Bourdieu's theory of structural constructivism has been transformed, in the works of his students, from theory to practice.

STRUCTURAL CONSTRUCTIVISM AS A RESEARCH PROGRAM

> Although truth has no intrinsic force, there is
> an intrinsic force of belief in truth, of belief
> which produces the appearance of truth.
>
> Pierre Bourdieu

The emphasis Bourdieu places on a reflexive sociology is revealed in the courses offered at École des Hautes Études en Sciences Sociales and the Centre de sociologie européenne, and especially in the research themes of the researchers trained by Bourdieu or having presented papers at Bourdieu's seminar. For instance, during the academic year 1986–87 the following courses were organized at Ecole des Hautes Études en Sciences Sociales: "Social history of the American social sciences from 1945," "Historical organization of French social sciences," and "Social history of the politics and techniques of the social sciences." At a more unofficial level, a few titles of papers presented at Bourdieu's graduate research seminar during the same year give light to the research interests: "The development of the market of political commentary in France,"

"On the sociology of socialist voters in the 19th century," and "Social history of the École Libre des Sciences Politiques." This general trend is also present in the review *Actes de la recherche en sciences sociales*, led by Bourdieu since 1975, and in his book series "Le sens commun" (Minuit), begun in 1965.

These publications have been effective forums for the popularization of sociological research. They enabled Bourdieu to compete with other sociological and intellectual groups for various symbolic and economic resources. One of the areas of emphasis of structural constructivism is—in distinction to the concerns of the dominant *Revue française de sociologie*—the sociology of culture and intellectuals. This reflects Bourdieu's position, which is closer to the literary pole and the human sciences. The social analysis of its own presuppositions has led Bourdieu to a specific kind of sociological history. What began to be applied was a sort of double reading, historical and structural, labelled by some Marxist scholars as impossible.[44] There is thus a constant interaction between the singular and the general, facts and theory, and through theory the generality of the singular is supposed to be revealed. But interactional analyses are surpassed with the assistance of Durkheimian principles, notably the construction of objective structures, to which the objects are related.

After the seminal *The Craft of Sociology*, there has not been another clear presentation of Bourdieu's method, apart from the less elaborate descriptions dispersed throughout the works of Bourdieu and his followers and associates in the form of empirical studies. The subject matter of these studies as examples of the use of structural constructivism range from the Church to agriculture, from the educational system to sports like tennis and judo, with special interest, for example, in the relationship individuals have to the body. Concentrating on the French case, these works are constrained in their form and content by prevalent discursive rules and by the division of labor in the French field of sociology. For instance, only specific statistical techniques are used and numerous areas of research, for instance, in political sociology, are not studied. The basic assumption on which these works rely is that of the education-based reproduction of a particular social system, the French one: the Republican school system is, despite official rhetoric, the vehicle of class domination. This element of disenchantment is visible in all these works.

In terms of sociological problems, some of the representative studies have examined the following questions: What social conditions made both possible Sartre's rise in the intellectual field in France after World War II and that of a new generation after Sartre?[45] Or how did philosophy's position as a scholarly and academic discipline change in the system of academic disciplines between the end of last century when the Republican school was founded in France, and the 1960s when a new generation of philosophers like Derrida and Foucault became influential?[46] Or how did the distinct social category of "intellectual" develop, beginning with the Dreyfus affair?[47] What is the relationship between literary schools like symbolism and naturalism, and the structural and morphological development of the literary field?[48] Louis Pinto has also examined the ways in which the media have proposed new models for intellectuals since the sixties, as well as the different national epistemologies in France and Germany; for example, through terms like positivism, considered blasphemy in Germany and perhaps elsewhere but a credo in France via Comte and Durkheim. Pinto's is the first attempt at comparative study of national epistemologies.[49] In one of their latest works, Monique Charlot-Rendu and Michel Pinçon deal with the lifestyle of the Parisian grande bourgeoisie and how this has changed.[50] One of the problems was the social mechanisms that permit groups to move from autonomy (in principle, free choice) to heteronomy, or which mechanisms regulate the social distribution of space? Monique de Saint-Martin has been concerned with the changing position of French nobility in the French class structure and the strategies it has applied to maintain its distinctive position in French society.[51] Bourdieu himself has compared where members of the Académie française and some of the writers of the avant-garde publishing house Minuit live in Paris.[52] Other questions treated in Bourdieu's work on the schooling system center on the mechanisms that link equal opportunities in principle to class discrimination in practice and on how these mechanisms are reproduced. Bourdieu has also recently analyzed the French higher educational system and its shift from emphasis on literary excellence, embodied by the École Normale Supérieure, to the technic-administrative excellence of the École Nationale d'Administration. He has also examined the artistic field, especially Flaubert as a revolutionary in art.[53]

Although the idea of creating models, or the methodical construction of structured relations, is central to all of these studies, and brings the researchers close to Durkheim or Lévi-Strauss, the impact of Elias on them is also very important. However, in Bourdieu's own works, history has been and still is subordinated to structure. This is partly due to Bourdieu's institutional position in the École Pratique des Hautes Études, in the École des Hautes Études en Sciences Sociales (an institution dominated by historians a bit later), and at the Collège de France, as the representative of French sociology.

Structural constructivism finds its moral basis in the same pool as Durkheimian sociology: Republicanism. The aim is to give to the dominated the instruments by which they can free themselves from this dominance. Without doubt, this intellectual and political project has been successful, in this context, in effectively widening the legitimation base and appeal of Bourdieu's theory: it fits the *Weltanschauung* of the French social-scientific intelligentsia and the requirements of intellectual freedom tied to the ideals of French literary culture. Self-reflexivity and sociological explanation of intellectual discourse also satisfy philosophical criteria of finding a conceptual level which would enable a firm critique of other intellectuals. Bourdieu is constantly torn between two sets of requirements: Those of updated Durkheimian sociology, and those of the wide intellectual audience. What united these two sets in the 1960s were scientific optimism and political radicalism. This combination can be seen in all of Bourdieu's works, starting from *The Inheritors* and *Reproduction*.

If structural constructivism has succeeded in appealing to nonsociological portions of the French intellectual public with its sophisticated theoretical innovations, this appeal was for a long time dependent on the scientific credentials of Bourdieu's approach. One of the many points of dispute among students of French social science is the nature of Bourdieu's relationship to economics as a scientific discipline. In the 1960s, the leading social sciences were linguistics and economics. As I have shown in this chapter, Bourdieu updated Durkheim's sociology by incorporating into it innovations from structural anthropology and structural linguistics. In terms of Bourdieu's intellectual project as it was conceived in the 1960s, the relationship to economics was also crucial because of the theoretical sophistication of economics. Again following Durkheim, Bourdieu aimed at further developing a broad scientific sociology that would include economics as one of its parts. In this sense, Bourdieu's project is concerned with the sociologization (and anthropologization) of economics and the development of a general theory of value, not only of goods but of people. An analysis on the uses of economics in Bourdieu's sociology will shed further light on Bourdieu's sociology as the crystallization of numerous transformations in the French intellectual field of the 1960s. By developing a type of socioeconomics, Bourdieu renewed French social scientific traditions by updating them.

CHAPTER 4

The Uses of the "Economy" in Structural Constructivism

Structural constructivism is committed to a scientific social science. If its relations to linguistics are complex, it has also entertained an ambiguous relationship with philosophy and economy, the most respected of the social sciences. In Bourdieu's approach, sociology tries to succeed philosophy. But in order to be successful in this, it has to be scientific. Thus sociology's uses of philosophy guarantees it a wide audience, and its overcoming of economics legitimizes its scientific status.

How are "economic" terms and schemas used in Bourdieu's structural constructivism?[1] In structural constructivism, these "economic" terms and schemas—as a set of scientific instruments among other scientific instruments—have one practical goal and two complementary uses: to assist in creating a scientific discourse on social reality via the construction of properly scientific objects and the invention of new problems.[2] The "economy" has to be analyzed in relation to a general economy of practices,[3] which may take into account both "economic" and "noneconomic" goods and profits. Contrary to numerous theoretical readings of structural constructivism,[4] the role of scientific practices[5] will be emphasized here in order to understand the conditions of possibility of this approach.[6]

Bourdieu developed his general economy of practices in relation to analysis of ritual practices in Kabyle society. This general economy of practices analyzes practices as a form of economy that follow reason or rationality distinct from an "economic" reason. The term economic is also used by Bourdieu in this loose sense as synonymous with rationality. The origin of the practices is neither in rational calculus nor in exterior determinism.[7] In Bourdieu's approach, practices—"economic" or noneconomic—are generated through the interaction of fields—or social markets[8]—and individuals' dispositions. This approach—reduced to economism by some readers[9]—strives to incorporate the "economic" into an economy of practices. Dispositions are seen as being created in relation to specific social structures, which are reproduced and transformed by the individuals. The habitus is the social mechanism which mediates between these two structures. It makes orientation and action possible without the presupposition of a rational, conscious, and utilitarian individual, and without recourse to abstract and universal laws when analyzing the social world. It brings to the fore a complex subject of practices. Using the concept of habitus is a way to avoid postulating either a Lévi-Straussian structural unconscious or a rational calculus following rational choice theory.

Capital—the most common "economic" term in structural constructivism—means any social value: it can mean attributes, assets, endowments, possessions, or qualities. Any disposition or quality can become capital once certain social conditions exist—that is, once a group of people begins to value it for some reason.[10] But the quality can cease to be a social resource if the modalities of consumption and values attached to certain goods change. Capital can also be defined—in opposition to definitions in theories of cultural heritage—as internalized or accumulated labor. A term such as cultural capital makes it possible to isolate specific social groups and analyze these groups in relation to different forms of social power. The concept of cultural capital was devised in order to create an intermediary between social class and access to higher education. Introduction of cultural capital emphasized that the parents' economic revenue was not a determinant in assessing the childrens' success at school: instead, cultural capital has to be taken into account. This poses new problems, for instance in the relationship between transfers of cultural capital and high university positions. Capital has also been divided into incorporated, objectified, and institutionalized capital.[11] In Bourdieu's work, the recognition or misrecognition (or, as it has also been translated, misconstrual) of a specific type of capital as capital, that is a social product, is crucial in the sense that for cultural capital to dominate, its arbitrary nature has to be misrecognized. This often leads to the use of Hegel's schema of trick of reason. Capital can also be acquired or inherited.[12]

The explicit analogy between economic capital and noneconomic capital enables Bourdieu to analyze areas of social activity systematically and enlarge the area of social scientific research. However, the differences between economic capital and cultural capital have to be emphasized. First, cultural capital is effective only if it is incorporated (*fait corps*), detached from the apparent or artificial and incorporated into the being, that is, essentialized. But in order to be directly converted into economic capital, cultural capital has to be objectified and institutionalized, for instance, in educational degrees. Cultural capital can also indirectly converted, that is, without being objectified. Indirect conversion seems to be the more usual case. Economic capital does not require interiorization, or more actively appropriation, for it to be a social force. In order for cultural capital to be socially valued, it has to be transformed from a social product of specific social groups into intrinsic properties of the members of these social groups. When misrecognized in this way—and this is the social condition for the effectiveness of cultural capital as a social force—cultural capital will be present in a disinterested form, not as a social product or a social privilege.[13] Second, cultural capital has to be detached from history and the inheritance mechanisms of social groups like families and kins, for instance, and made part of the individual and his/her "innate" properties.

What are the implications of the differences between cultural and economic capital for a general economy of practices? The first, obvious consequence is that one does not acquire or possess a symbolic good in the same way as one acquires or possesses an economic good. The value of a symbolic good as a whole cannot be quantified. A symbolic good such as "good manners" cannot be acquired by the unmediated conversion of economic revenue. One cannot free oneself from a symbolic good as one would free oneself from any economic good. In order to acquire a specific symbolic good, certain values have to be interiorized following specific social rules, a process which often takes a lifetime and requires the mobilization—as in the case of cultural capital—of a stock of diverse capital transmitted by the family. According to Bourdieu, the second characteristic is that for a symbolic good to be considered capital it has to be misrecognized as such—a social product. Cultural value requires a secret like gifts and talent, which are in opposition to economic value, which is crude, transparent, and measurable. Cultural value is personalized and unconditional, and for this reason alone a sociological analysis of cultural values is a delicate matter. The third crucial point is that these different types of capital have to be separated and kept socially separate. Accumulation and conversion have to be controlled. Distance from material necessities is the condition for the development of cultural capital and taste.

Even from this simplified presentation of the two main types of capital, it is clear that temporality is a very important aspect in Bourdieu's thinking.[14] For instance, in France, "real" culture and taste cost a lot in time because they contain a specific built-in and socially reproduced conception of time and complexity, and demand the mobilization of diverse capital. For example, it is necessary to start very young in order to acquire good judgment in wine tasting, comprised not only of knowledge, but also know-how, familiarity, and the right kind of respectful attitude. There are no shortcuts to this type of capital; in this sense, it is very rigid. Groups with a low volume of inherited cultural capital will have very slim chances of ever acquiring the cultural competence that groups with a high volume of inherited cultural capital have.[15] If wine tasting is learned in adulthood, an element of unfamiliarity will probably remain. This unfamiliarity can manifest itself suddenly and lead to awkward situations. Only those that are born into it can take shortcuts. The anticlerical jokes of the archbishop are supremely clerical, but not those of the parish priest. Because of the temporal aspect of this cultural competence, and the specificities of French cultural capital, inherited capital takes on crucial meaning. Perhaps culture does not require the same sort of temporal investment in cultures where economic capital can more legitimately be converted into cultural capital; that is, where the social values attributed to diverse capital are distributed in a different way and complexity is of a different kind.[16]

CONSTRUCTING SCIENTIFIC FACTS

In structural constructivism, meaning is produced by transferring instruments from other disciplines and then redefining them. For instance, the term "capital" came from political economy, "habitus" came from philosophy,[17] and "field" from the history of religion. Some instruments of analysis—such as social indexes of intellectual celebrity—were invented in order to give a new light to specific problems, for instance, the uses of power in the academic world.[18] In this way, the local requirements of intellectual excellence, notably of conceptual novelty, were met.

All the conceptual developments in Bourdieu's work have taken place over a span of more than thirty years of diverse empirical research.[19] Accordingly, the meaning of the terms have changed. For instance, in his works on Algeria, the term "capital" was used both in its "economic" sense and to refer to the prestige and power of a family's name. In this sense, symbolic capital is close to Weber's concept "status." Later, economic capital became just one special case of a larger category, capital,[20] which started to be considered a category comprised of a variety of social fields. The term "strategy" was introduced in order to reinsert the social subject into research, although problems of definition persist.[21] Until the second half of the 1960s the terms "field" and "habitus" did not exist as they are understood today.[22]

Bourdieu defines instruments of analysis loosely, to enable flexible use. Metastases are the result. The magic of words, or the creation by words of symbolic boundaries and limits, is a recurrent theme in Bourdieu's work, already present in his first book, *Sociologie de l'Algérie*.[23] The instruments developed in connection with a specific study not only represent reality, but also create it, within the limits of specific social constraints.[24] Conceptual instruments are not necessarily of little scientific value, or bad, simply because they are not defined in a precise way in relation to something which is external to them. Rather, for Bourdieu, the researcher reconstructs reality from bits and pieces using open concepts: scientific objects are constructed objects. The use of sociology is also always a use of power. As Bourdieu puts it, his conception of theory is that of "a program of perception and action—a scientific habitus."[25]

In order for the instruments to give access to a more objective knowledge of reality, they must be capable of creating relational information, making possible the move from the "I" to the "We," from preconstructed to constructed objects, from the self-evident to reflexivity: this is the criteria of a good instrument. Sociology has to be provocative and Bourdieu is a representative of critical French sociology. Words have the power to create social ruptures; they do not merely represent reality.

The most fruitful way to approach the terms developed by Bourdieu and his associates is to take them as relational concepts which are closely tied to specific empirical research projects and to the local criteria of excellence. For this reason, a reading of Bourdieu's work requires an archeological or genealogical, rather than theoretical, reading. A theoretical reading leads to the forced creation of artificial differences such as Marxist/non-Marxist and idealist/objectivist at the expense of differences which have to do with the interaction of instruments and research problems. A theoretical reading, while missing the research logic, will always leave something out, which explains the frustrations of some readers and the misunderstandings of others.[26] As with other local products, a contextual analysis clarifies by relating institutions to symbols. In Bourdieu's scientific practice, as opposed to other approaches, the world of theory is the world of the "as if," because there is a constitutive difference between the world created and the existing world, or as he says in one study, between social classes on paper and social classes in reality.[27]

By developing specific instruments, such as "supply and demand," "inflation," or "capital," "economic" theory creates information on social events, information which enables us to distance ourselves from the individuals and relate them to more general processes. "Economic" instruments create a break from the previous, individual-centered approaches—the substantialist mode of thinking—by producing relational information, a move which has affinities with Foucault's slogan "man is dead" and with other endeavors that share the same Bachelardian epistemology. Heuristically these instruments are very useful. Bourdieu has been inspired by neoclassical economics or human capital theory, but his critiques of neoclassical economics are numerous.[28] According to Bourdieu, the basic problem with human-capital theory is that it does not examine economic capital as a specific form of capital within a larger social context, in relation to other types of social valuations. When studying education, human-capital theorists cannot take into account abilities and educational investments in an adequate way because they do not explore investment in education within a more general set of educational strategies and strategies of social reproduction. The social value of education or of a specific type of capital depends more generally on the capital structures and volumes of individuals and groups. Thus, the expectations of symbolic and economic profit for a specific investment cannot be taken into account, as the various markets or fields and the structures and volumes of capital of different groups are not specified. To illustrate with an example related to those presented above, important cultural capital will probably make possible advantageous symbolic and economic revenues from future investments in cultural capital or types of subcapital such as literary capital. According to Bourdieu, it is very difficult to acquire cultural competence in an area, for instance, art history, relatively quickly without inherited cultural capital. Capital attracts capital.[29]

In Bourdieu's studies on Algeria, the term "economy" was also used—mostly in relation to a symbolic economy of "sentiment of honor."[30] In these studies, Bourdieu used different terms, in French and Kabylia, to describe this sentiment: prestige, fame, authority, respect, honor, and so on. In this work, the term "credit" was also used to point to "economic" rationality as opposed to honor and prestige. The social value of the family's name, which had to do with the peasant's status in society and the respect the family could acquire was later labelled by Bourdieu as "symbolic capital," something which can also be described—via a Weberian twist—as a nonmonetary means of acquiring status or revenues. In this analysis, symbolic capital forms an integral part of the overall social mechanisms by which economic capital is accumulated and is analyzed mainly in relation to economic capital.

The pair "supply and demand" has been used by Bourdieu and by his students and associates since the 1960s, especially in relation to studies of university diplomas and their relative value. Value has to do with rarity and with symbolic and legitimacy profits—symbolic and legitimacy hierarchies being homological. In fact, supply and demand, and schemas such as the devaluation or inflation of educational titles—or more precisely the idea Bourdieu has of them as a heuristic device—are omnipresent in his later texts.[31] In a way, supply and demand is an important element in the structuring structure of Bourdieu's sociology, part of his sociological habitus. More generally, demand is seen as being tied to specific social structures and their differential character:[32] following Bourdieu's holistic approach, demand has to be analyzed in conjunction with supply, a set of strategies in relation to all other strategies of the period, a social group in relation to all other social groups of the moment, and so on. For instance, the inflation of educational capital, that is, the breakdown of the social mechanisms which until then have guaranteed the scarcity of specific skills, can favor social capital and the nonscholarly part of cultural capital.

In order to further specify the status of the "economy," the specific research logic has to be clarified.[33] Intellectual reproduction is created by systematic means: in Bourdieu's approach, by terms and schemas such as positions, dispositions, fields, strategies, and habitus. But in a structural constructivist approach the research process does not proceed from a deductive model toward reality, as some commentators have suggested, or from facts by induction toward a model. The idea is not just to create a hypothesis and test it, or to create a theory and apply it, although elements indicating such an approach are present in some of his early works (*The Inheritors*, for instance). Theory and practice are complementary, as the titles of Bourdieu's work show (for instance, *Outline of a Theory of Practice*).[34] These restrictive options are represented by subjectivist and objectivist knowledge. No doubt most works in economics would belong to the latter. This same multidirectionality and flexible use of instruments can clearly be seen in the relative polysemy of the instruments, such as capital or habitus. New instruments are invented, such as the "portfolio of relations" (*portefeuille de relations*), in order to clarify a specific problem—in this case the quality and quantity of social capital.[35] There is thus a consistency in the use of terms, a consistency which has to do with epistemological premises such as the idea of dialectical generalizations, intellectual criteria like the need to be original, and the various empirical problems encountered.[36]

A more concrete example frequently raised will illuminate the focus of Bourdieu's approach. The rationality of the tennis player lies in a capacity for split-second improvisation. It would make no sense to ask the tennis player why, at that precise moment, s/he had decided to try a lob instead of a smash or some other stroke. There is no perfect information: no time for complicated analysis. The right thing to do will be the result of years of investment and of internalization of the rules of the game, of practical knowledge, which is distinct from theory or logic. It is the world of the approximate, or "the more or less."[37] According to this heuristic model, when watching a tennis game the spectator would be thinking analogically of something else and would transfer schemas accordingly. The point of focus of a general economy of practices is precisely the different practices in different fields in relation to the structures of these fields on the one hand and the individuals' dispositions on the other hand. Its direction is toward comparing this specific activity with other activities in order to find similarities and differences between them. It is no accident that the title of one of the books by Bourdieu and his associates is *The Craft of Sociology* (1991).[38]

"ECONOMICS" AND THE GENERAL ECONOMY OF PRACTICES

I have so far emphasized that the "economic" is one element in a more general heuristic device, which itself is embedded in a specific social epistemology and intellectual tradition. However, in order to be able to see the deep structure of the work of Bourdieu and his students, a multidimensional mental apparatus ("coordinates") which is applied to very different objects of research, has to be examined.[39] This apparatus or heuristic map has itself changed gradually and has been applied in different ways, but it constitutes the common ground—the *topos*—of these works.

Analogical reasoning takes the form of homological reasoning.[40] The relational character of reality also takes a particular form. The reality created by the researcher is structured and different social spaces, or fields in Bourdieu's terminology, are in homological relationship to one another at different levels. Heuristically this means that one set of problems—for instance, the consumption habits of artists—can be read through other variables, their positions in any other hierarchy, for instance, that of their "artistic styles." These two distributions— consumption habits and artistic styles—are spatially compared. Divisions in individual dispositions and social structures coincide. This type of reasoning facilitates movement in the research process from manifestations of a habitus or dispositions to the level of the structure of the dispositions themselves. A homology is postulated, and the strategies, positions or dispositions of individuals or groups in a larger social structure are analyzed as effects of homologies. Similarly, actions and their effects might be viewed as effects of asset structures. The political opinions of artists on a left/right axis are interpreted as a structural equivalence which can give clues as to their positioning on the axis of monetary means (rich/poor) and their dispositions toward other things. The dichotomy light/heavy can be a practical equivalent to right/left, and to other pairs: frivolous/serious, sweet/salty, night/day, and so on. Weber's definitions of priest and prophet have been transposed into works on art and literature.[41] The priest will be the representative of the artistic Establishment, the prophet, the avant-garde artist. Following this schema, which produces two opposed and, in contrast to Lévi-Strauss, hierarchical terms and their relationship, we can isolate two distinct styles, value hierarchies, and object hierarchies; two types of relationships to the body; two interpretations of material necessities; and so on. For instance, in *Distinction*, the main organizing duality is vulgar/distinguished, which is reproduced in the analysis by dichotomies such as sensuous taste and reflexive taste, popular theater and avant-garde theater, substance and form, and so forth.

This research method maximizes the determinations of a small number of elements by an external dialectical generalization, to use Bachelard's term. It leads to circular reasoning, visible even in the structure of Bourdieu's books, which are not constructed in a linear way. In France, such linear construction would be too scholarly, following the line of the classical structure—thesis-antithesis-synthesis. Reading Bourdieu, one realizes that he constantly refers back to certain relations, for instance, the structural opposition between priest and prophet, to enlighten them from different points of views. For a French reader this method bears resemblance with the one used by realist writers of the nineteenth century, Balzac and Flaubert notably.

Analogical reasoning and homologies[42] are tied to other devices, which all point to a characteristic discursive feature: the use of intermediate terms. Habitus is another intermediate term invented in relation to Pierre Bourdieu's research on young men's conditions in the Béarn region; however, the seeds of the idea can be found in his works on Algeria.[43] The term "field"—which combines previously separate elements in another way—was created in its present meaning in relation to research in Max Weber's sociology of religion and to the creation of a sociology of interests.[44] The term had been used previously in a phenomenological sense as the field of possibilities: the influence of Husserl and Merleau-Ponty here is clear.[45] Retrospectively, in the concept of the field—a structured whole—a whole array of subjects and authors like the magnetic field, phenomenology, Max Weber, and Lévi-Strauss can be studied. These constitute a geological whole composed of different layers.[46]

In its present meaning, the term "field" was partly created as a reaction to Marxist political-economic definitions of social phenomena and represents the systematization of Bourdieu's structural approach. The field is composed of capital, an *illusio*, and consists of certain pertinent features. The concept contains some very Marxist elements: for example, the opposition dominant/dominated. In accordance with yet another use of homologies, a field will be divided into dominant and dominated groups, and the dominant groups will themselves be divided into dominant-dominant and dominant-dominated (a:b; b1:b2; etc.). There is a definite tendency to construct a system—not surprising for a French intellectual who has been trained in philosophy.[47] And this predisposition for analogical construction or practical schematism is transposed into different areas of research.

Economics as an academic discipline does not examine the conditions under which economic thinking in the modern sense has developed. This lack enables Bourdieu to move to a deeper level than economics does. Surpassing economics legitimizes sociology as a broader and more fundamental approach. Bourdieu's aim, following philosophical habit patterns, is to conquer the place of the unsurpassable surpasser. In order to take succeed in this, the term "general economy of practices" was developed by Bourdieu. From the point of view of this discussion, the economic but noneconomistic[48] approach is close to what could be a sociological version of a socioeconomic approach, which would analyze the social values of individuals in "noneconomic" terms.

In Bourdieu's later uses of "economic" concepts—that is, once the concepts of field, capital, and habitus in their present meanings had been developed—there are two sorts of economics: the field of economy and the general economy of practices.[49] It would be too easy to reduce this to economism[50]—especially if one is committed to the theoretical notion of "Bourdieu's uses of the economy"—and to thereby classify the work as Marxist or utilitarian.[51] In order to do so, many elements that simply are not in Bourdieu's work would have to be attributed to it.[52] In my view, a more nuanced view has to be adopted. In France, following the tradition of authors such as Auguste Comte, François Guizot, and Augustin Thierry, it is possible to talk about social classes without evoking Marx.[53] In this tradition, class is defined in relation to the volume and structure of capital and the social structure, not in relation to production. Bourdieu's work may be viewed in this perspective. His contribution must also be calibrated to the context of his research in anthropology and with respect to his positions in the field of French anthropology, to Mauss's studies on primitive exchange and the body, and to Lévi-Strauss's works. Merleau-Ponty's work on the body is also relevant. Bourdieu's early works can be read as reactions to Lévi-Strauss's structuralism and in opposition to other influential intellectuals, such as Foucault.[54]

Modern economics tends to define "economic" interest very narrowly, leaving outside its domain symbolic profits and losses.[55] For the purposes of modern economics, precapitalist societies are "noneconomical" in the sense of being irrational. A general economy of practices analyzes economic, cultural and symbolic exchanges rationally without giving in to homo economicus. In these societies can be found unwritten laws, practices and common sense. This is a very common critique of anthropology and as such offers nothing new. However, the novelty of Bourdieu's work was to adapt this general economy of practices to the analysis of French society in the 1960s and to create a host of terms which could take into account the complex relations between "economic" and noneconomic social processes and "economic" and symbolic profits. In 1966, in conjunction with economists and statisticians, Bourdieu declared— following in Durkheim's footsteps—that economic facts are a subcategory of social facts.[56] Bourdieu's work is thus distinct from sociological research on the "economic" aspects of culture or the cultural aspects of economics. The idea is that the whole social structure has to be analyzed in order to examine shifts in the symbolic consumption patterns of one group or in the value of economic capital adequately.

An important work by Bourdieu which explicitly uses "economic" terms and schemas is *Language and Symbolic Power* (1991). For the economist, the linguistic market analyzed by Bourdieu may be a strange one: there is no transfer of property, no validation internal to the market. Seen from this perspective, it does not make sense, and the specific meaning of the work as a whole is lost. It must be approached in a different way in order to access its deeper elements. The use of "economic" models makes sense in relation to Bourdieu's more general social epistemology and heuristics. Delving under the surface, an economy of linguistic exchanges or of symbolic goods is meant to create, some would say by a theatrical operation, the effect of a break, of distancing. An economy of linguistic exchanges emphasizes the objective processes involved in language use or symbolic production and consumption. Terms such as "market" point to the social conditions of existence of linguistic exchanges. Accordingly, the market does not have to be subjected to mechanistic laws of free enterprise.[57] Perhaps it would be more accurate to speak of a social market in which the agents, for instance, the families in the case of matrimonial strategies in peasant society, have some control over the transactions. The two apparently contradictory dimensions—the market and other "economic" terms, and the Weberian notions of recognition and imposing authority—are wedded. For instance, this kind of double reading can illuminate the social purposes of the family, which is both a social market and an institution, as an instance of reproduction of cultural capital. Behind the relative chaos of linguistic exchanges specific social regularities can be found; these might have to do with implicitly favoring a verbal style, or the implicit discouraging of local dialects, manners, and so on. Secondly, the use of a term such as "market" or "field" paves the way for examination of social measures and values.[58]

For instance, the value of a review in the academic world could be conceived in terms of concentration of specific capital—a position in the hierarchy of legitimacies specific to the social space composed of specific academic reviews. This position can be seen as the result of the accumulation of the recognition brought by past contributors and by the mobilization of diverse capital. It would be too simplistic to argue that social value would be predetermined.[59] Specific capital is unevenly distributed in this space. But negotiations—or, more precisely, symbolic struggles—take place all the time, especially when a new individual enters the field or an old one leaves the field. These struggles mold the future value of an individual investment, and determine its value in the sense that the individuals anticipate certain symbolic profits in relation to their own capital structure and volume. In Bourdieu's later work, the concept of "field" is clearly the most developed instrument in the process of objectification, although terms such as "economy" or "market" fulfill a similar purpose.[60] For agents in a field a whole range of rules of the game exist. These individuals have to accumulate specific capital, adhere to certain norms of conduct and commitment, defer the accumulation of other capital, and adhere to certain rules of capital conversion. Further, the field has its own institutions, a symbolic police force, instances of reproduction and so on. A social space which is not constituted in this way is not a field,[61] and a systematic analysis using a Bourdieusian approach would prove difficult in such a case.

In Bourdieusian analysis of intellectual production, neoclassical economics is criticized in a number of ways: the agents are presented as socially constituted, they are not rational in the traditional "economic" sense of the term, and their rationality will depend on the fields and their positions in them. Individuals are also constrained by specific deontologies: they have preferences and metapreferences.[62] To postulate a zero-sum game ("if I win x, you lose x") is in my view again too simplistic.[63] The composition of a field changes constantly—in some periods faster than in others—and a specific skill, which enables individuals to win in some respects and lose in others, can suddenly become capital, something socially valued in a specific field. An example of this is the fate of Russian language in the French intellectual field in the 1960s. In fact, symbolic revolutions take place exactly in this way: what had previously been small becomes large and what had previously been large shrinks. A social resource's, like the knowledge of Latin or classical Greek in today's France, value can decrease,[64] but this decrease can be very gradual and take centuries, because of multiple anchorings in institutions. Or else the decline can be sudden, especially if tied, under exceptional circumstances, to only a few dozen individuals—such as the area of Soviet plant genetics in the Stalinist era.

In the concrete construction of an object, be it a tennis club or an artistic movement, the use of "economic" terms would be part of the objectification process.[65] After this objectification, the researcher would come back to the object—by incorporating testimonies into his/her work for instance. From this angle, two textual layers can be isolated: the structural, which is a social topology of the positions, or a Leibnizian *analysis situ*, and the ethnographic, which combines the positions and the habitus. Basically, this method is a variation of Marx's research method, presented most clearly in the introduction to *Grundrisse*.[66] Chronologically—that is, in the actual research process—the researcher would first "relationalize"[67] and then "essentialize" according to the limits of the first operation. This includes evaluating what the individuals say themselves about themselves and what others say about them, for instance. To argue that Bourdieu applies a deductive model or that *Distinction* can be considered basically an ethnographic work is to limit the work to only one phase of the research process, for instance, the phase of provisional objectification. This sort of reading prevents one from seeing the synchronic layers of Bourdieu's texts, which can be adequately grasped by examining Bourdieu's theory diachronically in its own context.

INTERESTS AND CAPITAL CONVERSIONS

There are other interests than the one capitalism has produced. In Bourdieu's work, there are self-interests and disinterest, understood in an economic and psychoanalytical way. An individual invests in something—for instance, the development of good artistic taste—and invests him- or herself in this activity psychologically and socially. There are as many forms of interests as there are fields[68] and the common interest of individuals in a field is to invest in specific capital and invest themselves in a specific activity. A multiplicity of practical interests are substituted for an abstract interest. An agent in any field, by acting, simultaneously does a variety of things: presents his or her own interest, the interest of the field in which the individual is acting, the interests of that specific social group in which s/he belongs in that field in relation to other groups of the field, and the interests of individuals in homologous positions in other fields. To reduce any action to mere self-interest, ultimately monetary and selfish, is too simplistic and does not take into account this multiplicity of interests. Interest in the field often takes the form of personal disinterest. Furthermore, every act of consumption, be it material or symbolic, is an action which will lead to multiple interpretations by others. Through one's possessions, or the things which are temporarily in one's control, or even through the people one knows, one's personality, values, and potential actions may be read. Through positions in a field, positions in other fields—provided we have the key to the transformation mechanisms—can be anticipated, generating a high or low level of "credit" from the others. How far can one go before this credit is taken away? To use a linguistic metaphor, one is not—as a social being—a noun, but rather a verb. Each position is composed thus of a complex set of complicities and inconsistencies. As the individual is defined in social terms, s/he must be more than simply a self-serving egoist.[69] For instance, few who know painters or artists would disagree (although some will) with the statement that an artist is obsessed by his/her art and cares little about anything else. Other profits or revenues are seen as merely instrumental. But at the same time altruism, dedication to and belief in art, in a socially legitimate higher goal, is the social condition for this egoism. The paradox is that in order to succeed one has to be sincerely disinterested.

The value of economic capital—as a category of a general economy of practices—itself depends on many factors which have to do with capital structures, the rarity of capital, conversions, and the social values attributed to different types of capital in different fields. In Bourdieu's sociology, paradigms of social value are all but abstract, as some have argued.[70] For instance, in academe there are constant symbolic struggles—struggles having to do with definitions and limits—over the exchange rate of economic capital into capital of university power. What does this mean? That there are specific mechanisms, dependent on context, by which money is transformed into specific university posts. In some academic cultures, one can directly buy positions or chairs. In others, only public money, as a specific kind of money, can be used. In the latter case, conversion of economic capital is indirect. The individual can use private or public money in order to invest in academic capital. That is, money can be used to buy time in order to work. The individuals who will get certain posts can be those who have enough money to wait a long time, and circulate around research institutions or seminars for years.

The value of investment in academic recognition or artistic legitimacy is unequally distributed among social groups. If this investment is seen as a definite value, inherited cultural capital can be mobilized. In this case, predispositions for this sort of investment exist in the individual's social group, probably a group with important cultural capital. In order to climb in the social ladder, a "friend of a friend" working in institution "x" can help in one culture by introducing the novice to important people. In another culture, s/he is not supposed to help, at least not directly. In the latter case, the convertability of symbolic legitimacy into academic legitimacy through accumulation of social capital will be more indirect, will take a longer time, and will probably be relatively low. The social value of economic income thus varies greatly, as the accumulation of specific resources is regulated by either implicitly or explicitly raising barriers in the form of tests, interviews, or *numerus clausus*, for instance, or by prolonging time of acquisition (or both). For instance, in a culture where conversions are strictly regulated, made indirect, and social promotion is dependent mostly on accumulated specific legitimacy, individuals will develop more complicated ways of converting capital, one of the most usual being economic investment in educational time. When monetary value enters this social space in a new way,[71] this complex set of regularities will change. In France in the nineteenth century, one of the few legitimate ways, apart from inheritance, for a university professor to get rich quickly was to marry into wealth.[72] Another, more recent way, is to write short, popularized texts and publish articles in the cultural press: conversion happens faster, the amount of time required can be quantified, and monetary and symbolic rewards are relatively high. By accumulating intellectual fame, which is accessible and profitable, the social mechanisms of accumulation of cultural capital are modified.

The primacy of economic income—which is an empirical and not a theoretical fact—has mainly to do with the fact that it can be quantified, rationalized, transformed into something else, stored and transmitted, something possible only in a culture where accumulating economic income for its own sake is seen as acceptable.

In Bourdieu's later works, "economic" schemas and terms are used as part of a larger sociological approach in order to create a scientific sociological discourse which would include the economic world as one of its objects of research. Bourdieu's intellectual project relies on an expansion into new research topics, such as culture and education, and surpassing other approaches in theoretical sophistication. The term "capital" is understood as a social value. In this way, its scope is considerably enlarged from its "economic" meaning.

As such, economics cannot define a measure for nonmonetary exchange and for its own relative social value.[73] Nonmonetary means—which can be used to accumulate different types of resources, including economic income—

comprise social capital, educational capital, and cultural capital. The general economy of practices, which not only adopts a formal approach but has the ambition of taking into account qualities, lacks a common measure of the relative values of different capital. Rather than a weakness, this can be considered an advantage in the sense that it enables the invention of instruments by which qualitative differences between resources can be taken into account and different socially guaranteed and imposed measures can be created by the individuals. One fundamental difference between economic and symbolic capital[74] is that the former can be accumulated by external appropriation, whereas the latter requires interiorization. The monetary value of cultural capital is difficult to measure quantitatively, except in its most objectified and institutionalized forms. For instance, the value of an educational title as objectified and institutionalized[75] cultural capital can be measured on a job market. Investment time will be measured and quantified, and the diploma will be evaluated in relation to other diplomas. These two types of capital emphasize two different modes of appropriation, different temporalities (short-term and long-term accumulation) and relations to quantification (high- or low-level of objectification), transmission (economic heritage versus cultural heritage), and conversion of capital.[76]

Bourdieu's reflexive sociology indicates new paths for a general economy of practices. These include the analysis of socially guaranteed mediums of exchange, capital structures, and volumes of social groups; conversion mechanisms; and the social values attributed to economic capital, for instance, in different fields and contexts. This reflexive sociology frees sociological analysis from both the iron cage of rational choice theory and the forced choice between theory and empirical research, individual and social, and other antinomies. However, the limitations of this approach have to be taken into account as part of local rationales and discursive practices, of institutions and the processes of integration of individuals into them. Intellectuals reproduce in their activities certain institutional dichotomies, transforming them into symbolic boundaries and constraints; for instance, those created by the dichotomy structure/agency. Bourdieu's integration into the École Pratique des Hautes Études most probably encouraged him to develop a critical, nonscholarly sociology tied to the interests of the larger intellectual public, which explains the relative symbolic heterogeneity of his texts.[77] Conceptual novelty and theoretical radicalism made Bourdieu one of the heroes of the leftist student movement, especially with the publication of *The Inheritors* (1964), written with Jean-Claude Passeron. Even today, Bourdieu is known for his iconoclasm, theoretical sophistication, and leftist approach.[78] For many of his admirers, the sociologist king has taken the place of the philosopher king. But this has required meeting the criteria of excellence handed down by tradition and updating them with scientific optimism.

Following the deaths of many leading intellectuals of the second postwar generation, Bourdieu is, with Lévi-Strauss, the most visible social scientist in France.[79] I hope to have shown in Bourdieu's case that what is needed in order to succeed is a delicate balance between inherited models and canons and innovation, a balance which requires a high level of mastery of the game.

Apart from sociology, and especially the sociology of culture, another rapidly developing area of cultural creation was semiology. Like sociology, semiology developed in relation to specific institutional and symbolic changes, which enabled its rapid integration into academe. In the next chapter, I will examine the constitution of semiology in the 1960s in the French intellectual field. Many of its representatives, notably Roland Barthes and Julia Kristeva, became members of the local intellectual nobility, despite the fact that they did not fulfill some of the old criteria of nobility (*normalien/ne* and *agrégation* in philosophy).

CHAPTER 5

Semiology and the Dynamics of the Intermediate Space

> He [Barthes] writes every day in front of his
> table, but finds the task difficult, advances
> very slowly and is not satisfied with the
> *tone*. He fears the text will be too boring and
> painful to write. He fears he will be caught
> in a work of *écrivant*.
>
> Louis-Jean Calvet[1]

Apart from restrictions created by institutional divisions, there are numerous theoretical obstacles for an analysis that attempts to combine theory and empirical research. These discursive obstacles derive from the difficulty of generalizing about empirical results and theoretical premises from one creation context to another without a preliminary critique. How are empirical results generalized from one context to another and what public criteria and mechanisms regulate this activity? If the status of these context-bound results and instruments is not revised, the illusion of theoretical advance is easily created, an advance which is then seen as independent from empirical research. This illusion in its turn liberates sociological theorists and other professionals of the universal from painstaking and unpleasant[2] studies of specific cases, of the complex relations of these cases with their contexts and their own conceptual and technical limitations. The weaknesses and advantages of specific approaches, such as those developed by semiologists or sociologists of culture, have to be examined contextually, not in relation to a formalized and dead—because decontextualized—theory. The danger of a critique of such a "parade theory" as structuralism, created for the purpose of endless theoretical debates, is that it will lead, even involuntarily, to the elaboration of an alternative and equally panoramic theory. On the contrary, what is needed is a language of particularity[3] which would simultaneously be conscious of the interaction between particular and universal.

The frequent confusion between semiology and semiotics as specific historical categories on the one hand and semiology and semiotics as theoretical categories in the context of larger "isms" ("structuralism," "poststructuralism") on the other hand is the first obstacle. Until now, most works that use terms such as "sign" or "signifier" have been quickly labeled as "semiotic" or worse "structuralist." In order to clarify this confusion, semiology or semiotics have to be analyzed in situ, especially in relation to the local institutional characteristics of intellectual work.[4] A second obstacle has to do with comparative sociology of science and its theoretical premises. Semiology in France is not "comparable" *as such* to semiotics in the United States, as some observers—eager to promote a comparative sociology of the humanities—would have it. Semiology in France is not "the same as" semiotics in France, although in some dictionaries semiology and semiotics are defined as interchangeable, and contributing to the confusion. And if an element such as "semiology in France" or the "Tartu-Moscow school of semiotics" can be isolated in their respective contexts, this does not mean that in another context a "similar" element, such as "semiology in the United States" or "the Finnish school of semiotics," can be isolated. One cannot assume that if an element is present in one context it has to be present in some or all other contexts. This problem is tied to the transposition *as such* of a point of view from one context to another—where the division between semiotics and semiology does not exist, for instance—irrespectively of contextual embedding. What still needs to be shown is presumed to be. To analyze semiology in France as if it were a relatively autonomous area the same way as one would analyze psychology in Germany at the turn of the twentieth century, that is, from a strict sociology of science perspective—whose principles have been molded in relation to specific empirical presuppositions—is misleading. This kind of science of urgency forces the object of research into a mold which hides basic differences, for instance those between semiotics and semiology—and, worse, takes them for basic similarities, enhancing the legitimacy of all-encompassing generalizations.

In order to avoid this confusion, a holistic point of view has to be adopted. In France and elsewhere, specific academic disciplines, especially intellectual disciplines such as semiology, have to be related first and foremost to the larger intellectual field and its characteristics. In accordance with this point of view, the crucial points to consider in a particular context include the position of the humanities, the formation of intellectuals and the dominant intellectual habitus, the changes in the quality and quantity of the public, the multiple constraints this public imposes on the new discipline, and so on. This is the single most important step before one can even start talking about semiology or any other academic discipline in any context.[5] Only in this way can the meaning of semiology at a specific point in time be determined. In France in the 1960s semiology as an intellectual approach relied on Saussurian principles, a subordination to general psychology, a dyadic approach, and an emphasis on codes and empirical research, in opposition to Peircian semiotics, which applies a logical and triadic approach.[6]

The intellectual field and its relation to academe is very different in the United States than in France. Compared to France, in the United States the impact of this larger entity on academic work is perhaps slighter or takes different forms, as it is slighter in many other national academic fields, such as the German.[7] To analyze semiology in France in the 1960s as if it were a natural science,[8] and to transpose models from other contexts to that of France, seriously simplifies the problem of research. This point of view assumes that the internal logic of the "semiological field" is necessarily the primary determinant of the development of the discipline. This approach erases as exterior and intruding major explanatory elements, namely the role of the third public and the larger social and intellectual conditions for the development of radical intellectual discourses and disciplines. Thus, the object of comparison and the relationships between the entity and the specific contexts have to be clarified before generalizing. A sociology of science cannot be reduced in all cases to a strict sociology of academic science.[9] For this reason, an analysis of the larger context of an intellectual field can be seen as a necessary preliminary step for any comparative research in the humanities or in social theory.

Semiology was one of the most visible novelties in the 1960s, and it has, perhaps more than any other body of knowledge, shaped the symbolic tools by which modernity has been analyzed. As in Bourdieu's sociology, in semiology scientific optimism merged with popular appeal. The scholars and dilettantes who succeeded in creating this seemingly unlikely combination rose to prominent positions and became members of the local intellectual nobility in the 1970s. Many of its representatives, cultural creators in the full sense of the term, abandoned science after the radical years of the 1960s.[10]

Next, I would like to examine semiology and semiotics in their birth context in order to trace the specific constraints that influenced their development in the French intellectual field.

The scientific innovations which were later regrouped under the heading "semiology" were integrated at the end of the 1960s into a more or less unified body of knowledge.[11] If linguistic terms were unfamiliar to the intellectual public in the 1950s,[12] in the 1960s they became a commonplace for all intellectuals.[13]

The combined effect of the growth of the intellectual population and the creation of new university chairs meant that young academics could get tenured positions without having to wait for the older professors to retire. The development of new, semiological ideas and the influx of money necessary for the creation of new posts were synchronized. Some sectors of the intellectual field were more dynamic than others. In the field of linguistics, Romance philology, the history of the French language, and lexicology declined. Some examples will illustrate this trend. The late A. J. Greimas finished a thesis in lexicology in 1953, and in the 1950s Roland Barthes was also working on a thesis in lexicology. Before the 1950s, French linguists were mainly grammarians.[14] However, Greimas did not find financing for his research: he was forced to seek financing in other areas of linguistics.[15] Barthes, meanwhile, moved closer to more dynamic disciplines like anthropology, which was represented by Lévi-Strauss, and social history, with names like Fernand Braudel and Lucien Febvre, where funding was available. For French lexicologists, experts in literature and philologists, semiology also presented an international alternative to purely local endeavors.[16]

Greimas's and Barthes's cases exemplify a more general evolution: the reconversion of some linguists with a traditional formation to new, more dynamic areas of linguistics, where new intellectual tools were created, mainly structural linguistics. Greimas writes about a colleague of his, Pierre Guiraud: "This evolution which brought him [Pierre Guiraud] from historicism to an increasingly pronounced structuralism . . . is the fate of nearly all French linguists of this generation: having received traditional training, we had to give in little by little to the requirements of the new methods, to remake our own education by ourselves."[17] This collective reconversion to other fields forced scholars to improvise. This "wavering" can also be observed in the career of Barthes, who switched from lexicology to linguistics, socio-semiotics, and literary theory.

Where did this new submarket, relative to the production, distribution and consumption of "semiology," take shape? The main institutional foothold of semiology was the Sixth Section of the École Pratique des Hautes Études. Founded in 1947 by the *Annales* historians Fernand Braudel and Lucien Febvre, and with the financial assistance of the Rockefeller Foundation and the French government,[18] the Sixth Section "inherited" a position of intellectual radicality from the Fifth Section, the Department of Religious Studies, which had been the focal point of radical thinking between the wars, associated with names like Georges Bataille, André Breton, Georges Dumézil, Alexandre Kojève, Alexandre Koyré, and Marcel Mauss.[19] The Sixth Section of the École Pratique des Hautes Études delivered new diplomas such as the *doctorat de 3ème cycle*, which started to compete with the traditionally dominant *agrégation*.[20]

This structural continuity is best described by the term "marginal."[21] What does it mean in this context? To start with, no degrees were required at this time in order to attend lectures at the École Pratique des Hautes Études, in contrast with the dominant University of Paris. When we take into account the importance in France of the para-academic intellectual and artistic circles and the various cliques, salons, journals, and so on where the cultural heroes of the moment are born, we can say that the section was structurally positioned in such a way that it favored face-to-face contacts between academics and writers, bridging the gap between academic and literary networks. Thus, one particularity of the French intellectual field is the existence of institutions which have structural relations with the traditionally very important para-academic public.[22] This enables the interaction between marginal parts of both the academic and literary fields, usually composed of young intellectuals.

A second specific feature of the École Pratique des Hautes Études was that it did not confer diplomas. For students and researchers in search of academic recognition, attending courses there was not a good investment. Thus, the only way the school could compete with other units of the university system, mainly certain parts of the University of Paris, was to be at the vanguard of intellectual development, just like the Fifth Section had been in the interwar period. Indeed, in the 1950s the faculty of the Sixth Section included names like Lévi-Strauss, Fernand Braudel, Lucien Febvre, and in the 1960s in semiology, Barthes, Greimas, Christian Metz as Barthes's assistant, Barthes's student Gérard Genette, Oswald Ducrot, and Louis Marin.

Some more specific institutional changes also took shape at the beginning of the 1960s. In 1960, SELF (The Society for the Study of French Language) was founded by a group of young linguists (Jean-Claude Chevalier, Jean Dubois, Henri Mitterand) only to disappear in 1968.[23] The organization aimed to revitalize French linguistics, in order to attach it to innovations in other fields.[24] The same year a Center for Studies and Research in Mass Communications (CERCAM) was created at the École Pratique des Hautes Études. Its first director was the Marxist sociologist Georges Friedmann, who was also, with Lévi-Strauss and Braudel, a member of the administrative council of the school. Friedmann, Barthes, and Marin also directed the Research Center for Trans-disciplinary Studies (Sociology, Anthropology, Semiology). In 1968 Julia Kristeva and Tzvetan Todorov, both Bulgarian linguists, and Genette participated in the works of the CERCAM, which published the review *Communications* (1961). The watchwords of the center were interdisciplinarity and openness, reflecting its policy of combining sociology and semiology and creating a forum for all the new approaches.

In the 1960s, the Sixth Section of the École Pratique des Hautes Études, and institutions such as the Institut Henri Poincaré in Greimas's case, became the main forum in which avant-gardes from all sectors of intellectual activity gathered to create the melting-pot effect which is typical of this part of the French university system. In short, the institution facilitated unusual encounters. In Barthes's seminar, for instance, one could find avant-garde writers like Philippe Sollers lecturing on the poet Stéphane Mallarmé. Sollers represented a hybrid intellectual type, both writer and self-proclaimed expert in linguistics and literary theory, a true product of his time. He reiterated the type embodied by Bataille. It may be too simplistic to say that Sollers was a parody intellectual, but certainly his arsenal consisted largely, though not entirely, of smoke and mirrors.[25] In this respect, he was not far from Barthes, who wavered between academism and the fashionable hunger for effect. The main difference is that Sollers was first a writer, then a theoretical essayist, whereas Barthes moved from academe to literature.

Marginality meant more in this context than just an institutional position. For some of the intellectual warriors who embodied intellectual radicality,[26] marginality was also a psychological stance. Because the intellectual field was very hierarchical, centralized, rigid, and highly coded, being outside the local academic elite led to an acute awareness of one's otherness or even of one's intellectual inferiority.[27] This feeling arose partly from certain institutional characteristics of a valued academic career. Attending the École Normale Supérieure was a "must" for access to the dominant positions in the university system. Further, as been noted earlier, such an education did not favor scientific specialization. Both Barthes and Greimas, for different reasons, were deprived of this qualification: Barthes had serious health problems, which had prevented him from taking the entry exams,[28] and Greimas was originally from Lithuania—an outsider from the beginning.

Educational deprivation, stemming from the dual model which traditionally structured academic careers (Écoles Normales Supérieures vs. the others), was a characteristic shared by many intellectuals who were to become world-famous: the sociologist Lucien Goldmann and the literary theorists Tzvetan Todorov and Julia Kristeva, who were all foreigners; the anthropologist Lévi-Strauss; and the psychoanalyst Jacques Lacan, who had a doctorate in medicine. But the new intellectual generation was not limited to the intellectuals who either had not made it to the École Normale Supérieure or were foreigners. Indeed the very elitist system of training French intellectuals gave birth to insider rebels, who became the ferocious enemies of established practice and the precious allies of the "others," acquiring for the latter an indigenous legitimacy. Due to the increase in their numbers, *normaliens/nes* did not enjoy the same prospects of social promotion as they had previously. Access to the ranks of the local intellectual nobility was not as rigid as before. A hybrid composition was characteristic of the intermediate space of the intellectual field, and of institutions like the Collège de sociologie (1937–39), founded by Georges Bataille and others. At the same time, the *normaliens/nes* found in outsiders allies who were not raised according to the local intellectual code of etiquette and its rituals.[29] This combination proved to be explosive, as the non-*normaliens/nes* were eager to break the rules, and the *normaliens/nes* were ready to partly legitimize this revision.

Beside Greimas and Barthes, the foreigners, and the ones who had not attended the École Normale Supérieure, some members of the intellectual elite who had a philosophical formation, intellectuals such as Jacques Derrida and Michel Foucault, could also be found in the modish Parisian intellectual reviews like *Tel Quel* or *Critique*. They were in a way the legitimate successors, the future marble busts, who could theoretically access the highest positions of the university system, a path traditionally closed to their intellectual companions. For Derrida and Foucault, being radical was more a result of their structural position in the field, and of the expectations of the others, than a personal characteristic. They created their own symbolic "systems," even "anti-systems," as a result of their training. From the viewpoint of their intellectual values and their criteria of excellence, only the invention of a "system" consisting of "new" concepts or "anti-concepts" and of the relations between these concepts could be elevating. Only the development of a new system would bring them up to the same level as their scholarly models. This goal was central to their behavioral strategy.

Taking into account the characteristics of the social conventions relative to cultural creation in this locality, it is no wonder, in this phase of accrued mobility of ideas and individuals, that semiology found collaborators in a variety of academic disciplines. The most important of these were the declining field of philosophy and the ascending fields of history and the social sciences. Semiology, at this initial stage of development, fulfilled the internal criteria of excellence of the French intellectual field and the expectations of the new young public. It made possible an *aggiornamento*, an updating of the French intellectual habitus. Its representatives, armed with a basic philosophical and literary formation and threatened by the scientization process, could now legitimately incorporate into their discourses terms and schemas from linguistics. This time, this process of assimilation from the human and social sciences was not interrupted, as it was in the 1930s by World War II. On the contrary, it was encouraged by multiple changes. From the point of view of the criteria of intellectual excellence, semiology was a self-service restaurant in a rapidly deteriorating environment. Semiology presented rarities like translations of the Russian formalists and Mikhail Bakhtin, and for intellectuals in a feverish search of newness the investment was totally disproportionate to the symbolic and even economic revenues thereby gained. Economic revenue could be accumulated by presenting lectures and publishing articles in the cultural press. Here was an intellectual Eldorado: Derrida's and Foucault's uses of semiology demonstrate this. Also, because the field of semiology and semiotics was relatively uncodified the chances of being labelled a "pioneer in the field" were higher than in other, more established fields.

Because the transformation in the structure of social conventions[30] depended on various advances in more specific subareas like the philosophy of language or theoretical linguistics, the image that specialization in linguistics was not incompatible with a radical intellectual profile was reinforced.[31] Intellectuals saw linguistics as a radical science, yet the constraints of the literary norms of behavior guided the interpretations of linguistic innovations. Technical presentation and empirical analysis, for instance, were definitely "out." Continual updating was for this generation an internal necessity for legitimate symbolic creation, because the challenge of past achievements, those of Sartre especially, had to be met.

FROM INVISIBLE TO VISIBLE

Semiology aimed at elaborating "a unified methodology for the Humanities and the Social Sciences," based on "the Saussurian postulate of a structured world, apprehensible in its signification."[32] This ambition, which can be seen in numerous other works than those of Greimas and his followers—for example, in Julia Kristeva's early writings[33] and Barthes's works of the 1950s and 1960s—enabled the creation of a vast and panoramic perspective on language and society, a view which began to rival the rapidly declining Sartrian humanism, which was being ousted from the intellectual pantheon. It also gave rise to boundless theorizing on a limitless topic: language. According to local rationales, science was the only viable alternative to Sartrian existential pathos.

Retrospectively, the institutionalization of semiology can be characterized as the combining of different subareas and formations into a more or less uniform pattern, a pattern which however was very heterogeneous.[34] This heterogeneity, considered in the context of a rapidly expanding university, explains the process whereby the the social cohesion of the discipline was constructed: the semiologists were against the dominant parts of the university, philology and the traditional humanistic studies, which still reigned supreme in the intellectual game and its reward system. For a certain time, identifications followed this dual model: redefinition of self-image followed opposition to the previous historical type. These negations were enhanced by a whole network of services[35] that undermined the hegemony of the dominant institutions and approaches. But through resistance, the revolutionaries were able to construct a new academic orthodoxy, which paradoxically radicalized the main structural oppositions of the new space, already present when rapid institutionalization occurred: oppositions such as literature versus science, soft science versus hard science, Parisianism versus cosmopolitanism. These oppositions were homologous to those of the intellectual field.

Both poles of the new space in formation[36]—Barthesian literary semiology and Greimasian "scientific" semiology—could benefit from the influx of money, students and academics in the initial period of the "scientization" of the social sciences. While both Barthes and Greimas,[37] as directors of studies at the École

Pratique des Hautes Études in the first half of the 1960s, were giving lectures on Hjelmslev's linguistic and semiotic theories,[38] the results of their endeavors differed radically.

Barthes's seminar was entitled "Sociology of Signs, Symbols and Representations."[39] Participants in Barthes's seminar included the philosopher and sociologist Jean Baudrillard, the psychoanalyst Jacques-Alain Miller,[40] and the linguists Thomas Aron and Paolo Fabbri. Barthes, in contradistinction to Greimas, was perceived by many as an artist, who spoke about literature to "all":[41] reception required only general knowledge, French culture, and acquaintance with modish philosophy.[42] Thus, he fulfilled the criteria of a legitimate intellectual: he was both a creator and a scholar. And by combining Durkheimian sociology with semiology, his seminar also met the requirements of the École Pratique des Hautes Études.[43]

Barthes was more literary than Greimas and was close to modish writers, like Philippe Sollers, director of the review *Tel Quel*. In fact, according to Philippe Sollers, Barthes had a definite interest in collaborating with the very visible and well-known review *Tel Quel*, which could also protect him from attacks by other semiologists, such as Georges Mounin and Luis Prieto.[44] "I think he experienced *Tel Quel* as a coldly calculated hysteria. . . . The two parties had an interest in this. It is certain that *Tel Quel*'s type of agressive mobility favored him a lot, following the ten years after *la chose* Picard."[45] The importance of networks as connectors of individuals having similar interests is clear in Lévi-Strauss's evaluation of the first, scientific Barthes compared to the second, literary Barthes. "I never felt close to him, and my feeling was confirmed by his later development. The later Barthes did the contrary of what the earlier Barthes had done, something which, I am convinced of this, was not in Barthes's nature."[46]

Barthes along with Foucault and Derrida, to some extent incarnated the French intellectual ideal. They were literary and creative artists versed in modern intellectual discourse. The difference was that Foucault and Derrida were *normaliens* and philosophers by training, whereas Barthes had a degree in literature. At the beginning of the 1960s, Foucault's research was simultaneously historical, literary, philosophical, and psychological. His research topics were specific sociopolitical institutions like prisons and asylums. He later added a left-wing political touch to his work at the end of the 1960s. Derrida was almost entirely philosophical, but also heavily literary in his first works: later, he moved closer to Saussurean linguistics and Lévi-Straussian anthropology. In these fields, he was a complete amateur. But because of his philosophical training he was considered by the other producers, intermediaries, and producers as a legitimate interlocutor who could engage in a legitimate dialogue with Lévi-Strauss about representations of "primitive" societies or with Benveniste about the relation of Greek language and Greek philosophy. Derrida's discourse, a subtle combination of anthropological, linguistic, literary, and philosophical subcodes, was ultimately linked to very general and abstract categories, "speech" and "writing." He had his own style, consisting of neologisms and an original conceptual system—a "must" for success in this context.

No matter how these authors are classified, their common characteristic is that they combine different registers and process specific innovations in a general manner and in language accessible to a large intellectual, Parisian public. Greimas, due partly to his philological training,[47] was more rigid and more strictly academic, striving to create a systematic and scientific approach to the study of signs. Compared to Barthes, he represented the diametrically opposite pole, the academic and specialist, more or less an underdog in the intellectual field. The qualities associated with this type were "pedantry," "dryness," and "dullness"; Greimas's seminar was attended at the end of the 1960s mainly by linguists (Michel Arrivé, Jean-Claude Coquet, Julia Kristeva, and Tzvetan Todorov, among others).

A few examples will illustrate the different constraints relative to the two poles. In 1964, Barthes published *Eléments de sémiologie* (one of Barthes's more scientific texts), and Greimas published *Sémantique structurale* in 1966. Most of Barthes's works came out in the collections of the fashionable publisher Le Seuil, which published Derrida, Lacan, and Sollers, whereas Greimas's work was published by an academic publisher, Larousse. Barthes's work was intended for wide and rapid circulation, whereas Greimas's work was highly technical and terminologically complex, subject to slower and more restricted circulation. Greimas's academic works did not have access to the cultural press. Barthes was reprinted in paperback; Greimas was not. In fact, Greimas's lexical inventiveness lead to the existence of a highly esoteric lexical field, which created a science effect at the expense of large circulation. This allowed the new discipline to accumulate recognition at the academic pole. As an American literary theorist has expressed it, when reading Greimas's work "one looks with frustration at the forbidden and promised lands of mathematics or symbolic logic, or of musical theory."[48] But to the young Parisian public, used to literary effects and to the brilliance of the literary formula (often at the expense of logical coherence), Greimas was deceptive, too academic, and in a certain way, too clear. He did not meet the criteria of implicit taste. In contrast, one can certainly not say about Barthes and Derrida, "ce qui n'est pas clair n'est pas français" [what is not clear is not French] (Antoine de Rivarol): to consumers lacking specific competence obscurity was not obscurity—it was a sign of profundity. Neologisms were the main index of this originality and profundity. Clarity was not socially encouraged in this context of accrued competition. Although Greimas did not promise enough to the audience, to the *literati* in search of newness Greimasian semiology offered a variety of theoretical, lexical, and methodological innovations and as well as an example to follow.

The symbolic revolution in the French intellectual field could not have combined tradition and innovation without reactivating the long-term cultural memory of the French intellectual model, the "man or woman of letters." It was the simultaneous evolution of scientific and literary discourse and the expansion of the university that made possible the rapid institutionalization of semiology. This reactivation also explains why many intellectuals, like Lévi-Strauss (in *Anthropologie structurale*, 1958), Barthes, Derrida, Foucault, and Sollers, for instance, wrote essays from a new perspective on Rousseau, Mallarmé, Lautréamont—authors known to the cultivated, essentially Parisian public versed in the classics of French education. Sugar was administered with the arsenic. This is why Randall Collins's comment on Foucault's success among sociologists tells only half the story: "The amateur sociology of the Paris philosophers and literary theorists is impressive mainly to people who lack much grounding in what sociology has already achieved."[49] Indeed, these ideas were not conceived for a sociologically—or linguistically—competent public. The only competence required of the public was mastery of the local cultural conventions, that is, the knowledge and good manners relative to French literary culture.

Science, by transposition from phonology[50] or from Lévi-Straussian anthropology,[51] was mainly promoted by linguistics, which presented new intellectual instruments, and by the social sciences, which offered new objects of research such as tourism or mass communications, and in this way legitimized new products. This division of symbolic labor between linguistics and the social sciences inevitably led to the dominance of linguistic methods in the social sciences, a dominance which is currently being revised in disciplines like anthropology.[52] Greimas combined Lévi-Strauss and Propp, a synthesis he willingly describes as the result of a *bricolage*,[53] or of "practical logic." Greimas did in linguistics what Lévi-Strauss had done in anthropology and used "figuratively terms appropriated from the natural sciences."[54] He sought to formulate the elementary structure of signification[55] following Lévi-Strauss's *Structures élémentaires de la parenté* (1949), a work largely inspired by the ideas of the linguist Roman Jakobson. For Greimas, as for many other social and human scientists, the logic of scientific discovery was analogous in the natural and the linguistic sciences. For Lévi-Strauss, the logic of scientific discovery had been analogous in linguistics and the social sciences.

In some sense everything that was not valued by the accepted approaches,[56] could become valued as a reaction to the dominant hierarchies: the inside, the hidden side, became the outside, the visible side. Empirical problems could be accepted to a certain extent because of the requirements of a radical, leftist political profile, and of the rising numbers of social science students. Bourdieu's sociology profited from both of these. Existential Marxism gave way to the theoretical, structural Marxism developed by Althusser and his students at the École Normale Supérieure. Greimas was influenced by Lévi-Strauss and Dumézil in anthropology, Barthes in literary theory, Lacan in psychoanalysis, Merleau-Ponty in phenomenology (especially *Phénoménologie de la perception*, 1945), and Saussure and Hjelmslev in linguistics. The coherence of this list of names stemmed from redefinition demanded by the new positions. The list was more or less shared by other representatives of semiology. The multiple contradictions inherent in the structural position of the new discipline were not felt as such, mainly because of the structural lack of differentiation of semiology and the multiple networks between the individuals.

FROM REDEFINITION TO DIVISION

Without doubt the most influential work in semiology was Greimas's *Sémantique structurale* (1966). Deductive and systematic, it created the impression that a new science had been born.[57] Barthes's scientific response to Greimas's *Sémantique structurale* was *Système de la mode* (1967), dedicated to Greimas. In 1966, under the protection of Lévi-Strauss, the Semio-linguistics Section of the Laboratory of Social Anthropology of the Centre National de la Recherche Scientifique, the École Pratique des Hautes Études, and the Collège de France gathered together a heterogeneous group of semiologians. These included logicians (Oswald Ducrot), rhetoricians (Gérard Genette and Tzvetan Todorov), specialists in visual semiotics (Christian Metz, Anton Zemsz), linguists (Jean-Claude Coquet and Yves Gentilhomme), and philosophers of language (Julia Kristeva).[58] The new discipline's richness was in its diversity. It was a melting pot, which is characteristic of a dynamic discipline that attracts scholars from other declining subareas.

The Sixth Section of the École Pratique des Hautes Études started to organize doctoral training in semiology the same year, and in 1969 the Cercle sémiotique de Paris was established. Founding members were the linguist Émile Benveniste (president), Barthes, Lévi-Strauss, and Greimas. Barthes, with Derrida and Foucault, also took part in the orientation commission in charge of founding the new university, Paris VIII–Vincennes, in 1968. In this "Parisian village," proximity characteristic of the French intellectual field,[59] was intellectual, social, and institutional; and symbolic invention was coupled with institutional invention. Friendship also led to the exchange of ideas, services, and references. According to Greimas, "I accompanied Barthes the day he asked Lévi-Strauss to direct his thesis. Lévi-Strauss refused, but mentioned to Barthes that there existed an American translation of a certain Vladimir Propp. Barthes gave me the reference."[60] Barthes noted, that "I got into linguistics because of Greimas,"[61] and that "I owe a lot, I have said this, to conversations I had, beginning in 1950 with Greimas, who acquainted me very early with the Jakobsonian theory of shifters and the importance of certain figures, such as metaphor, metonym, catalysis, ellipsis."[62]

Benveniste was one of the examiners present at Lévi-Strauss's dissertation defence at the Sorbonne and he became a member of the editorial board of Lévi-Strauss's review *L'Homme* (1960). He was also, with Braudel and Merleau-Ponty, Lévi-Strauss's colleague at the Collège de France. Dumézil backed Lévi-Strauss when he tried to get a job at the Fifth Section of the École Pratique des Hautes Études[63] and Febvre invited Lévi-Strauss to give a lecture at the Sixth Section. Thanks to them, Lévi-Strauss worked at both sections. Greimas was appointed to the post of director of studies at the Sixth Section with the assistance of Lévi-Strauss.[64] Barthes owed his post at the school to Braudel, who was able to raise sufficient finances for the creation of sixty new positions in 1960,[65] a crucial event in the development of the human and social sciences in France.

The importance of social relations can hardly be overemphasized in this context. But forced proximity and dependence also led to brutal breaks. Moreover, as administrative rules were loose, leaving ample room for the use of personal influence, the creation, by former friends, of new groups and cliques was frequent. In Lévi-Strauss's words, Braudel was an "enlightened monarch" at the Sixth Section,[66] which he helped found. Lévi-Strauss founded the Laboratoire d'anthropologie sociale. Both he and Braudel had their reviews, *Annales* and *L'Homme*. Both were influential in publishing houses, Lévi-Strauss at Plon and Braudel at Armand Colin.

The relative lack of structural differentiation of the forming field of semiology, due to resistance to the dominant model and to the importance of common interests created by this resistance, was dominant until the end of the 1960s. This lack of structural differentiation enabled the initial institutionalization of semiology. Internal differentiation, a result of the crystallization of the diverse and often antagonistic networks, rapidly replaced multilevel alliances. This led to a loosening of the close relations between the intellectuals themselves, who were striving to create their own clientele, as well as between "their" reviews, "their" institutions, and so on. This larger fragmentation among the new generation led to a loosening of the personal relationships between major intellectuals. Lévi-Strauss's statement on his old friend Lacan testified of this process: "By then he [Lacan] had become a kind of guru, and our ties had weakened a great deal."[67]

Semiology was in a "marginal" position in the intermediate space between the literary and academic networks, and thus positioned in the most dynamic part of the field. The paradox is that this facilitated the very rapid and efficient initial development of the discipline[68] but became an obstacle to its evolution into a full discipline. The radicality of the student audience did not fit the requirements of academic respectability. In the 1970s, semiology was still largely a melting pot, where different perspectives met—"a rarely integrated discipline and methodology, more or less tolerated and most often excluded from higher education in the human sciences."[69] Thus the transition from non-existence to thorough institutionalization was interrupted, mainly due to diminishing financial investments and the resistance of the dominant sectors of the university. At the same time, the interaction between the two poles of the symbolic space diminished. The scientific pole became more and more isolated in the 1970s[70] and the cultural pole, the most dynamic part in the 1960s, boosted by the support of the cultural press, was subjected to more rapid and abrupt changes in orientation, following Parisian modes. Then, in the 1970s, Maoism and psychoanalysis became the hegemonic discourses.

For Greimas and his followers, semiology gave way to semiotics in the 1970s, leading to the separation of the discipline from the cultural pole. Meanwhile, Barthes abandoned science altogether, returning to his initial literary interests. Barthes's scientific activity has to be examined in relation to local rationales, that is, the multiple social pressures for adopting a scientific discourse, and not within the framework of an abstract construction such as "structuralism" which does not explain anything. Semiotics was semiology for the experts, a sign of disciplinary closure and monopolization of knowledge, whose discourse and objects differed from the more general cultivated discourse of the intellectual field. This led its representatives to adopt more clearly the deontology of the *savant*, thus of academic respectability, instead of intellectual radicality.

While semiology was slowly becoming semiotics, the philosophical style of most French intellectuals adapted in the 1960s to the requirements of the moment in the form of a scientific style. This scientific style had to be accessible to a young, nonexpert, intellectual audience that comprised the readership of movements such as "structuralism" and "poststructuralism." What forms did the symbolic continuity between philosophy and the human and social sciences take in the 1960s? In the next chapter, I will analyze the main tension inherent in the new approaches, that between philosophical past and scientific present.

CHAPTER 6

On Scientific Style: The Effects of Two Cultures

> Every page breathes a combination of
> logical paradox and metaphysical dramatics.
>
> Randall Collins

Institutionally, the human and social sciences were considered minor branches of philosophy until the 1950s. By being taught in secondary schools all over France, philosophy formed one of the building blocks of French culture. The problem for a philosopher-turned-human-or-social-scientist was to move from a way of thinking that emphasized the universal in the interaction between particular and universal to one which emphasized the particular.[1] In many ways, the scientific style of the 1960s was an updated philosophical style, because many human and social scientists were by training philosophers. Everyone who was a philosopher by training always had something to settle with philosophy and philosophers.[2] Otherwise doomed to remain secondary school teachers, these philosophers found in the human and social sciences refuge disciplines, in which they could use philosophical methods: "With philosophy against it!" could have been their motto.

Just as Sartre's literary works seemed to many outsiders, especially to those trained in the Anglo-American tradition, to be philosophical literature, and works such as *L'Être et le néant* and *Critique de la raison dialectique*, to be philosophical novels, even for some locals,[3] Lévi-Strauss's anthropology came across as a sort of philosophical anthropology. Foucault's history resembled philosophical history, and Bourdieu's sociology, a type of philosophical sociology. Deleuze's or Derrida's philosophy could also have been classified as "literary philosophy or philosophical literature." The tendency of all these thinkers who straddled two cultures was to adapt philosophical instruments to more specialized discourses. Colin Gordon has explained the success of

83

Foucault in France as being precisely due to "the relative richness of the relations between historical and philosophical registers in French thought."[4] But Gordon failed to go further, that is, to emphasize the role of the dominant intellectual habitus and the institutional framework—the mold—in which intellectual ambitions were created. In view of this institutional framework, it is not at all surprising that outside of France the doors to departments of literature have been open and those to departments of philosophy closed to many of these philosophers turned specialists. The difference between France and other countries is that specialized discourses are defined in different ways.[5]

Specialists who did not have two cultures appeared to resent the "short-cut" offered to the philosopher/specialist, viewing it as a way to avoid pain-staking work and getting one's hands dirty. For many of these specialists, the tone of the philosophers turned human and social scientists was too impatient. Not surprisingly, one of the main tensions of the human and social sciences was between specialists in these disciplines, who could engage in solving small problems analyzed with specialized techniques, and those having two cultures, for whom small problems were psychologically and socially unre-warding, unless they could be shown to represent big ones: the tensions between the *savant* and the *philosophe* were constant. Beginning in the 1960s, the latter could retreat into either philosophical or specialized styles, schemas of thought, or problems, thus always avoiding either specialized or philo-sophical critique.

According to philosophical criteria of excellence, every thinker had to start from scratch, from the beginning. This same back-to-basics effect appeared in the theoretical discourses of the 1960s, which referred back to Freud, Marx, Durkheim, Weber, by the minutest reading, following the classical *explication de texte*, of a few selected passages, translated into French. This tendency can be explained by the fact that there was no technique that could be transmitted from one generation of philosophers to another. There was thus no such thing as philosophical competence. Althusser's "technique" consisted of spontaneously contrasting and demarcating different elements and learning new ideas by hearsay from his friends at the École Normale Supérieure.[6] He admitted not avoiding the uses of paradoxes and provocations, "in order to awaken the astonishment, admiration (!) and unbelief of the third party, to my great con-fusion and pride."[7] Lévi-Strauss's style is described by Maybury-Lewis as "a sort of Chinese puzzle, full of diversions, false trails, metaphoric asides, and inconclusive perorations."[8] In the 1960s, the pressures of being original were especially strong, and every thinker wanted to present something entirely new, different, unthought.[9]

Philosophical discourse did not find real solutions to philosophical prob-lems, for instance, the "mind-body" problem. Usually pseudo-solutions were produced, or specific problems were just forgotten or displaced. Raymond Aron put this quite poignantly: "In order to solve the old problem of the unity of theory and practice, he [Althusser] calls theory theoretical practice."[10] According to local rationales, it was often enough to present a problem verbally or textually in order to create the illusion that a solution to the same problem had been produced. Confirmations and verifications or "proof," were found in concepts, not in events in the "real" world.[11] Also, simplistic theses, arguments, or whole "-isms," preferably in shocking formulations, were often attributed to previous thinkers or enemies, labelled as "naive thinking,"[12] formulated expressly in order to give a pretext for presenting the author's own thesis. "Naive thinking" was the precondition for the existence of "sophisticated thinking," usually one's own. In order to prevent criticism, the thesis of the author was presented as though it was necessarily going to be misunderstood and deformed.

Local philosophical and theoretical discourse was constructed against the background of imaginary "naive thinking" or "common sense," or, as in the 1960s in the human and social sciences, an "ideology," "event," or set of "pre-constructed objects." The myth of philosophical or scientific thinking required a countermyth, consisting of bourgeois or "naive" thinking. A more developed variation of this technique of prefabricated myths enabled the intellectual to attribute to others something which nobody has ever said. "You thought it was as "x" said? How silly . . . Well, it isn't!" The author could thus congratulate him- or herself for attacking prejudices nobody ever had.

The human and social scientific outlook of the 1950s and 1960s shared with nineteenth-century positivist worldview the ideal of scientific optimism which gave a license to write about anything to "solve" everything. In scientific discourse, experimental method legitimized the universalization of a single observation: a well-proven experiment was valid universally, as Durkheim had already stated.[13] If everyone used the same technique, no one could be blamed for using it. In the humanities, the technique used was the *explication de texte*, the cornerstone of the classical humanities, updated to suit the requirements of the moment through incorporation into semiological methods.[14]

In times of rapid social change and circulation of ideas like the 1960s, epistemologies of urgency[15] were needed. Intellectual ambitions were targeted at creating a "system"—this time not philosophical but rather scientific. Thinking in systems presented a double advantage: the creator of a "system" could avoid the painstaking and slow work of analyzing details or whole works, and a "system" was generally immune to attacks from specialists.[16] Further, specialized discourse could always be disqualified as trivial. Also, both the human and social scientists and the audience were used to dealing with universal problems, impressive in their sheer proportions. For minds used to systems,[17] details did not have any value. Analysis did not start from a specific problem—as it would in the case of a specialist—but from a universal principle like reason or inequality, for instance.[18] This tyranny of the universal which was in reality a particular, historically determined viewpoint, enabled the scholar to integrate all particular viewpoints into his/her framework, since from the point of view of the system all other viewpoints are particular viewpoints. However, the "system" did not necessarily refer only to a theoretical construction, but also to practical logic, to a way of doing things.

The example of Althusser illustrates such a "way of doing things." Before starting to read philosophical texts, Althusser would draw up a few formulas or sketches, reconstructing the general traits of the philosophy in question. Only after these preliminary operations, would he carefully read a few selected passages of the work in question.[19] Thus, in a sense what was sought had to be known beforehand. By presenting his "philosophical technique" openly and acknowledging his—and others—ignorance of many philosophical works, Althusser, probably due to his mental illness, in fact broke with a specific form of symbolic domination in the French intellectual field. Althusser's auto-biography is a unique document in the sense that in it a key intellectual figure reveals his and his fellow intellectuals' limits, anxieties, and fears, as well as the close relationship between institutional framework (the École Normale Supérieure) and discursive practices (criteria of excellence). The specific form of symbolic domination is based on a logic of the oblique, on the fear of ridicule, of the mask falling, and of ignorance and mediocrity being revealed.

> Of course my philosophical culture of texts was rather limited. Descartes and Malebranche I knew well; Spinoza, a bit; Aristotle, the sophists, and the stoics not at all; Platon, pretty well; Kant not at all; some Hegel; and finally, I knew a few passages from Marx very well.[20]

The type of philosophical habitus represented by Althusser was shared by the human and social scientists who combined two cultures. They transferred this habitus—these reflexes and habit-patterns—to anthropology (Lévi-Strauss), sociology (Bourdieu), or history (Foucault). For Lévi-Strauss, Bourdieu, and Foucault the "structure" was initially the main focus of research, which guaranteed scientificity. By boldly creating their own approaches and "systems" these intellectuals transformed points of discussion and deliberation into objects of acceptance or rejection. Once accepted, neologisms such as episteme, genealogy, and others, which got their meaning and function from this set of relationships and which formed this system, would be accepted with it. Acceptance of the system was almost equivalent to religious conversion, the opening up of a new vistas, new realities, and new problems.

The philosophical habitus had, however, disastrous effects on the relationships these individuals had with their work and with other intellectuals: their system was everything, all else was irrelevant. This rigidity supported other developments: the fragmentation of intellectual discourse, the ambitions of the politicized students, and the logic of the oblique, of the obscure, and of the secret.[21] Secretiveness and obscurity were favored over an open and straight-forward approach.[22]

Elusiveness characterized this literary-philosophical style:[23] nothing was ever explained, attacks were always indirect. In this shadow dance, enormous sentences were coupled with individual ticks, neologisms, analogies: these discursive rules were transferred to the new sciences in the 1950s and 1960s. But if the veracity of the ideas could always be questioned, their ambition was as such irrefutable.

The privileged mode of demonstration was the use of tautologies, an appeal to "internal coherence" and to a common fund of belief transmitted through education. This is why such a sweeping schema as the Bachelardian "epistemological break" between science and non-science fit the human and social scientific ways of thinking so well. Its premises were grounded mainly in nineteenth-century scientific discourse.[24] In fact, the transfer of this epistemology was the central part of the conceptual apparatus transferred from philosophy to the human and social sciences.[25] This epistemology was thought to guarantee scientificity. But it also reinforced the relegation of facts and quantification to an inferior position in relation to concepts,[26] although statistical techniques, for instance, were partially introduced in order to counter Anglo-Saxon dominance, which had a strong influence on the criteria of social-scientific excellence. For instance, in sociology, the reaction to Anglo-Saxon dominance led Bourdieu to combine French social science (Durkheim, Mauss, Lévi-Strauss) with French epistemology (Bachelard, Cavaillès, Canguilhem, Duhem, for instance) and French statistical techniques (Benzécri's analysis of correspondence).

In the scientific style of the 1960s, sweeping generalizations and abstractions relative to history or to the functioning of society were combined with speculation impressive in its sheer proportions. Philosophical problems were introduced with conceptual techniques of argumentation and in literary philosophical style.[27] Plato and Kant were more contemporary than Einstein or Heisenberg: chronology was just an illusion, as was progress of knowledge. Diverse slogans like "man is dead" or "the author is dead" and old philosophical techniques, like those which circulated among students in schools before exams, were also widely used. One way an author could treat a subject was to say, "This should be done," or, "This should be clarified," and then not do it but assume it had been dealt with. Another was to extrapolate from an individual example to a vast generalization, linked by a "Thus." The heuristic motto could be: Think about the particular such as an individual or a text, but write universally using terms like "idealism," "objectivism," or "psychologism." The incentive to theorize on the basis of one case, to develop "isms," was strong. Through rhetorical formulas, the author confused the readers and created specific effects among the readers, who were able to find confirmation from their own life experiences of these general and arbitrary arguments. It was very difficult to dismiss such disorienting "evidence": "Who is man anyway?" "Aren't we ruled by language?"

The incredible success of the human and social sciences in France from the late 1950s to the early 1970s has to do with the fact that the dual-culture philosophers could appeal to a large audience, become cultural heroes, and monopolize the highest positions; whereas those trained in specific areas remained "dry" academics, slow and conservative in their movements and thoughts. Further, by producing vast, all-encompassing theories—thus satisfying the intellectual, moral and political ambitions of the audience—the human and social sciences inherited the unrealistic pretensions and ambitions of philosophical discourse. The theoretico-political radicalism of philosophical style also fulfilled the criteria of journalistic language in its search for general and definitive answers, a crucial link in the 1960s. These generalizations helped to keep the media and laymen interested.

Typically, for a member of this social group, study of a specific problem in the French, or in some other context at a specific moment in time would only serve as a springboard for an abstract, theoretical exposition of the particular case, camouflaged by neologisms, tautologies, and complex philosophical side developments. The foreign reader was faced with a huge generalization, based on the minutest analysis of one case, a real abyss of Greek and Latin signs, of German speculative philosophy, and of references to French writers of the nineteenth-century. To a reader unfamiliar with this specific culture of the oblique and of originality these signs did not fulfill their role as sign-posts. For foreigners these signs were not indexical signs, but irrefutable and sometimes irritating symbols and allegories. One consequence of this has been the often uncritical reception of these ideas outside France. Creating one's own, preferably cryptic theory was the surest way to achieve a situation of irrefutability, which implied that the system's creator was its only legitimate interpreter. This power constellation, which was based on the dependency of the reader on the creator, was expressed by an outside observer, brought up according to different social conventions and rules of excellence, in the following way: "At a recent meeting hosted by the marxist journal *Arena*, a discussion about deconstruction and politics raised such conflicting representations of Derrida's ideas that it was suggested as a joke that he should be phoned and thus settle the issues with a definitive statement."[28] The prospect of a straight answer becomes a joke. But from the point of view of a celebrated French intellectual, any particular objection to one's own theory must be a sign either of incomprehension or of an unwillingness to understand.

One of the discursive conditions of possibility of this kind of discourse was that there be no control mechanisms between particular and universal. Unusual encounters were a criterion of intellectual excellence in theoretical essays. The tendency to abstraction relied mostly on the intuition of the observer or researcher, not on the explicit use of rules and research techniques and their reproduction. This artistic and Romantic posture also implicitly disfavored extensive fieldwork or any kind of complex comparative study. This attitude toward detail was found in the philosophical stances of some French sociolo - gists, who also thereby reproduced a certain implicit psychological theory. Their anti-empirist epistemology and essentially conceptual cosmology would lead them to perceive phenomena using a few variables and seeing each case as a totality, a total social fact, often in opposition to Anglo-Saxon epistemologies, which were labelled naive empirism. Following this Spinozism, the whole could be seen in the part and the part gave the key to the whole. A specific case would be formulated in universal terms, from the title and down to the finest detail. *Homo Academicus* could not be titled *Homo Academicus Gallicus circa 1968.* Foucault's *Surveiller et punir: naissance de la prison* (1975) was based on selected French material but pretended to analyze a general case. This was the only mode of existence for the particular, the particularities of the particular being uninteresting.[29] Thus it was not surprising that many human and social sciences have remained at the level of theoretical programs, aspiring to found scientific approaches.[30]

SCHOLARLY AND AVANT-GARDE MODELS

Would it be generalizing too much to say that a similar discursive style can be detected in such a disparate group as Barthes, Lévi-Strauss, Foucault, Lacan, Bourdieu, and Kristeva? I think not, because to varying degrees, common socio-historical characteristics and constraints—explored for specific areas in earlier chapters—united these intellectuals. Their discursive strategies differed from one another, for obvious reasons. But they had this is common: in their works they combined literature with emotion, wit, rapidity, and suggestiveness, and science with precision, the quest for truth, and stylistic heaviness, thereby fulfilling the requirements of grandeur. To varying degrees, the dilemma of this second postwar intellectual generation—a transitional one between those of *philosophe* and *savant*—was that it had to say something new and interesting in such a way that would satisfy the criteria of reception and the criteria of their intellectual heritage. For this generation, cultural celebrity was the solution to succession. If the "intellectual," as opposed to "academic," dimension became preponderant in social scientific texts, formal models and statistics could still be used, but lightly.

Accessibility to a scattered audience was an important characteristic of the most visible intellectual works created in the 1960s. The role of accessibility to a wide public also varied for the texts of specific thinkers at different times. For instance, sociological works analyzing literature could be constructed so as to appeal to the specialized audience (for instance, most of Robert Escarpit's work), or to the large intellectual public.[31] In the latter case, symbolic heterogeneity was greater. Criteria of reception explain why sociological texts destined to a wide public (cultural sociology or sociology of the intellectuals) tended so widely to re-use the French literary-philosophical heritage, authors such as Flaubert, Leibniz, Spinoza, Kant, Balzac, and Proust. Literary culture was essentially scholarly culture, which for a long time had challenged, in the form of literary realism,[32] the social sciences.[33]

Schematically, the social constraints imposed by the large public on discursive practices could be the following: the topic under scrutiny had to be a familiar one, that is relative to French education or culture, or to a universal problem such as freedom or death; the style had to be literary and the argument—presented in a simple, suggestive, and often tautological form—had to be convincing morally, politically, and intellectually. The intellectual cosmopolitanism[34] of French cultural discourse did not encourage the use of technical language. The style had to minimize sociological and/or historical aspects—that is, to stay at a conceptual level which could be understood irrespective of personal situation. It was often necessary—especially in situations of urgency as the 1960s—to be interesting at the expense of being precise.

The wide use and misuse of terminology drawn from structural linguistics by authors such as Roland Barthes and Jacques Lacan was a reflection of these local discursive constraints. In postulating a structure as an *a priori* of research, as was done in practice, it was impossible to separate cases in which a structure was an adequate presupposition from those in which it was not. Structures would have been everywhere if the definition of a structure had was not been related to the material under study. Further, it was impossible to differentiate structure and event from one another, an isolated case or manifestation from a more general pattern. Likewise, if a structure was postulated, it would not be possible to discriminate between indices of the existence of this structure and non-indices. Everything became a manifestation of the existence of the structure. To postulate a "hidden level," be it structural or unconscious, was disastrous if control mechanisms were not introduced. And they were not. Anything could become an index of the existence of structures. Thus structures and indices would be nowhere. However, from the point of view of intellectuals, this discursive condition was ideal for innovation, for it enabled them to use their imagination and culture.

In the drive for abstraction and profundity, a few older philosophical techniques were widely used in relation to an "other level."[35] One consisted simply of isolating a few characteristics, declaring them part of a structure, and of explaining their existence using a structure. The problem of course is that this kind of tautology does not explain anything; yet, at times, authors such as Lévi-Strauss do come very close to this. A second technique, widely used by social scientists, consisted in asserting that the proof of the existence of certain characteristics was in the denial of their existence by the individuals to whom they were attributed. This was very dangerous, because anything the scholar wanted to believe—for instance, that a particular social group was exerting dominance—could be legitimized, especially when it was denied by those it concerned. All these techniques must to be viewed, I think, in relation to the imperatives of inherited universal philosophical discourse, the "local cultural habit of rhetoric and abstraction,"[36] and the intuitive universal genius behind it. Prisoners of an illusory grandeur, thinkers brought up with these illusions did not usually see them as illusions.

Linguists' and semiologists'—specialists'—evaluations of the uses of linguistic terms and schemas by the most visible members of the human and social scientific intelligentsia have been devastating.[37] Georges Mounin analyzed the discourses of Lévi-Strauss, Lacan, and Barthes from the point of view of the misuses of Saussurian structural linguistics. Adriaens strongly criticized Julia Kristeva's use of formal models in her semanalysis.[38] These—and other—critiques have not been popular, however. Sweeping generalizations and intellectual excitement have much more appeal than meticulous reading, especially when the intellectuals under scrutiny had gained worldwide recognition and when the audience shared their cultural taste.

Creating interest and effect in a work were crucial for a thinker seeking recognition among the large public. Accordingly, terms and schemas were borrowed in seeming disorder from other disciplines. Examples abound of thinkers combining specialized with philosophical or linguistic terms. Bourdieu relied heavily on economic and philosophical terminology using concepts like capital, investment, credit, doxa, and habitus. Greimas drew upon physical chemistry for terms like isotopy and modality. Kristeva and Lacan borrowed terms from logic[39] and Heideggerian philosophy, Foucault looked to historical and linguistic discourse for his episteme and discursive rules; and Lévi-Strauss adopted a linguistic and psychoanalytical vocabulary.[40]

All the discourses also had to satisfy the requirements of the leftist political profile of most of the young intellectual audience. In Vincent Descombes's words, "Until 1968, epistemology was broadly to the left and metaphysics to the right."[41] This political profile explains the superficial uses of terms such as dialectics, which usually meant interaction, diachrony (which meant history), or the transfer of sociological categories (like "bourgeois art") into research on art and literature. The use of metaphors of diverse kinds tended to be implicit. These metaphors were rarely developed, outside of superficial similarities.

Thinkers favored the search for effect rather than deep conceptual development in terms of identity and contradiction. In order to be effective, analogical reasoning, which facilitated unusual encounters, demanded the suppression of obstacles between particular and general cases. For philosophical purposes superficial similarity was enough, and it enhanced the widespread imaginary scientism.

Many intellectuals, especially the ones that were the most market-oriented—like Roland Barthes, Jacques Lacan, and Philippe Sollers—used polemical tactics to combine politics and culture. Numerous representatives of the human and social sciences developed a stylistic mannerism,[42] especially because of the political ambitions of their audience. The most subtle stylistic combination used was the defensive offensive, a technique mastered especially by Lacan in his *Écrits*. Here, he first very aggressively attacked his opponents, then retreated into defense of the validity of his own method, and this followed with sweeping generalizations. Alternating between aggressive attacks and ultracomplex syntax developed by Mallarmé and Breton, Lacan effectively combined academic syntax and literary-political effect. This type of polemical discourse interested the media. Such also enabled intellectuals to accumulate visibility in the media.

Another technique was to incorporate possible counterarguments in order to dismiss them in advance. Terminological synonymy and neologism were also used, because these were the most obvious and most superficial ways of showing novelty. It was not necessary to understand the status of the term "diachrony" in Saussure's linguistics in order to use it in one's own research as a synonym for "history" or "change." For instance, instead of using the normal term *significatif* ("meaningful"), during the 1960s Barthes increasingly began using the term *signifiant* as its synonym.[43] In the eyes of the readers, this made Barthes's work even more semiological. Under closer scrutiny, its "scientificity" could easily be denied, but voices of protest against the uses of semiology were quickly and effectively—that is, collectively—silenced. Critiques such as those of Mounin or Fougeyrollas seemed to just spoil the fun.

In structural constructivism a whole array of terms were developed: habitus and field, for instance. Additional colorations were added, new terms invented in order to anticipate critique and to guarantee irrefutability and originality, leading to a veritable terminological jungle, as I have tried to show earlier. Greimas was a master at transferring complex terms and redefining them.[44] Derrida "invented" différance and grammatology; Kristeva semanalysis,[45] intertextuality, and dialogism;[46] and Foucault genealogy, archeology, and a host of technical terms borrowed from linguistics. For avant-garde writers, these academics legitimized a scientific and objective critique of old literature and Sartrian philosophy. This path quickly became the only legitimate way to be modern, leading to collective censorship and self-censorship.[47] For marginal academics, these writers offered broad support for a moral critique of the academic establishment.

Common to all these intellectuals was the use of terms such as isomorphism, homology, diachrony, synchrony. These were mostly used purely metaphorically, as *a priori* of "scientific" research. Following local rationales, there was no need to demonstrate that a homological relationship effectively existed between two structures: it was enough that it be postulated. Sophisticated thinking required depth. "Structures" enabled one to organize the research and claim a scientific status for the work. In order to distance themselves from the linear and scholarly formal construction thesis-antithesis-synthesis, some authors further developed the technique of circular construction in their works and in their argumentation, a trick inherited from philosophical discourse. However, these techniques and terms such as "isomorphism" and "structure" were more than formal characteristics of the discourses. These forms were at the core of specific habit-patterns and thus part of sociopsychological properties of these individuals.

The results of the intellectual and scientific endeavors of the thinkers of this generation have been totally disproportionate to their declared ambitions to create the "science of the text" or, reveal "the structure of the mind." The act of faith represented by intellectuals' *oeuvre* was—and still is—nourished by the anticipation that they would become, if not in this life, then at least in the future, *post mortem* scientific pioneers, *savants*. Prisoners of the past, their only master could be the future.

REPUBLICAN EDUCATION AND THE INDIVIDUAL CREATOR

Differences between works, their subject matter, styles and the information they convey are clear and unambiguous. It is easy to recognize a text by Foucault, or one by Lacan. Explaining in a general way the ideas conveyed by some works, and even introducing local aspects and contradictions in the works, does not pose problems. What outside observers may miss is the ambitions and educational background of the works—the mold in which these works were produced. Ideas can be exported, but the sociopsychological mechanisms, the imperatives of grandeur, are not exportable. Just as wine turns into vinegar, these sociopsychological mechanisms turn into something they are not, namely, individual characteristics of individual intellectuals. Instead they should be clarified as belonging to the sociohistorical characteristics of a specific culture.

Socially reproduced by the education systems, the ambitions of thinkers vary according to different cultures. It is no surprise that intellectual activity would take a total moral and intellectual character in a sociohistorical context such as the French intellectual field where education took on total character. For the students at the Écoles Normales Supérieures, or the *convicts* as Durkheim used to say,[48] the school was everything and gave everything. According to Alvin Gouldner, in some cultures and institutions thinkers have to have an "Olympus complex"[49] in order to be credible, in order to fulfill the requirements of intellectual legitimacy and emulate their models. In other cultures, this kind of style is discouraged. When discouraged, the differences between the nominal, declared value of a work or idea, and the real value will tend to be narrower than in a culture where the inflation of nominal value is the only way to point to the real value of the work. In France, the more prestigious the institution to which the author is affiliated, the more "added value" or "prestige" will be given to the work, the more likely it is that obscurity will become the sign of profundity and that incomprehension will be attributed to the receiver, not the producer. These modalities of belief have to do with the whole system of conventions and rules which govern the logic of symbolic power. In France, the sources of added prestige equivalent to American institutions such as Harvard or Yale have traditionally been the Écoles Normales Supérieures.

One element of the logic of symbolic power is the set of rules which control the position of a master *qua* master, of the individual creator. In the French intellectual field of the 1960s, where the "Olympus complex" was part of the codified definition of legitimacy, the position of the master *qua* master was very fragile. Pretensions and ambitions had to be affirmed continuously. This is especially true when the legitimizing ideology was science, which required openness. As in this context the rules of legitimacy included the nominal inflation of value,[50] there was no way for an intuitive universal genius or intellectual to devalue his/her position as a master through open self-analysis, for instance. Perhaps these rules are best illustrated by showing the limits of their applicability. For an established member of the social-scientific intelligentsia, the only form this self-analysis could take was an indirect, scientifically integrated self-examination, as in the case of Bourdieu's *Homo Academicus*. The differences between sociologists engaged in different national fields can be examined by comparing the positions of Alvin Gouldner in the United States and Bourdieu in France. Because of the sheer size of the U.S. field, its logic of straightforwardness, and the relative autonomy of each of its parts, Gouldner can name his opponents; whereas Bourdieu has to use more indirect ways of indicating his criticism.

In *Homo Academicus*, the narrator, the individual with a body, is separated from the narrator's sociological identity, which is integrated as a specific position in the framework of the sociological reconstruction of the object of research.[51] The only way for the narrator to speak of himself in his own sociological reconstruction is by the introduction of a *Doppelgänger* to analyze the social group of which he is part. Although the introduction of this literary and artistic innovation[52] into social-scientific discourse is not satisfying as such, it has to be taken as a courageous attempt if not to transgress social limits at least to point to them indirectly and displace the center of attention to the relationship between subject and object. Instead of being considered only as a traditional scholarly study, as a simple object, *Homo Academicus* can thus also be analyzed as an indexical sign and a work of self-analysis.

In Bourdieu's work, the object of research—which includes a rationalized subject of research—is necessarily approached transversely, not frontally. This logic of the oblique cannot be decoded by applying a logic of the straightforward, with the rules relative to a different logic of symbolic power. The conception by the author of *Homo Academicus* is placed at the center of a contradiction, that between the autonomy of the sociologist and the socially bound actions of social subjects, including the sociologist himself. Most of the reviews published on *Homo Academicus* have missed the point of the dynamic between subject and object of research, as well as the traces of this dynamic in the text itself. As the relationship between subject and object is not frontal, it would be counterproductive to dismiss the work for not being frontal, as an empirist—whose set of research assumptions include the separation of subject and object—might be tempted to do. The question of objectivity is, according to Bourdieu's point of view, a question of the relationship of the subject to the object. A simple frontal constellation is replaced by a more complicated relationship, born of a consciousness of complicity, of similarity: a Proustian inspiration. Even at this level of an individual work, the logic of symbolic power directs the elaboration of the text in complex ways. Everything cannot be said, and the little that is said is said obliquely. Bourdieu's own opinions are presented by characterization of the social group to which he belongs and whose members have two cultures. Does the position of the subject require constant affirmation of a position external to the object? To a degree, yes, but not as much as in a frontal constellation. How is mastery shown? Can it be shown by the introduction of even contradictory material into the text? These are a few questions which comparative intellectual history or sociology might try to answer.

If French intellectuals cannot unravel portions of the discursive rules relative to intellectual work, except indirectly or in exceptional circumstances, it is because they are the prisoners of their Republican education and because they have accepted a whole set of assumptions, about themselves, their peers and the "outsiders" as unquestionable facts. Open denunciation of grandeur would go against everything they have been taught. Self-denial would mean denial of their own positions and of the ideology governing intellectual work. It would relax the hold of all the social bonds that form these subjects as they are: it would be worse than the crumbling of illusions. Accordingly, in order to dominate symbolically, Bourdieu has to conform to his creations, to construct his own life as it has been constructed in his works. In this way, scientific meaning is given, transforming contingencies of time and space into necessities of time and space. However, the narrator's appearance has to be concordant with the public image he gives of himself. In this way, he is the first to conform to the image he constructs of himself: in order to be convincing, he must start acting that way.

Further, by presenting choices as necessities Bourdieu clears his conscience. If education gave everything, it has to be blamed for everything. The disappointment felt toward Republican education, "hypnotized by an illusory grandeur," is parallel to a feeling of inadequacy nourished by illusion, that of scientific discourse, which has become Bourdieu's own illusion. By denouncing this "illusory grandeur," Bourdieu denounces the others, and he denounces himself indirectly by naming the group to which he belongs. He points to "it"— to himself: *de te fabula narratur.*

In the 1960s, the avant-garde was redefining itself in opposition to Sartre and the literary establishment. What forms did the complicity between the various academic and literary avant-gardes take? I will try to clarify this problem in the following part by examining the literary avant-garde, the *Nouveau Roman* and part of its "second generation," grouped around the review *Tel Quel.* If the scholars and academics of this new intellectual generation combined science and popularity, so did the writers and novelists. Following the example of the social- and human-scientific intelligentsia, writers sought to be scientific[53] and objective. Also, by specializing in theoretical essays, they combined literature and theoretical reasoning, thus filling the gap between science and literature. This enabled them to distance themselves from writers such as Paulhan and Sartre, members of the previous generation of intellectual nobility.

Part III

Iconoclasm and Parody: The Literary Avant-Garde Against Sartre

> It was first concerning commitment that the
> *Nouveau Roman*—and this time I am also
> talking on behalf of my friends, including
> Duras and Pinget—would confront Sartre.
>
> Alain Robbe-Grillet

CHAPTER 7

System of Succession and System of Coronation

> A group exists when it is named.
>
> Jérôme Lindon

From a sociohistorical point of view the *Nouveau Roman*, like other modern intellectual movements, was in large part the creation of cultural journalists. The academician Émile Henriot was the first to use the term "nouveau roman" in *Le Monde* in 1957. However, he used it only to refer to the novels written by the young, which he considered obscure and incoherent. By using this term Henriot could review in the same article two very different works, Nathalie Sarraute's *Tropismes* and Robbe-Grillet's *La Jalousie*. Robbe-Grillet and Lindon, who was Robbe-Grillet's publisher, had the idea of capitalizing on the first letters of the term invented by Henriot. In this way, the term "nouveau roman" was consciously transformed[1] into a sign, the *Nouveau Roman*, which made possible the creation of a new literary identity based in a scientific literature. With the creation of a sign composed of indexical, iconic, and symbolic relations, a new literary school, the *Nouveau Roman* was born. From an arbitrary name it became a social force, drawing new authors to the publishing house Minuit.

This unity between some writers and their works was further enhanced by the objectifying power of a photograph taken by the Italian Mario Dondero, who worked for *L'Espresso*, in front of Minuit. Cultural journalists were eager not to miss anything in the Parisian literary scene and the coining of the phrase was an instant success. In August 1958, *Esprit* published the first special number on the new school, which was also called the "new realism," "the school of refusal," or even the "anti-novel."[2] In fact, the name itself was both completely unimportant, that is, in terms of what it actually said, and extremely significant. A literary school does not exist without being named. But the reason for the success of this sign went deeper than the modish search for a new name because of the use of the term "new," which could also be found in other areas of French social life, like cooking (*nouvelle cuisine*), wine (*Beaujolais nouveau*), art (*art nouveau*), and philosophy (*nouveaux philosophes*).

Labelling or the creation of an order of succession by creating a conceptual pair like "structuralism-poststructuralism" or "modernism-postmodernism" contributes, through a process of social magic, to the transformation of current novelties, known by the few, into future myths. The success of the *Nouveau Roman* is a result of the combination of literary succession and of literary creation or transgression. The hegemonic literary school is declared old and relegated to a distant past. The *Nouveau Roman* both had common properties with previous literary schools and referred to—in an ambiguous way—new works and writers. As a sign, the *Nouveau Roman* was part of a complex set of stylistic, thematic, philosophical, and political relationships. It is from this cluster that its power stemmed. If unity of literary style was not found between certain works, it was imposed on them, despite even the protests of their writers, because the symbolic death of the old (pre-, proto-) was the condition for the existence of the new (post-, new). According to one critic, "Butor is the anti-Proust."[3] This radicality was also emphasized by Barthes, the most visible pro–*Nouveau Roman* literary critic of the moment:

> Here too we must recall the traditional background against which Robbe-Grillet's endeavor occurs: the novel long established as the experience of a depth: a social depth with Balzac and Zola, a "psychological" depth with Flaubert, a memorial depth with Proust. The novel has always determined its terrain as *interior* to man or society; and there has always been, in the novelist, a corresponding mission to excavate, to mine out.[4]

As the term *Nouveau Roman* became more and more commonly used to refer to specific individuals and to a certain literary style, the anticipations, disappointments and hopes drawn from literary and intellectual history were quickly mobilized behind the new sign and what it represented. The lack of understanding of Marcel Proust's and the Surrealists's contemporaries was reminisced about[5] and interviews and reviews of the new *enfants terribles* of French literature followed at an incredible pace.[6] When Robbe-Grillet's *Gommes* was published, the names of Kafka, Simenon, and Graham Greene were invoked.[7] This chaos of stories, judgments, true and false anecdotes, glorifications, and comparisons worked as a powerful mechanism whereby certain qualities, or literary gifts, were celebrated collectively. The hygienic and surgical side of this revolution[8] and the absence of moral preoccupation and of man were emphasized.[9] Philippe Sollers, a newcomer at the end of the 1950s and today one of France's leading writers, described in the following passage what recognition meant to a beginner:

I was surprised. I had done, like that, a few scales, and everybody applauded: I was disturbed. . . . Almost everybody seemed to think I was gifted, in advance, although I didn't feel ready yet, I still felt behind.[10]

Struck by the magic wand, he became himself the most zealous believer in his talents. Past literary achievements—the glory and greatness of French literary tradition—had to be surpassed, which created a constantly precarious situation. Were the young writers worthy or not? Thus, the primary function of signs such as *Nouveau Roman* was to present as novelties events which, for the writers implicated in them, often did not amount to anything special. Publicly presented as breaking with the past, the writers were literally caught up in the struggle between past achievements, present necessities, and future glorification, a struggle in which all writers were implicated. A successor to Malraux could not be of lesser caliber than Malraux. Grandeur required grandeur.

If the *Nouveau Roman* was a complicated phenomena—was it just a publisher's invention to keep up the rhythm of literature and the succession of important happenings and charismatic figures?—a concept like "the second generation of the *Nouveau Roman*" could seem even more difficult to grasp. The first generation is already difficult to analyze because of referential ambiguity.[11] If that which precedes has not been defined in a satisfactory way, how can one define that which follows, the "second generation of the *Nouveau Roman*"? If the similarities between that which follows and that which precedes—the successor and the predecessor—have not been established, how can an order of succession be constructed?

In fact, the second generation does not simply succeed the first generation, come after the pioneers, follow their footsteps, or stand on their shoulders. The second can either reject the preceding, as the *Nouveau Roman* rejected traditional novel, or legitimize the preceding as the first, the original—or in other terms, the category of reference and symbol of a new order (old novel–new novel). Thus, from the point of view of literary succession, the second generation is indeed even more important than the first generation. A literary revolution like the *Nouveau Roman* can succeed only if it is followed by a group of various legitimizers and followers. These have to be more the bodies of a literary language than the creators of a new one. They ensure the passage from objectifications as signs to signs as literary canons. For this reason, succession without creating a new literary group has serious drawbacks for the reputations of the young writers who will form the second generation.

In the French literary scene of the 1950s, certain mechanisms of symbolic and economic recognition, which due to morphological changes mainly in the literary public had not existed before, started to exist at the avant-garde pole of the literary field. For young writers, conditions had never been better. They were given credit before even having shown their skills as writers, which was possible only in a context where literature is the focus of attention of all those interested in culture. It had been decided that some of these unknown writers would be geniuses.

The most important of these mechanisms was new literary prizes. The most visible of these was the Médicis, which was created by the writer and editor Alain Robbe-Grillet in 1957. Robbe-Grillet was the best-known member of the new literary movement, the *Nouveau Roman*. The jury of the Médicis Prize included writers and critics close to Robbe-Grillet, such as Nathalie Sarraute and Roland Barthes. They were opposed to traditional French literature, the representatives of which saw Robbe-Grillet's works as "devilishly simplistic" or even "an imposture."[12] In a 1955 review of *Gommes* in *Critique*, Barthes, on the other hand, emphasized Robbe-Grillet's novelty, which was in stark contrast to classical standards:

> This mode of iteration is quite different from the thematics of classical authors. The repetition of a theme postulates a depth, the theme is a sign, the symptom of an internal coherence. In Robbe-Grillet, on the contrary, the constellations of objects are not expressive but creative; their purpose is not to reveal but to perform; they have a dynamic, not an heuristic role; before they appear, there exists nothing of what they will produce for the reader: they make the crime, they do not betray it: in a word, they are literal.[13]

If the Médicis Prize began as a small prize compared to important prizes like the Renaudot or the Goncourt, today it is one of the most prestigious. An indication of the working of the literary field and of its temporal structure is that the Goncourt was itself created in the nineteenth century to promote young writers as a reaction to the Academy: its fate was also to become, slowly but surely, a consecrator of traditional literature. The Médicis Prize, by pointing to quality, enabled young, unknown beginners, to be recognized by a wide public as being talented and promising writers. This widely publicized prize superseded the narrow, specialized recognition which had previously been the lot of young writers in avant-garde circles, thus creating a totally novel situation. As the dimensions of both economic and symbolic recognition changed drastically and as the size of the literary market grew, a writer could be both an iconoclast and a recognized author, just like Lévi-Strauss and Foucault in the human sciences. The distance between iconoclasm and anonymity on the one hand and literary fame on the other hand became very short as the rhythm of production accelerated. Iconoclasm, through systematic presentation of what is current as already outdated, became the most rapid way to attain literary recognition. The social visibility of iconoclast artists was far superior to those of other groups.

The condition for this change in the temporality of the field[14] was the structural transformation of the literary field as a whole due to the gradual rise in

"November 1990. Sade enters La Pléiade. Hell on parchment paper. La Pléiade—the voluptuous pleasure of reading." Catalogue Pléiade, Gallimard, no. 90, 1990, p. 4. Reprinted with permission of the publisher.

Illustration 3. Consecration of literary iconoclasm. Advertisement for Sade's complete works.

the number of products, writers, journalists and readers. This system of prizes was also a system of transfer of symbolic legitimacy to the chosen ones, who would become the legitimate successors and, by a detour, legitimize the first generation as a first generation. It is no accident that five writers from Minuit were awarded the Médicis.[15]

Literary events have implications not only for the past in the form of modifications of canons and noble traditions but also for the future in terms of the authors and styles which are on the coronation list. In addition to the Médicis, the Fénéon literary prize was also created in the 1950s. Like the Médicis, its function was to encourage literature by young writers. Young writers who were awarded the Fénéon and are well-known today include: Michel Butor (1956), Philippe Sollers (1958), Jean Thibaudeau (1960), Marcelin Pleynet (1962), and Denis Roche (1965). Philippe Sollers also received the Médicis Prize in 1961.

LITERARY PARODY AND INTELLECTUAL ICONOCLASM

For semiology, literature does not exist.

Julia Kristeva

In the search for young talent, certain groups were definitely favored in this system of succession. The most important of these were the young and unknown writers and poets grouped around Philippe Sollers, director of the review *Tel Quel*, which was financed by Le Seuil. Sollers had been hailed by both Louis Aragon and François Mauriac as a gifted writer, but he was too "radical"[16] for the directors of *La Nouvelle revue française* and of the publishing house Gallimard, the most prestigious literary publisher in France. Le Seuil, on the other hand, was expanding rapidly, and needed new names and faces for its team. Two young writers of the *Tel Quel* group, Jean Thibaudeau and Jean Ricardou, came from Minuit. At Le Seuil, they were known as the eyes of Minuit. Both had been discovered by Jérôme Lindon, director of Minuit, and Robbe-Grillet. By joining Le Seuil and *Tel Quel* Ricardou and Thibaudeau enhanced the public image of the review and of the young writers grouped around it. Soon they were labelled by cultural journalists as the "second generation of the *Nouveau Roman*."[17] Succession was created by the physical transfer of a few writers from Minuit to Le Seuil.

One function of cultural journalism is to give form to the multiple events of the literary field, to select and promote. As such, it must also search actively for legitimate successors and give novelty acceptable forms, for example via a label like the experimental novel. Works thus need to be explained in relation to previous works, accepted canons of literary art. At the same time, these works have to present something new, which distinguishes innovation from old recipes. Another group of individuals specializes in this search for new names: editors and publishers. If both the editors and the journalists are the literary field's gatekeepers, internal legitimation also comes from fellow writers, who, as writers, always need new models and examples. Early in their careers the unknown young writers who were grouped around the review *Tel Quel* and would become the "second generation of the *Nouveau Roman*" were the legitimizers of the *Nouveau Roman* as a symbolic revolution in the literary field. By promoting the *Nouveau Roman* these young and promising writers and poets in fact indirectly promoted themselves.

It was clear that the members of *Tel Quel* were reiterating what the members of the *Nouveau Roman* had done.[18] Comparing them to Robbe-Grillet, the critic and future member of the Académie française Pierre-Henri Simon noted, "they have constructed their rhetoric before their masterpieces."[19] In particular, Ricardou's work *L'observatoire de Cannes* (1961) was widely considered an imitation of Robbe-Grillet's works.[20] Michel Foucault, already a known literary critic, wrote that in Ricardou's and Thibaudeau's writings there were "objects which owe their existence and possibility of existence only to Robbe-Grillet."[21] Sollers's Médicis-winning *Le Parc* (1961) was judged by many a parody of the *Nouveau Roman.*[22]

In the first half of the 1960s, Ricardou published numerous reviews on books by Claude Simon (*La route de Flandres*), Claude Ollier (*Le maintien de l'ordre*), Michel Butor (*Répertoire I* and *Degré*), Robbe-Grillet (a general article about the importance of his work), and Sollers (*Le Parc*) in important reviews such as *Critique* and *La Nouvelle revue française*. Thibaudeau published abstracts on works by Beckett and Robbe-Grillet in the review *Tel Quel* (3/1961). Abstracts were also published in *Tel Quel*: in 1960, the best-rated books were by Robbe-Grillet (*Dans le labyrinthe*), Nathalie Sarraute (*Le Planétarium*), and Maurice Blanchot (*Le livre à venir*).

Other members of the group *Tel Quel*, such as Jean-Louis Baudry and Jean-Pierre Faye, also started to write novels in the same style as Robbe-Grillet, Butor, and Sarraute. "Objective literature," a label invented by Roland Barthes, was the most promising alternative to traditional literature and Sartrian existentialist pathos. Emotion was replaced by pure technique, "a purely intellectual conscience."[23] Such was the impact of scientific culture and the imperatives of modernity. In their statements to the cultural press these writers revealed that their greatest literary influences were the works of Butor, Robbe-Grillet, and Sarraute. By reiterating the style, the themes, and the ideology of the works of the members of the *Nouveau Roman*, these writers presented themselves as the second generation of the *Nouveau Roman*. This imitation elevated them to the status of promising young writers via the new prizes, and allowed them to surpass the anonymous mass of young beginners. Their literary and theoretical works can be classified broadly into three categories: poetic works, a genre largely forgotten and neglected by the first generation (Marcelin Pleynet, Denis Roche); experimental novels and even anti-novels (Jean-Louis Baudry, Jean Ricardou, Philippe Sollers, Jean Thibaudeau); and theoretical essays (Jean Ricardou, Philippe Sollers). Their literary works were conceived in the same style as those of the first generation of the *Nouveau Roman* and their theoretical studies concentrated on the theory of the *Nouveau Roman*. This complex dependency of the *Tel Quel* group in relation to Robbe-Grillet, the *il* [*he*] and the father, was clearly expressed by Michel Foucault, who asked himself what novelties *Tel Quel* had really brought:

> People are in the habit of placing (putting forth and putting before) Robbe-Grillet before the writers of *Tel Quel* (the existence of this review has changed something in the domain we are speaking about, but what?). Not to reproach them or to point to excess but to suggest that in this supreme, so obsessive language of Robbe-Grillet's more than one who thought escape possible, has got lost in his labyrinth. In this father, more than one has found a trap where he remains captive, captivated. And, after all, if the writers of *Tel Quel* themselves can hardly write in the first person without referring to and leaning on this major He . . .[24]

The *Nouveau Roman* was surpassed through theoretical speculation, in accordance with the trends of the moment. By creating the theory of the *Nouveau Roman* as a separate, competing literary style, the young writers of the second generation emphasized their own uniqueness. Following the transformation of the traditional humanities into the human sciences, literary criticism became literary theory. This made possible a metadiscourse on the *Nouveau Roman*: a process of theoretical explanation most clear in Ricardou's work *Problèmes du nouveau roman* (1967), a reinterpretation which received Robbe-Grillet's blessing. The collective work *Théorie d'ensemble*, published in 1968, was the *summum* of the theoretical activity of the *Tel Quel* group. But even in this work, the first three articles were reprinted from other reviews, and were written by well-known intellectuals like Barthes, Derrida, and Foucault, who were not members of the core group of *Tel Quel*. Real literary succession—the use of certain literary conventions for the creation of a group's own style—was replaced by theoretical speculation, which undervalued purely literary endeavors in favor of theoretical essayism.

In French literary reviews and journals, the members of the review *Tel Quel* (especially Faye, Ricardou, Sollers, and Thibaudeau) were the most visible young writers writing in the style of the *Nouveau Roman* at the beginning of the 1960s. They also began to canonize this movement as a new literary school by producing literary criticism and theory on works by Robbe-Grillet, Sarraute, and Butor. In this way, they legitimized the *Nouveau Roman* as something unique in literary history. But their fate, like that of the other members of *Tel Quel* who would follow in their footsteps, was to be stigmatized as a second generation, coming after and therefore being less important than the first generation, the pioneers.[25] Foucault emphasized this dependency, euphemistically due to his proximity to Sollers, in his review of Sollers's (*Le Parc*), Thibaudeau's (*Une cérémonie royale*), and Baudry's (*Images*) works:

> Without doubt, some figures (or perhaps all) in *Le Parc*, in *Une cérémonie royale*, or in *Images* have no inner volume, relieved of this dark, lyrical core, of this receding but insistent center of which Robbe-Grillet had already warded off the presence.[26]

Foucault emphasized the similarities between Sollers's, Thibaudeau's, and Baudry's novels to Robbe-Grillet's work. None of the works of the members of the second generation could match the novels of Robbe-Grillet or Butor, although writers such as Faye or Sollers were recognized with such prizes as the Médicis. Exceptional circumstances and the frantic quest for young talent in the late 1950s and early 1960s had resulted in premature literary consecrations.[27] Abrupt recognition replaced slow maturation and in this way the old—the *Nouveau Roman*—stayed current: no alternative literary order was even considered. Sollers attacked Robbe-Grillet mainly on a personal level, ridiculing his idol and literary mentor.[28] The group *Tel Quel* similarly became, in the eyes of most of the literary journalists and writers, the "second generation of Surrealism."[29] Later, the theoretical works of the members of the group *Tel Quel* followed closely the works of more illustrious intellectuals such as Barthes, Derrida, Foucault, and Lacan.

In tracing the literary origins of the *Nouveau Roman*, and of any literary order of succession, it is necessary to examine more than just what happened before the creation of the literary school. Perhaps even more important is what happens after it, because cultural origins, a dangerous word if ever there was one, are always created *a posteriori* not only by historians and theorists of literary and intellectual life, but also by young writers and poets in search of models to follow. These interpretations and retrospective rationalizations, the possibilities created by language at a point in time, shape our perception of literary history and its important events.

In the next part, I will examine the conditions that made possible *Tel Quel*'s succession to the *Nouveau Roman*. I will argue that forums such as *Tel Quel*, by popularizing scientific works and theorizing about literature, were the crucial element in the changes affecting the intellectual field in the 1960s.

CHAPTER 8

The Conditions of Possibility of the New Avant-Garde: The Case of *Tel Quel*

Tel Quel, a literary and intellectual review founded by the publishing house Le Seuil in 1960, is considered, along with certain Italian intellectuals, to be the most important representative of the so called neo-avant-gardist movement.[1] In the French intellectual field, *Tel Quel* was also one of the most influential diffusers and legitimators of the new sciences, mainly semiology and semiotics, which were developing in the 1960s. From the beginning, it took the previous intellectual avant-garde, the Surrealists, as its model. This to a certain extent enabled the writers to prevent the label "under Robbe-Grillet" to be applied to them, despite the fact that their literary works owed everything to the members of the *Nouveau Roman*. Following the logic of symbolic struggles, *Tel Quel* began to distance itself from the dominant intellectual models of the early 1960s: in literature from the *Nouveau Roman* movement and in the intellectual field from Sartre's doctrine of political engagement. After a short period of literary success the review found itself in a phase of multipositionality[2] which was particularly effective for intellectual domination.

This position made possible *Tel Quel*'s synchronization of the mutations in different spheres of intellectual activity: in literature (Michel Déguy, Jean-René Huguenin, Alain Robbe-Grillet, Philippe Sollers), in serial music (Pierre Boulez, Gilbert Amy), in philosophy (Jacques Derrida, Michel Foucault, Pierre Klossowski, among others), and in semiology (Roland Barthes, Gérard Genette, and Christian Metz), for instance. Structural linguistics quickly became the watchword and *Tel Quel* and its most important collaborators contributed to the crystallization of a new intellectual style, "structuralism" and later "post-structuralism." Symbolic police of the avant-garde movements, *Tel Quel* took part in the intellectual and institutional revolution that was beginning at that time.[3] "Mere" writers, its members aspired to become intellectual stars recognized by the growing intellectual public. In *Le Figaro littéraire*, Sollers was labelled Sollerspierre, the literary judge of the *Ancien Régime*, by the cartoonist Maurice Henry.

TEL QUEL

Francis Ponge, *La Figue (sèche)*
Claude Simon, *La poursuite*
Jean Cayrol, *La presqu'île*
Jean Lagrolet, *L'écrivain désamorcé*
Boisrouvray, *Une vallée sous les nuages*
Philippe Sollers, *Requiem*

Pensez-vous avoir un don d'écrivain?
32 réponses à une enquête.

Virginia Woolf, *Le moment : soir d'été*
Jacques Coudol, *Le voyage d'hiver*
Jean-René Huguenin, *Adieu*

Jean-Edern Hallier, *Un visage à part*
Jean Thibaudeau, *L'attentat*
Renaud Matignon, *Flaubert et la sensibilité moderne*
Francis Ponge, *Proême*

Albert Camus
Notes de lecture

Printemps 1960

Cover of *Tel Quel*'s first issue, Spring 1960. Éditions du Seuil, 1960. Reprinted with permission of the publisher.

Illustration 4. Classical form and innovative content are combined.

Moreover, the social conditions of the production of this new avant-garde as well as its strategies for maintaining an avant-gardist public image while at the same time accumulating symbolic power were fundamentally different from those of the Surrealists. Many Telquelians were not only "free intellectuals" (essentially writers), but worked simultaneously as publishers, academics, journalists, and other institutionalized producers, that is, market-created intellectuals. The cultural press, publishers, and other professionals of intellectual marketing began to play an increasingly important role in the process of fashioning ideals and models. Many intellectuals of the new generation had access to this press, while the consumers themselves were no longer the "bourgeoisie" but rather humanities and social science students. The first and second developments can be explained by the specialization of cultural creation, and the third by the dramatic rise in the number of students, especially in literature, humanities, and the social sciences.[4] In the works, the "slogans" of the Surrealists were repeated. However, according to Peter Bürger[5] this repetition could only mean a loss of their efficiency.

REVIEWS AND PUBLISHING HOUSES

Why analyze intellectual reviews, like *Tel Quel*, instead of studying individuals? Intellectual authority, unlike folklore, is usually associated with a surname— Lévi-Strauss is a notable example. By a complex social process having to do with the constitution of intellectual stereotypes, first names and middle names become irrelevant. An intellectual review on the other hand, is usually a collective, something not very personalized or valued and, *a priori*, not a very interesting object from the point of view of the dominant values in cultural research.

Yet on the intellectual and critical levels, the analysis of reviews offers many insights. First, as relatively informal social formations they constitute the material and symbolic space where symbolic revolutions take place. The Surrealist or Russian Bolshevik reviews are good examples. A review is an agent of symbolic power—the voice of a group, with a certain structure. At the same time, as specific social formations and places of sociability and integration, reviews are forums for avant-garde movements in politics, the arts, and the sciences. From this viewpoint, during the twentieth century the review has played a role similar to that of the princely court in the sixteenth century, the literary salon in the eighteenth century, and the circle in the nineteenth century.

Second, by analyzing reviews we can partly circumvent an individualistic ideology of culture that often forces proximity to a name, taking the necessary distance from this individualistic ideology in order to examine the mechanisms of symbolic domination with fewer subjective and objective constraints. The disadvantage is that because the populations under study are usually small compared with those of certain cultural professions, for instance, statistical methods cannot be applied.

Intellectual works, usually by individual thinkers and incorporated in individualized "-isms," have traditionally been analyzed from one angle: as symbolic entities. The "material" dimension is usually neglected. Studies in cultural or intellectual history, not to mention in the history of philosophy, separate the two dimensions. The symbolic entity is associated with certain intellectual and/or artistic values, the material entity with price. In the eyes of most of the intellectuals themselves, the material entity is irrelevant and vulgar, having nothing to do with art or creation. However, the material dimension of these products is also related to a certain general level of material and physical accessibility, to the means of production and to the distribution of the merchandise by libraries and book clubs, for instance. Therefore, from a sociological point of view, the two dimensions cannot be totally separated from one another, except conceptually.

Cultural consumption is linked to adequate perception categories which must be clarified as part of different cultural practices and which are not independent of the material dimension. Demand, which is based on cultural consumption patterns of different age groups, develops in response to changes in supply: cultural "needs" are always socially created.

With these two dimensions in mind, the analysis of reviews—or other relatively informal social formations in the cultural domain—can be used both to describe a specific type of domination relative to a particular symbolic economy and also, especially in regard to individualistic ideology, to reveal certain deep-rooted beliefs. The review and group *Tel Quel* will be examined herein as part of a complex web of social relationships: first, that between the review and its publisher Le Seuil's position in the space of publishers; second, that between the review and the intellectual public, the consumers; and third, that of the review and the global arts and humanities market. These relationships will clarify *Tel Quel*'s position in relation to the institutional and symbolic changes underway in France.

Intellectual products are financed by publishers in competition with other publishers, and in cooperation with the cultural sections of newspapers and intellectual programs on radio and television. Publishers are usually part of larger economic and/or political conglomerates, which are often dependent on banks and foundations. Publishing houses also vary in size and investment structure. Generally speaking, small publishers like Minuit have a small budget and staff and invest for the long term, whereas large concerns such as Gallimard will produce on a large scale, employ a large staff and possibly an in-house press relations department, and invest more for the short term. A medium-sized house like Le Seuil may in turn favor a mixed investment structure, financing avant-garde products with revenues from best-sellers.[6]

A review is an intermediary between the publishing house and certain specific segments of the public, and its investment strategies depend on the publisher and the consumers. The investment strategies of publishers, who shape the raw material, cannot be independent of the processes by which symbolic domination evolves, through written and oral products like reviews, books, articles, lectures, and interviews, for instance. The success of certain thinkers, such as Michel Foucault in the 1960s, would not have been possible without considerable investment by publishers like Gallimard and more generally, without the publication by commercial houses of academic works, something which was not possible immediately after World War II.

Tel Quel's publisher, Le Seuil, was situated in the intermediary space in the publishers' field. *Tel Quel* was a medium-sized intellectual review compared with *Critique or Les Temps modernes*. At the beginning of the 1960s its publisher, Le Seuil, began to diversify its investments, particularly toward the human sciences, by recruiting editors with expertise in related domains[7] and by financing new works, for instance, works by Roland Barthes which had been refused by Gallimard. This reorientation was partially made possible by profits from certain popular novels such as *Don Camillo*. In this way, Le Seuil also participated in the larger, local symbolic revolution.

Le Seuil's characteristic trait was its personalism: that is, the relatively high degree of autonomy the publisher allowed individual editors. The house began to publish avant-garde works. Contrary to a small publisher like Éditions de Minuit, Le Seuil could mobilize the marketing and financial resources of a medium-sized house. Thus, *Tel Quel* was in a unique situation: integrated within the intermediary space, it also followed an avant-gardist consumption pattern. This allowed full exploitation by Le Seuil of the changes in the consumers' space. Republication of works in paperback collections, for example, was a new development aimed at bringing "culture to the people": an attainable goal as a result of the rise of the general schooling level. Some works came out in paperback quite soon after their initial publication. For example, the paperback edition of *Logiques* by Philippe Sollers, leader of the *Tel Quel* group, was available three years after the hardcover version. Paperback reedition was becoming one of the main factors in the constitution of an intellectual avant-garde in this specific context. The paperback system made high print runs of hundreds of thousands of copies possible.[8] These paperbacks were sold at affordable prices, a key element in attracting younger consumers.

The creation of Le Seuil's leading reviews *Tel Quel*, *Les Cahiers pour l'analyse*, and *Change* coincided with a process of specialization and scientization of certain academic disciplines. Works in the "human sciences" included Le Seuil's so-called "leader productions," particularly in psychoanalysis (Jacques Lacan), semiology (Roland Barthes, Gérard Genette, Julia Kristeva), and linguistics (Julia Kristeva). These works were in a complementary relation, in terms of consumption patterns, to the review *Tel Quel*.

Although *Tel Quel* was in a stable financial situation, unlike the avant-garde reviews between the world wars, the size of the public affected the volume of intellectual creation (i.e., the size of print runs), while the composition of the public influenced the substance of the group's ideas. In this local market, the readers of *Tel Quel* were the younger members of the intellectual public, concentrated in the schools of arts and letters of the Parisian universities. This placed certain constraints on ideas: a writer was supposed to be dangerous, and to escape ruling dichotomies without being too technical, and to present symbolic ruptures. The products had to be both economically accessible and symbolically desirable. *Tel Quel*, for example, presented excerpts of radical products, and its collection of books published "theoretical essays." Its members were ready "to harmonize their rhythms with the movements which pulsated through the ethical and political avant-garde of the student world."[9]

The review's editorial policy was influenced not only by its publisher and by the public but also by the strategies of the dominant group among its staff members—a situation related to the group's power structure. This affected the quality of the review as a material and symbolic space, and in particular, its efficiency as a mechanism of transformation and accumulation of different kinds of social resources, especially intellectual fame. The two principal groups among the Telquelians were the writers and the academics.[10] Thus to a certain extent, the review combined two modalities of cultural creation. Moreover, the division was becoming increasingly complicated for instance as some avant-garde writers began to double as editors—specialists in the diffusion of symbolic goods—and as other, more complex, combinations developed, especially in relation to the media.

The editorial staff's power structure was monopolistic. The distance between the position of one of its' members, Philippe Sollers, and the review *Tel Quel* itself was short. Sollers was simultaneously the editor of the "Tel Quel" book collection, the unofficial director of *Tel Quel*, and a well-known avant-garde author. Sollers's position of proximity to the collective *Tel Quel* enabled him to use a strategy of substitution. Had the editorial staff's power structure been oligopolistic, it would have been more difficult for him to present himself more or less convincingly as the group's legitimate representative. In such a case, the social conditions for access to a "collective language" would have been less favorable.[11]

Within the group, the specific investments of *Tel Quel*'s members depended on their social properties. The most keen to transgress the limits, to be daring and dangerous, and to present as yet unclassified products, were those with origins in the dominant classes but who lacked official signs of intellectual excellence. A prime example in this context was Sollers, who had neither attended the École Normale Supérieure nor passed the *agrégation*. His paradoxical situation— simultaneous recognition and illegitimacy—was possible because conditions for reversing this stigma and turning it into an enhanced identity existed. A lack of signs of cultural achievement could be converted into a position external to institutions and authority. As 80 percent of the review's readership was within the universities but rebelling against them, incentives to create intermediate forms— like lectures, public seminars, and informal bulletins—were strong. The review's position also led it to recruit marginal academics as collaborators and to create a "science effect" through the publication of so-called scientific works.

In fact, in the power structure of the group, the ones who contributed most to the review's prestige were the ones who depended on it the least: the academics Barthes, Derrida, and Foucault. For these academics, *Tel Quel* worked as a mechanism of social metamorphosis, making the ordinary university professor, presenting routine lectures, into an extraordinary cultural hero capable of intellectual extravagance. From quiet and modest assistant professors or lecturers, they became imposing and dominating heroes, real princes of thought. This metamorphosis was possible only in institutions such as the Sixth Section of the École Pratique des Hautes Études. Barthes, Derrida, and Foucault did not belong to the editorial staff of *Tel Quel*, but their importance as bearers of intellectual credibility led to a fragile power structure: the writers were dominant within the editorial staff but the academics were dominant within the *Tel Quel* group itself.

THE DEVELOPMENT OF NEW LEGITIMATION CIRCUITS AND NEW AVANT-GARDES

If the journal was "the cemetery of ideas" (Proudhon) in the sense that its function was to simplify ideas to the extreme, forums for diffusion like the journal or the review became indispensable for intellectuals seeking recognition among the wide intellectual public. Because of the rising importance of the wide public in the 1960s, the importance of reviews like *Tel Quel* also grew. The changes outlined above permitted a growing number of marginal academics to use new channels of legitimization: reviews that worked as forums for wider diffusion like *Critique* and *Tel Quel*, journals like *Le Magazine littéraire* (1965), *La Quinzaine littéraire* (1966), and *Le Nouvel Observateur* (1964), and institutions such as the Écoles Normales Supérieures, the Collège de France, and the Sixth Section of the École Pratique des Hautes Études, which were situated at the research pole of the university field.[12] In this way, a whole range of new channels for social ascension and strategies for the accumulation of symbolic power were developed which combined the two poles of the intellectual field, the pole of the creator or free intellectual and the pole of the professor. The accumulation of symbolic power was the result of a social process of accumulation of recognition, carrying with it certain expectations and associations felt to be legitimate. Used to grandeur, grandeur was sought and found in a few individuals who became "the new Gide" or "the Sartre of the 1960s." These changes provided the marginal writers that made up most of *Tel Quel* with the opportunity to present themselves as the promoters or producers of new intellectual styles. They became a new avant-garde movement whose new form of literary practice linked to the "science of the text"[13] enabled them to wield "the sword of scientific objectivity."[14]

In fact, with the enhanced importance of "commentaries"; the development of the paperback book industry, which more rapidly conferred to avant-garde works the status of classic through wider and more rapid diffusion;[15] and the creation of alternative legitimization and diffusion circles, it became possible to introduce a certain work in a new way and at the same time present the reasons why it should be considered avant-gardist. Simultaneous presentation of the text and its right and legitimate reading protocol[16] created an ideal reader, who was constructed now relatively independently of scholarly legitimation, although necessarily in relation to it. Thus, the social value of a text might be constructed as follows: the producer could be an editor in a publishing house whose good friend would write a critique in the cultural press, and who would be invited to an alternative seminar at the École Pratique des Hautes Études to present his work. In this case producer and legitimator belonged to the same legitimization circle, thus guaranteeing the cumulative process of symbolic power.

It became possible to produce avant-garde works just by declaring that one was producing them. In other words, with the invention of a new economy for accumulating cultural celebrity and academic power, the text and the categories according to which it was to be legitimately evaluated were produced simultaneously. As the consumers were no longer only a writer's peers, able to evaluate the value of a text within a certain discipline and tradition, it became structurally possible to present old wine in new bottles and label them "avant-garde."[17] In foreign countries, notably the United States, which were very important for *Tel Quel* financially as well as in terms of symbolic prestige, these intellectual products were restricted in the process of their symbolic consumption only by association. They were associated with Paris, Sartre, the Surrealists, French "chic" philosophy, and the "newest new," for instance. An analogy can be drawn between the status of French ideas and other French luxury products, like wine, perfume, or fashion.

The products themselves, with their "alternative" profile, found consumers among young university students who, incidentally, purchased the most paperbacks. Unrestricted by the traditional rhythms of social life and divisions like work/leisure, night/day, and week/weekend, eager in their search for new idols, and dreaming of breaking off symbolically with the world, they became the base for new investment strategies not only by intellectuals but perhaps more significantly by publishing houses and the media. As their numerical importance grew, the material and symbolical profits that could be attained by appealing to this group accrued and competition intensified.

Indeed, it is generally in the interest of intellectuals to create something new and subversive. However, at this time, the social production of "newness" had itself changed. Paradoxically, the new was now presented as both easily attainable and precious or rare. The paperback book industry found in the apprentice-intellectuals, the students, fertile ground for the cultivation of symbolic subversion and for a back-to-basics effect: everything must be started again, back to the sources; for instance back to Marx and Freud in the cases of Althusser and Lacan. This ambition coincided with the criteria of excellence reigning among French intellectuals, an aspect neglected by many analysts.[18] In this case, from the standpoint of the producers, going to extremes in order to prove one's talents and keep and widen one's audience was imperative. At the same time, all young intellectuals had to become market-oriented to a certain degree, in order to comply to social necessities.

In the beginning, the social value attached to *Tel Quel* consisted of two elements: its own value as a group of young intellectuals, which was negligible because of the group's low social age as intellectuals; and the symbolic power the review's members had inherited from the Surrealists, which surpassed in value the former's own legitimacy. From the start, *Tel Quel* lived on credit, appropriating for itself the label "avant-garde" with minimal investment. This is not surprising, as the functioning of the intellectual field is based on credit. But in situations of urgency credit is given on lesser grounds. The public image of the avant-garde was largely created by other writers and by the cultural press, all of whom were eager not to miss anything and to present cultural products as precious symbols following the implicit ideology—and not as commodities. The literary success of *Tel Quel* was largely due to the demand for new and young producers of ideas. In literature, realism had given way to formalism and to the search for distinguishing profits in the world of theory, as can be read in the words of Philippe Sollers:

> Straightaway, by emphasizing the *text*, its historical determinations and mode of production, by systematically denouncing the metaphysical valorization of the concepts *"oeuvre"* and "author," by questioning the subjective and so-called objective aggressivity, we have touched upon the nerve centers of our social unconscious and, more generally, upon the distribution of symbolic propriety. In relation to "literature," what we propose strives to be as subversive as Marx's critique of political economy.[19]

As can be deduced from the above, the textual strategies used in the texts themselves, as well as in retrospective rationalizations[20] such as that of Sollers, have to be related to more general changes in the strategies of reproduction of the whole intellectual field, changes largely due to a modification in the division of symbolic labor[21] and to structural changes in production, diffusion, and consumption. The development of an intermediate space in the intellectual field favored the theoretical essay as a mode of universalization of interests, because the theoretical essay enabled young thinkers to combine outrageous ideas with wide diffusion, contrary to the traditional academic thesis, doomed to technicality and exclusivity.

Analysis of textual strategies, restricted by an internal reading protocol—leading to the classical problem of *ars nova* and *ars antiqua nova*—has little relevance without an evaluation of the concrete creation context. Even an approximate analysis of the global situation gives a more coherent view of these strategies. The creation of a certain social image or label is a collective process which involves, at different levels, all intellectuals. Semantic struggles over cultural "authenticity," or, in other words, the struggles for the legitimate domination principle, are resolved by innumerable social processes working at different levels. The "real" avant-gardist intellectual is the agent who, first, believes him/herself to be a member of the avant-garde; second, is able to convince a significant portion of the consumers—in whose interest it is to be convinced of this as well—that s/he is;[22] and, third, can accumulate the support from legitimization circles necessary for defense of his/her claims from accusations of arbitrariness or illegitimacy. In short, there is no asocial definition of the avant-garde, and semantics is thus always power politics. The textual strategies themselves, in the case of an avant-garde, are reduced to different innovation strategies for presenting something as the "newest new"—that is, as surpassing its predecessors, the "old." The "old" becomes a curse relegated to an obscure and largely irrelevant past. The avant-garde is, by definition, destined to produce something unique continuously and to repeat the unrepeatable incessantly, or in other words—and more relevantly from my perspective—to be constantly young.

What kind of strategies did *Tel Quel* use to maintain its image as a new intellectual avant-garde and increase its own power and credibility? In the case of *Tel Quel*, legitimization came about through its participation in the implantation of structural linguistics in the French intellectual field of the 1960s and additionally through its invention of new discourses and social positions.

TEXTUAL STRATEGIES OR STRATEGIES WITH TEXTS?

Many of the new master thinkers, in marginal positions in the university system, found in *Tel Quel* a way to widen their base of legitimization, and to diffuse their ideas via attachment to external legitimization circles as opposed to internal ones, "professional" or academic circles. The impact of external circles in the intellectual field was stronger, which meant an increase in the review's intellectual fame. In 1965, for example, the Bulgarian linguist Tzvetan Todorov translated some texts of the Russian formalists, prefaced by Roman Jakobson, under the title *Théorie de la littérature* (1965). By introducing the works of the Russian formalists to a broader public in France, *Tel Quel* popularized texts whose interest in other countries was limited to specialists, thus making possible the merging of the new sciences and the new symbolic power accumulation economy. Roland Barthes also published some of his texts in *Tel Quel*, as did his assistant Gérard Genette. Finally, in 1965 the philosopher Jacques Derrida wrote his first article in *Tel Quel*, on Antonin Artaud's theater.

At the same time Philippe Sollers, a writer and the editor of the review, and Jean-Louis Baudry were attending the seminar, which started in January 1964, of Jacques Lacan, the father of "structural psychoanalysis." Louis Althusser, who had invited Lacan to the École Normale Supérieure at the rue d'Ulm,[23] had begun his work on structural marxism, and Michel Foucault had already published *Folie et déraison* (1961). In the years that followed all the major publishers started to publish authors that were part of the new intellectual generation.[24] In 1968 *Tel Quel* published a special issue on modern Soviet semiotics (*Tel Quel* 35/1968), compiled by another Bulgarian linguist Julia Kristeva.

Certain social conditions specific to France made possible this presentation of formalism as "new": the relative impermeability of certain parts of the intellectual field;[25] the small number of individuals acquainted with these texts; the growing number of dominated academics; the transformation in the structure of the publishing field with the emergence in the intermediary space of houses such as Le Seuil, for example, making possible investment in the human and social sciences; the evolution of new legitimization and diffusion networks; and the quantitative and qualitative changes in the audience. These developments made new investments—for producers, diffusers, and consumers alike—symbolically and materially profitable. For the dominated intellectual a certain type of knowledge—linked to structural linguistics and its major concepts and schemas—became indispensable, and the multiplication of its value favored those individuals that had already invested in the newly forming disciplines. Aside from Barthes, Genette, Todorov, and Kristeva, these individuals included students and/or associates of intellectuals currently in vogue. In this reinvestment process, *Tel Quel* assisted in the universalization of certain intellectual schemas and intellectual evaluation hierarchies, which acted as an implicit orientation mechanism. For example, through a certain terminological hierarchy, terms such as "theory," "signifying practice," and "structure" were on top, while "subject," "consciousness" and "intentionality" were on the bottom. Disciplines were subject to hierarchization in similar fashion in the 1960s: semiology, linguistics, Lacanian psychoanalysis, and neighboring developments that were labelled as "theory of the text" came first, followed by history and ethnology, and finally sociology and psychology, which were considered equivalent to "empirism" and "positivism."[26] This changed at the beginning of the 1970s with the relative devaluation of textual analysis.

Tel Quel's appropriation of Russian formalism and semiological developments was possible because it had within its reach the necessary "human capital" and could serve as a forum for popularization and legitimization. For *Tel Quel* this connection with East-European studies was crucial. Among literary practices literary theory occupied a dominant position in the alternative value hierarchy, largely due to the influence of Barthes, who was appointed director of studies (*directeur d'études*) of the Sixth Section of the École Pratique des Hautes Études in 1962 and who had access to the new legitimization circles. At the same time *Tel Quel* participated in the process of institutionalization of a new academic orthodoxy.

With the expansion of new disciplines such as semiology and the symbolic revolution these disciplines set into motion, it was possible to present new products and research areas by adopting dangerous and daring profiles. Existing terms were used in new contexts and terms were created to indicate intellectual radicality, such as Foucault's "archeology" and "genealogy," Derrida's "grammatology," Kristeva's "semanalysis," Goux's "numismatics," Baudry's "materiology," and others. The multipositionality of *Tel Quel* and its members allowed the transposition of models both from one subfield to an other, thus increasing their interaction, and between the two poles of the intellectual field. Theoretically speaking, the strategy of innovation could combine Saussure's structural linguistics, whose main concepts were popularized in France mostly by Barthes; Freud's psychoanalysis revised by Lacan; and Althusser's Marxism. In a lesser-known example, Goux saw in his new "science," numismatics or the general analysis of values, structural homologies between the functions of the signifier, work, and the unconscious.[27] Goux's evaluation hierarchy in action consisted of, on the one hand, the signifier, work, the unconscious, and the proletariat, and on the other hand the signified, idealism, logocentrism, and the bourgeoisie. In practice this hierarchy led to endless metonymy and metaphor chains and to a multidimensional reading process. Another example, Kristeva's semanalysis, which aimed to analyze the process of production of meaning, consisted of combining—in the same fashion as Goux's numismatics—Marxism, psychoanalysis, and linguistics, the three "revolutionary" theories. However, Kristeva distinguished the production of meaning from meaning itself: the first, mobile and open, was presented as not participating in logocentric language, which was ruled by dichotomies like right or wrong, and as being anterior to meaning, which was qualified as tyrannic, monovalent, idealist. Thus, she "went beyond" structuralism's immobility, integrating it as an anterior part of her new science: the theoretical dichotomy was a reversed chronological dichotomy. But more importantly, this innovation strategy was a theoretical double movement: Kristeva radicalized certain aspects by separating the production process of meaning from the meaning itself, declaring her new discipline and the evaluation hierarchy that "lived" in it as the only legitimate evaluation criteria.[28] This meant that potential critiques—for example from the point of view of linguistics or psychoanalysis—would be "old" or illegitimate and largely irrelevant.[29] The creation of new labels was thus an example of the struggle for the ultimate distinction profits—a struggle for the "new" on the ruins of the "old."

By combining Marxism, linguistics, and psychoanalysis, it was possible for the members of *Tel Quel* to practice the intellectual game in many different registers at the same time: linguistic critics' objections were devalued by psychoanalytic arguments, psychoanalytical arguments by linguistic arguments, and all of these by evoking the historic mission of the new political and intellectual avant-garde.[30] In fact, with respect to the legitimacy of the works of *Tel Quel*'s members, it was the Communist Party (Parti Communiste Français, PCF), along with the new student audience, which in the last instance certified and guaranteed the radicality of the new symbolic luxury goods. For *Tel Quel*, positioned at the intersection of different discourses, the Party brought credibility, a good historical conscience and an image of disinterestedness, integrated new consumers that were activists and sympathizers of the Party, provided access to the Communist cultural press,[31] and most of all, legitimized *Tel Quel* as the new avant-garde—the delegated institution. In return, *Tel Quel* enhanced the Party's cultural appeal and increased its legitimacy in the symbolic marketplace. The function of political credibility was of crucial importance from many reasons. It permitted the patching of "theoretical holes" created by the relative indeterminacy of the disciplines in formation. Furthermore, it allowed these structurally illegitimate (for the moment) disciplines and intellectuals with low scholarly credentials to present themselves as the political judges of the "new" academics as well as, in literature of the dominant reviews (for example, *La Nouvelle revue française*) and of the *Nouveau Roman*. Specific scientific competence could be forgotten by referring to the revolutionary mission of *Tel Quel*, a mission targeted to the large intellectual audience. This gnostic schema was recurrent in the discourse of the review. The function of the representation of a new morality, which was characterized by consumerism and ethical radicality, was linked to an always young profile, in opposition to the institution. Writing[32] became for *Tel Quel* the primary means for the transition to a socialist and communist society.[33] Obscurity in the texts had to do with the existence of a multiplicity of partly conflicting, simultaneous value hierarchies. Literature, philosophy, politics, ethics, and science were all mixed.

The subordinate position of *Tel Quel* in relation to the dominant intellectuals and to the codification of the new sciences led to two specific illusions: a retrospective one which made anachronistic the old genres in literature to which the legitimate researcher in literature was tied, and a prospective one.[34] While the first declared that "poetry is dead," the second announced that *Tel Quel* was to create literature. The function of the creation of new labels was to hasten the disappearance of established disciplines and approaches. Such destruction was in the revolutionaries' interests. Their innovation strategies were characterized by the constant use of hyperbole, to emphasize—with the assistance of conspiracy theory and double-language—*Tel Quel* as the possessor of the "right" knowledge. This forced the others to define themselves, via the cultural press, with respect to *Tel Quel*. By doing so they in effect accepted or even ratified the review's importance. The Telquelians innovation strategies were sustained by the group's anticipation of a certain future and the "incomparable" recognition that this future would inevitably bring with it. The illegitimacy of the new positions was projected into the future, where real intellectual justice lay. A striking example of this type of discourse is Sollers's text "Support/Surfaces (bloc)/Conflits."[35]

For these marginal intellectuals whose positions contradicted their growing fame inside and outside France,[36] the scientization process led to a double game in literature and science, and to the creation of a new economy of discourse. This new economy of discourse sought to escape from the traditional dichotomies of theoretical discourse, such as inside and outside, objective and subjective, and so forth. The "new reason" in fact led to the proliferation of relatively obscure terms, like "wake," "nonknowledge," "différance," the "margin," and the "plural," which were presented as definitely outside the ruling discourse and its dichotomies identified with "idealism," "logocentrism," "repression," and so on. New terms were believed to offer an escape from conceptual divisions. This new discursive economy became the truth for certain academic marginals, who were in a position analogous to that of the students: that is, inside institutions like the École Pratique des Hautes Études or the Écoles Normales Supérieures, but resisting them.

For the Telquelians and their followers, the social order was considered *a priori* as something aberrant and repressive. Consequently the social and historical conditions for the possibility of discourse were left unexplored and salvation from intellectual mediocrity was sought in abstract and extreme solutions. With the systematic mixing of different registers, subversion and its new legitimization discourse were considered the only profound discourse, and were often assimilated to the obscure. The "new reason" was legitimized by its collusion with the "science of the text" as distinguished from academic knowledge and labelled, following Althusser, "the scientific ideology." This was due to the contradiction between the academic specialization of the new sciences and the illegitimacy of the scientific works of *Tel Quel*'s writers. The only way to safeguard the specific literary recognition and maintain the initial credit was to create illegitimate sciences. This way the impotence of these epistemological knights could be momentarily forgotten.

Internal analysis of *Tel Quel*'s avant-garde works—guided by an intertextual reading process—does not take into account either the social conditions that allowed for the strategies themselves (in other words what was legitimately felt as being allowed) or the existence of many conflicting legitimization hierarchies. The strategies, which were mostly not conscious, were themselves governed by key concepts that carried within themselves certain distinguishing profits,[37] by certain canonic thinkers (Althusser, Derrida, Lacan, and Saussure, for instance), and by certain organizing schemas and value hierarchies ("theory-empirism," "subject-structure," etc.). In the case of *Tel Quel*, analysis is complicated—if one wishes to analyze cultural creation as a whole—by the difficulty of isolating the numerous field-effects at work. This is due first to the multi-positionality of the review, which itself underwent changes; secondly, to the multiple modifications, each with its proper temporality, of the intellectual field; and thirdly, to the blurring of different discourses and the inventions of labels in the works.[38] The social conditions for this symbolic revolution were the existence of marginal academic institutions, especially the Sixth Section of the École Pratique des Hautes Études, the means for diffusion and legitimization—such as *Tel Quel*—and the aspirations of social sciences and literature students. The main sociological explanation for *Tel Quel*'s upholding of its public image as avant-garde and for its accumulation of symbolic power was the introduction of new concepts and texts—"theoretical innovations"—that also permitted the development, via the new channels of accumulation of symbolic power, of new academic disciplines linked to the expansion of the linguistic and human sciences and to the process by which they detached themselves from legitimate disciplines.

Thus, the Telquelians strategies with texts have to be related to the different innovation strategies available in the intellectual field which maintained and increased the initial credit of *Tel Quel* by virtue of its role as an object of multiple identifications. The innovation strategies can be grasped—in their specificity—when analyzed in relation to the structural possibilities offered. However, this does not lead to sociological "determinism" in the pejorative sense of the word but to analysis of the sociological and historical context that made possible the emergence of new revolutionary sciences and disciplines.

GLOBAL CIRCULATION AND VALUE HIERARCHIES

Two movements have dominated the importation and exportation of ideas in the human and social sciences between Europe and North America since World War II. The first movement was the exportation from the United States into Europe of empirical social science, which today is symbolically and institutionally dominant in most European countries. The second movement was the exportation from Continental Europe into the United States of philosophy and the human sciences.[39] French theory was especially central in the second movement. What was *Tel Quel*'s relationship to this transatlantic exportation and importation in the arts and humanities and to global mechanisms of symbolic domination?

A connection was established between the local and global markets via the review's bimodal reception structure. Although French consumers generally bought *Tel Quel* on an individual issue basis, it was purchased by subscription outside the local market, especially by universities in the United States. These subscriptions provided the publisher with an essential, stable financial base. However, the relationship between the local market and the foreign universities was such that this very significant financial dependency was accompanied by only a slight intellectual dependency. The "global diffusion" of the *Tel Quel* group's products can be verified empirically using, for instance, the *Citation Index in the Arts and Humanities*[40] and also by comparing references used in different national intellectual debates. However, *Tel Quel*'s global circulation was connected to specific stereotypes relative to French culture and to the fact that Paris was a European cultural center.

Preestablished value hierarchies and presence in intellectual centers[41] facilitate the diffusion of symbolic goods, through a system of publishing houses and reviews like *Tel Quel*. The latter are used to reproduce certain problematics and beliefs. At the same time, an intellectual can more easily become legitimate—that is, develop the self-assurance necessary for speaking about universal concerns—when s/he occupies a high position in the cultural value hierarchy and is also located in an intellectual center like Paris. The best example of this type of legitimate intellectual is certainly Sartre.

The preestablished value hierarchy has to do with unregistered trademarks. The French intellectual is considered a luxury good. The trademark of the French intellectual as a symbolic good has at least three key characteristics. First, it has been constituted historically by association and via the social construction of specific beliefs—for example, the concept of French intellectualism, starting from Voltaire—by French education and foreign Francophile milieus. Second, the "trademark" has been maintained because it has become priceless and is itself a mechanism of multiplication of value. Finally, once established it can be revoked only through a very slow process, because the name or trademark has been detached from the good, and circulates more rapidly, in different forms. In addition, the "merchandise" it refers to consists of more than a single item, which means the name can be attached to numerous "individual" creations; and the name will not disappear physically.

In the 1990s, the value hierarchies of some of the products developed in the 1960s are still in an ascending position in certain small and large national cultures, such as those of Finland and the United States. As a result of a collective urge among intellectuals to update and be modern, the products circulate without the context in which they were produced. Local, French characteristics, prejudices, and values are taken by intellectuals, who appropriate French models outside France for universal ones. The current global circulation of these goods, which favors abstract theoretical thinking, prevents, among other things, analysis of the transformation mechanisms between the local and the global, between the structures conditioning cultural creation and "-isms" like "structuralism" and "poststructuralism." These "-isms" have become the real creeds of intellectual modernity.

To sum up, the following ingredients characterized *Tel Quel* as an intellectual product, while comprising a system of constraints upon it: the review's integration within a medium-sized publishing house which was in close proximity to the paperback industry and maintained a policy of "personalism"; *Tel Quel*'s intermediary position among intellectual reviews; the review's seemingly chaotic inclusion of avant-garde works from many domains and its combination of two modalities of intellectual production; the editorial staff's monopolistic power structure, combined with a fragile power structure within the group; and *Tel Quel*'s focus on the expanding youngest segments of the intellectual public, leading in these ideas to the primacy of symbolic ruptures.

The social processes involved in the constitution of an intellectual avant-garde, in the case of *Tel Quel* and in this local market, were determined by the structural and morphological factors illustrated above, that is the publisher, the public and the position of the review. More generally speaking, the *Tel Quel* group was positioned at a crossroads.[42] Important modifications in the systems of symbolic domination were occurring, linked to evolving cultural practices like the expansion of the audiovisual media and intellectual canons. Although the *Les Temps modernes* model worked in the 1950s, its success was limited during the 1960s when it was in a descending position and was partly challenged by the *Tel Quel* model, then in an ascending position.

Complicity of avant-garde literature and social and human sciences took thus numerous forms in the post-Sartrian French intellectual field. Resistance to Sartre translated on the symbolic level into avoidance of terms such as "subject" or "praxis" and an obsessive concern with "scientific objectivity." This double movement of rejection and embracement led to reappraisal of French classics such as Rousseau and of more avant-garde writers such as Mallarmé and Lautréamont. The search for a new vocabulary and for a fresh view of the common cultural heritage united these dominated writers and human and social scientists. At the same time, numerous changes created new conditions for social promotion and for the formation of the next generation of intellectual nobility.

In the epilogue, I will examine first the symbolic constraints created by French cultural heritage and then the social constraints created by the structures of the intellectual field. From these characteristics I will sketch a processual model of the transformations in the French intellectual field in the 1950s and 1960s. This model will make possible systematic examination of the ways in which, starting from the 1950s, a French intellectual nobility was formed in contrast to previous elites in the same locality and to other national intellectual nobilities.

Epilogue: The Emergence of a Tripolar Structure

Even today, in order to make students
understand the theoretical couple
connotation/denotation, it's better to have
them read Barthes than Hjelmslev.

Louis-Jean Calvet

Until the 1950s, the French intellectual nobility revolved around two figures that formed a structure: the dominant man or woman of letters and the dominated scholar. The large majority of both were men. In the 1950s, three separate but interrelated processes coincided. First, the rise of the social and human scientific intelligentsia enhanced the legitimacy of the scholar. Second, a relatively autonomous third dimension—the media—expanded, which enabled the rapid ascension of certain groups to high academic and literary positions. Third, women started to occupy more positions in the French intellectual field than ever before, especially as university professors and in the new media professions.[1]

The deontology of the French intellectual changed: popularization became accepted on an unprecedented scale. A scholar aspiring to the highest posts had to take into account the wider intellectual audience. Some, like Barthes in the mid-1960s, sold their services to advertising firms. Market-conscious intellectuals such as Barthes or Sollers began to succeed by creating new, socially acceptable channels of ascension. These new intellectuals popularized discursive strategies used previously by avant-gardes such as the Surrealists. The traditional *dignité normalienne* also changed, in accordance with more general changes. If a *normalien/ne* was still "a prince by blood," to use Georges Pompidou's words, this *normalien/ne* was now fighting for visibility in the cultural press like everyone else. The definition of intellectual nobility changed: a thinker hoping to win a place in the higher intellectual nobility could link scientific pretensions to sophisticated popular appeal. This new combination aroused the indignation of members of the old nobility, old-style writers or scholars.[2]

127

The change in the structure of the intellectual field had far reaching and complex effects on scientific creation and on the ways in which new scholarly approaches were created in the humanities and the social sciences from the 1950s to the 1970s.[3] For anthropologists such as Lévi-Strauss, semiologists such as Barthes, and sociologists such as Bourdieu, who were among the most visible members of the human- and social-scientific intelligentsia, science was the criteria for intellectual excellence and offered a way to challenge Sartrian dominance, but within the social conventions and discursive rules of the intellectual field. The scientific model was found in the natural sciences and in a binarism inherited from information theory and cybernetics. To some thinkers, namely, those who were the most market-oriented, science was a metaphor. To others, such as the social scientists, truly scientific discourse was the goal. But both groups took advantage of the new social conditions. Some of their members became celebrated cultural heroes.

In the case of dominated writers, the same imperatives applied. For a certain time, they had to both theorize and popularize literature. The recruitment of the local intellectual nobility became more heterogeneous than ever, shifting emphasis from monopolistic institutions such as the Écoles Normales Supérieures to institutions that combined scholarly and literary networks, the École Pratique des Hautes Études and the expanding media enterprises. Instead of writers or philosophers, journalists were now in a position partly to shape the intellectuals' self-image. It was they that defined who was an intellectual.

Of the ten most important intellectuals in 1981, according to journalistic accounts, four were writers, five scholars, and one a philosopher.[4] Two of the four writers were women. The top representatives of the human- and social-scientific intelligentsia—Lévi-Strauss, Barthes, Foucault, and Lacan—had taken the top four places.[5] Nevertheless, from a gender perspective, surveys generally indicate the accrued importance of women in the French intellectual field compared to previous situations. Moreover, of the 448 responses which composed the material from which the ranking list was created, 107 (24%) came from women. Among the top thirty-six intellectuals, four (11%) were women (Simone de Beauvoir, Marguerite Yourcenar, Marguerite Duras, and Claire Brétécher). In addition, Beauvoir and Yourcenar, who were in the top ten, could hardly have been chosen only by women.

In 1989, after the deaths of Barthes, Foucault, and Lacan, Lévi-Strauss was still considered the most influential intellectual, sharing first place with the journalist Bernard Pivot, who had his own literary program, *Apostrophes*, on television.[6] Among the top ten, Bourdieu was ninth. In 1981, he had been 36th. With Lévi-Strauss, he was the only representative of the social sciences in the top ten. The deaths of Barthes, Foucault, and Lacan opened the way in the 1980s for the ascension of a mixed group of intellectuals: historian/editors such as

Foucault totem and worshippers Julia Kristeva, Gilles Deleuze, and Félix Guattari. Pekka Vuori, *Helsingin Sanomat* (Helsinki, Finland), 5 December 1993, p. B2. Reprinted with permission of Pekka Vuori.

Illustration 5. Totemism in the 1990s.

Georges Duby, François Furet, and Pierre Nora; the writers Angelo Rinaldi and E. M. Cioran; philosophers/editors Bernard-Henri Lévy and François Wahl; politicians like François Mitterrand and Jack Lang; philosophers/journalists such as Jean-François Revel; and so on.[7] Women also disappeared from the list: only eleven out of 147 (0.4%) were women. The physical disappearance of Beauvoir and Yourcenar and the male-biased composition of the jury might partly explain this phenomenon.

Both in 1981 and 1989, half of the top ten were *normalien/nes*. Many avant-garde writers of the 1960s, associated with the *Nouveau Roman* or *Tel Quel*, were part of the lower intellectual nobility in the 1980s. In the lower intellectual nobility I would include those thinkers who were not the most influential, but were influential enough to be sent questionnaires on intellectual power in France,[8] or to figure on a list of thinkers considered as important intellectuals.[9] These included members of both the *Nouveau Roman* (Michel Butor, Marguerite Duras, Samuel Beckett, and Alain Robbe-Grillet) and *Tel Quel* (Jacques Derrida, Michel Deguy, Viviane Forrester, Julia Kristeva, Bernard-Henri Lévy, Alain Rey, Denis Roche, Dominique Rolin, and Philippe Sollers). Their success was not, however, as spectacular as that of the scholars. How can this success be explained? What were the relations between social positions and ideas?

In the next section, I relate social mobility and changes in intellectual works to changes in the structure of the intellectual field.

BIMODAL SOCIAL ASCENSION

Based on this study on the most dynamic areas of the French intellectual field in the 1950s and 1960s, sociology, semiology, and avant-garde literature, I will present a projective model on the temporal and spatial patterns of the French intellectual field. This model exemplifies the redefinition of local rationales and discursive practices by the social- and human-scientific intelligentsia. Although the period has been widely studied,[10] it has not been analyzed systematically by highlighting French structural characteristics. In an essentially simplified way, it can be said that the main change was the transformation of the dual structure that had existed from the eighteenth century, into a clearer triadic structure that redefined the relations between state-created and market-created intellectual elites and legitimized to an unprecedented degree cultural celebrity as a social resource. This structural change had a major impact both on social mobility and on the substance of intellectual works. I will argue that this structural change is something unique that must be taken into account each time an element of the French intellectual field is analyzed—whether in itself or in a comparative perspective.

The basic problem when examining the relations between state-created and market-created intellectual elites is the relation between mobility and social resources. Capital structures of diverse social groups and the accumulation and conversion of capital over time must be linked.[11] When examining the social mobility of intellectuals, in addition to an individual's entrance into the intellectual field, a conversion period, in which his/her social assets are accumulated and converted, has to be isolated. The limits of this conversion period are linked to social age: on the one hand, to the period when the individual's social age is minimal and, on the other hand, to the point at which it is maximal; that is, at which conversion does not lead anywhere. These upper and lower limits are personified by two agents: the novice and the academician. An individual's conversion period lies between these two extremes. The rules governing entrance and legitimate conversion of resources in a national intellectual field are contextually defined.[12]

Before presenting more specific examples, let me clarify the modalities of social mobility in the French intellectual field that existed starting from the 1950s. In a simplified way, one can say that parallel to the "traditional" modality of social ascension, the accumulation of academic or literary capital, an "expressway" or alternative path of social ascension emerged, connected with the unprecedented expansion in volume of the intellectual market. The "express way" was linked both to the formation of the third pole, the media, and to the emergence of a large, nonspecialist audience for cultural goods. This third pole had for some time offered various dominated groups, for instance, women at the turn of the twentieth century, the opportunity to pursue an intellectual profession. The difference between the situation in the 1950s and that of earlier period is that in the 1950s this third pole, to which audiovisual culture was linked, became institutionalized as an integral part of the intellectual field. Instead of investment in specific recognition as a writer or scholar, and thus total dependency on a long-term investment in only one subfield and on the dominant agents of this subfield, an unknown individual could now make a career as a cultural celebrity in the media. The prime example is Bernard Pivot, who started at *Le Figaro littéraire* at the beginning of the 1960s and by 1989 had become, with Lévi-Strauss, the most influential intellectual in France. The following simplified diagram (figure 1) illustrates this long-term structural modification from a bipolar intellectual field to a tripolar intellectual field.

Instead of the bipolar structure that had existed from the eighteenth century,[13] a clearer tripolar structure can be isolated in the French intellectual field beginning in the 1950s. The intermediate area existed in an embryonic state until the 1950s, developing slowly or rather, via accelerations in the structuration of the field. Prior to the 1950s, the most extensive change had taken place at the end of the nineteenth century, a transformation widely studied by historians of French intellectual life.[14] The analysis of a tripolar structure, both spatially and temporally more complex than a bipolar structure, requires a processual per-

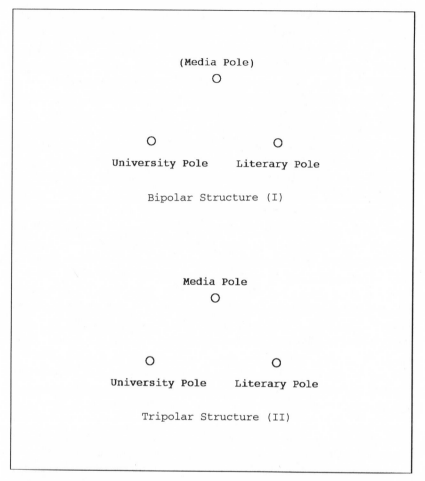

Figure 1. Bipolar structure (I) and tripolar structure (II)

spective rather than a structural one.[15] A processual perspective combines spatial and temporal analysis, keeping in mind all that has been said about the characteristics of the French intellectual field with regard to changes in the quality and quantity of the intellectual audience, and changes in the intellectual heritage, among other features.

The tripolar structure was tied to a tripolar asset structure. The intellectuals able to convert their specific resources into the most versatile and advantageous resource—that is, the less codified resource, cultural celebrity—were the most socially mobile: these individuals were found among the new intellectual nobility in formation, consisting of the social and human scientific intelligentsia and the avant-garde writers.

How did the relationship between the poles change in terms of conversion and flow of resources? In the bipolar field (I), literary, and to a lesser extent academic, recognition could be converted legitimately into cultural celebrity, but cultural celebrity could not be (re)converted easily into either literary or academic merit.[16] Cultural celebrity was still before Foucault's time, a temporally unstable social resource. Even stricter social conventions regulated relations between writers and academics. Literary merit could not be converted into academic power, and vice versa. In the tripolar field (II), all the unidirectional flows became bidirectional as social conventions changed: cultural celebrity could be transformed into both academic and literary legitimacy. Journalists could now become prize-winning authors or academics, and assume positions in the local intellectual nobility. The new sciences, such as sociology, semiology, and anthropology, had to be popularized in the form of "theoretical essays," most often, in order to be used effectively as a social resource. Relatively speaking, cultural celebrity became, with the development of new instances of legitimation and accumulation of fame, a temporally stable, yet still relatively uncodified social resource. When the status of intellectual fame was not codified—that is, not seen as a valuable social asset—its exchange rate was the greatest. Once stabilized, once social mechanisms were created to protect the value of this resource, intellectual fame lost its exceptional character.

In the tripolar field, literary recognition could be converted into academic distinction—many of the members of the *Nouveau Roman* were also university teachers—and academic distinction could be converted into literary recognition, as in the case of numerous philosophers.[17] The crucial element is, however, cultural celebrity, which, being easily accessible and very profitable symbolically and economically, dislocated the relations between different subcapital of intellectual capital. It became acceptable to popularize and to seek recognition among the expanding intellectual public. Starting from the 1950s, both scholars and the *literati* could join the ranks of the *glitterati*. However, once regulated, the formerly enormous symbolic profits found in this type of resource were lost. The points of least resistance for accumulation of this type of capital were to be found in positions occupied by intellectuals such as Barthes and Foucault. From the point of view of effective appropriation of cultural celebrity, the crucial period was when this resource was temporally stable enough to be accumulated but was not yet codified; that is, not yet subject to strict social regulation. During this time, probably during the first half or the middle of the 1960s, the value of cultural celebrity was at its highest. Figure 2 exemplifies these transformations.

What did this tripolar structure mean concretely for the human and social scientific intelligentsia and for the young writers? Let us take the example of

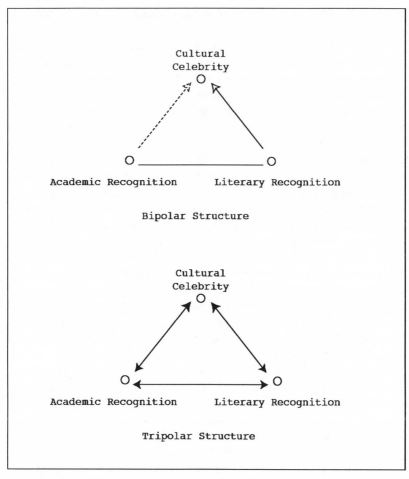

Figure 2. Resource conversions in a bipolar and in a tripolar structure

Michel Foucault, whose social ascension began at the end of the 1950s and culminated with his appointment to the Collège de France and to the higher intellectual nobility in the 1970s—an exceptional success.[18] Once he entered his conversion period, Foucault moved, after initial heavy investment in the university field,[19] toward the intermediate space and the literary field, converting his academic credentials into cultural celebrity. The best investment at this time, this kind of conversion was relatively easy during this phase of rapid expansion of the intermediate space: the new audience needed new idols and the publishers, radical ideas. A clear increase in Foucault's visibility in intellectual reviews and the cultural press can be observed from the beginning to the middle of the 1960s, especially in reviews like *Critique* (two articles in both 1962 and 1963, and one each in 1964 and 1966), *Tel Quel* (two appearances, in 1963 and 1964), *La Nouvelle revue française* (1961, 1962 and 1964, and twice in 1963); in the daily *Le Monde* (1961, 1964, 1969, and twice in 1970); in weeklies like *Le Nouvel Observateur* (twice, in 1960 and 1970); and in biweeklies like *Les Lettres françaises* (1966 and 1967) and *La Quinzaine littéraire* (twice, in 1966 and 1967).[20] In short, the value of cultural fame was the highest for young intellectuals during the relatively short period when its value was temporally unstable prior to the social codification and regulation of its accumulation and conversion.

During the period of conversion of his academic credentials into cultural celebrity, changes could also be seen in Foucault's works. Instead of academic texts, he wrote mainly theoretical and literary texts.[21] This period was then followed by a reversal, that is, his return toward the university. Foucault started to publish more academic works (such as *Les mots et les choses* [1966]). As of the second half of the 1960s, he distanced himself from the literary avant-garde—from writers such as Sollers, reviews like *Tel Quel*, and "-isms" such as "structuralism"—after having profited from close relations with them. This reversal coincided with the institutional reorganization of the university, especially after May 1968.[22]

In this period of reconversion, Foucault's conversion of his cultural celebrity into academic recognition proved to be as easy as the first period of conversion of his academic distinction into cultural celebrity. During a phase of redistribution of financial resources, the redefinition of academic legitimacy, as new departments in the human and social sciences were created, enabled Foucault, in the process of being appointed to the Collège de France, to oust agents who had invested only in the university field. Foucault's competitors were not known to the wide public, now used to a kind of "light science." It took Foucault, who in the second half of the 1960s was the most visible and famous intellectual hero, sixteen years (1954–70) to move from the beginning of his conversion period into a symbolically dominant position in the intellectual field. By comparison, it took Barthes twenty-four years (1953–77) and Bourdieu twenty-three years (1958–81) to move from anonymity to the Collège de France and a place in the intellectual nobility.

In Foucault's social trajectory—in which structural changes and symbolic investments coincide nearly perfectly—as well as in the careers of intellectuals such as Barthes, Bourdieu, or Derrida who occupied close positions and belonged to the same social group,[23] the "expressway" to social ascension mentioned above, can be recognized. In Barthes's case, cultural celebrity could not be converted so quickly into academic recognition. He did not have the traditional institutional attributes of the intellectual nobility (*normalien*-habitus, *agrégation* in philosophy) as did Derrida, Bourdieu, and Foucault. In a way,

Barthes was too literary[24] and too well-known, which worked for a time to his disadvantage. Although he combined peer recognition with recognition by the intellectual audience, Barthes also became an academic dilettante too soon, and for a long time did not strike the right balance between old and new criteria of excellence. Nevertheless, he also entered the Collège de France in 1977. Of this new intellectual generation Derrida exemplified the opposite case: he was not sufficiently known by the wide intellectual audience. His more rigid *normalien*-habitus prevented his access to the cultural press. Perhaps he was tied more than Foucault to the École. Meanwhile, Bourdieu stood between Barthes and Derrida: not as famous as Barthes, he was somewhat better known than Derrida in some circles due to the political implications of his scholarship.

Schematically, Foucault's trajectory can be presented in the following way: first, entry into the university field; second, accumulation of academic recognition over a period of six years; third, conversion and accumulation of capital with an emphasis on conversion of academic recognition into cultural celebrity over a five-year period; and finally, conversion and accumulation with an emphasis on conversion of cultural celebrity into academic merit over five years. The form and content of Foucault's works followed this same logic of two cultures. They consisted of academic works without academic form[25] and texts with philosophical content—discussing questions like reason, liberty, or man—combined with a human- and social-scientific form.

In order to highlight the specificities of this "express way" (b in figure 3) it has to be calibrated into a larger schematic process-sociological model of the modalities of social ascension (channels a1, a2, and b) and of accumulation/conversion of intellectual capital.[26] None of these modifications can be explained without combining in the analysis spatial attributes and temporal attributes, asset structure, and the multiple accumulation and conversion of capital.[27] Figure 3 presents a simplified visual image of these modalities of social ascension.

After this period of rapid change, stricter social control of the boundaries between the university and literary fields and the intermediate space could be observed.[28] On reading lists for the philosophy baccalaureate in the 1970s, structuralist authors gave way to the classics.[29] The philosopher, writer, journalist, and editor Bernard-Henry Lévy is a good example of an intellectual who in the 1970s was in a position to apply the same kind of strategy as Foucault. Fulfilling the formal requirements of a legitimate French intellectual (*normalien* and *agrégé* in philosophy), Lévy had good contacts with many leading intellectuals, was photogenic—at least compared to Sartre—and was able to communicate. He began very early working at magazines such as the modish *Globe* and in the publishing business as director of several collections at the publishing house Grasset. He also collaborated with the review *Tel Quel*. Academic-philosophers considered his writings technically mediocre and, in contrast to Foucault, he

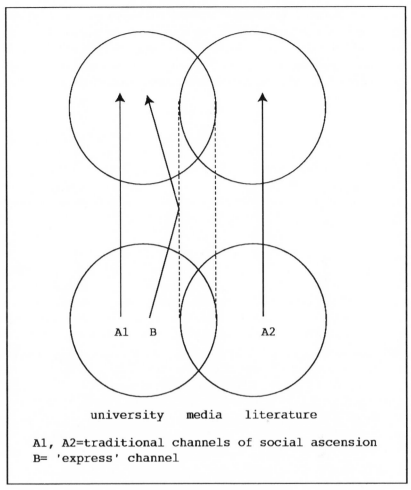

university   media   literature

A1, A2=traditional channels of social ascension
B= 'express' channel

Figure 3. Bimodal social ascension

never became a scholar. But Lévy had at his disposal a very efficient legiti-mation circle, which enabled him to become a member of the higher intellectual nobility in the 1980s and 1990s.[30]

In periods of rapid reorganization of the market for ideas—such as the 1890s, the 1950s, and the 1960s—short-cuts and new channels of ascension are created, which also lead to the redefinition of the mechanisms whereby the local intellectual nobility is formed. If expanding scientific culture and the media created models that enabled young intellectuals to contest established criteria,[31] they also channelled endeavors into certain directions handed down by Latin humanism: conceptual, abstract, and universal thinking, the use of a literary and philosophical fund of knowledge, and the logic of the oblique. The main problem for this second generation of postwar intellectuals was to combine the traditional roles of the *savant* and the *philosophe*, both state-created intellectuals, with the new roles tied to the expansion of the market for cultural goods.[32]

In Conclusion

As I hope to have shown, in the French intellectual field ambitions and values cannot be separated from transmitted institutional frameworks and the educational ideals of Latin humanism and Republican education. The unique features of works such as those of Barthes or Foucault are highlighted against the background of culturally biased criteria and habit-patterns. Sociocultural biographies should be painted by outside observers, free of the hypnosis of grandeur. Not in order to belittle the genius of these intellectuals, but to highlight individual nuances. Both the content and form of intellectual works must be examined in relation to local discursive rules and rationales that direct perceptions and evaluations, the behavioral strategies of the individuals studied, and the mechanisms by which intellectual nobility is socially created.

The previous chapters have stressed the institutional and deontological continuity in the French intellectual field that made possible structured change and constrained symbolic endeavors. Why did succession take place in institutions such as the École Pratique des Hautes Études, Écoles Normales Supérieure and the Collège de France? Because they were the only ones that permitted reconciliation of intellectual radicality with academic respectability. The human- and social-scientific intelligentsia, the core of the new intellectual nobility, succeeded in imposing new criteria of excellence that satisfied both tradition and the new criteria for access to the highest positions. In this way order could be restored.

Meanwhile, the *Nouveau Roman* succeeded traditional psychological literature. The *Tel Quel* group formed for some time the second generation of the *Nouveau Roman* but quickly abandoned literature for broader intellectual concerns. Writers like Robbe-Grillet and Sarraute formed the literary elite of the 1960s. At that time, the review *Tel Quel* played the role of symbolic police of the avant-garde. Noted intellectuals like Barthes, Derrida, and Foucault published in *Tel Quel*. In a certain way, the review *Tel Quel* continued the tradition of avant-garde reviews of the interwar period. Some of the Telquelians, notably Philippe Sollers, later returned to traditional literary forms.

The dominant French intellectual habitus has been defined by intellectuals, mostly men who have had a specific kind of informal and formal education. This education was tied to class and to specific educational institutions. The new intellectual nobility formed in the 1960s combined seemingly contradictory dimensions: popularized scholarly work, often conceived in binary form, and political radicalism. By colonizing the media, publishing theoretical essays, and creating new career combinations, this generation partly bypassed the traditional means by which the local intellectual nobility was formed.

The comparative dimension has been missing in cultural studies, especially in those inspired by Bourdieu's approach. This kind of comparative approach is urgently needed, in order to examine cultural creation in all its complexity. I have tried to present in this work an alternative, processual field theoretical model of French intellectual culture, which builds upon and contrasts with Bourdieu's structural approach to culture. A dynamic and comparative analysis of the asset structures of cultural creators and of the more general value of various resources can reveal important deep structures of intellectual life. This type of analysis enables the researcher to evaluate the relative values and mechanisms of accumulation and conversion of different types of social resources and to present instruments by which long-term analysis of intellectual fields can be assessed. In my view, a comparative historical view can refine the existing sociological approaches to the study of intellectuals—mainly, those represented by structural constructivism—and may prevent simplified comparative research and theoretical sublimation.

In order to compare cultural capital and elites in different contexts, I believe one has to generalize formally and individualize substantially; that is, to preserve the same loose terms—cultural capital, for instance—but redefine them depending on local characteristics. For example, language skills can be considered as being an important part of cultural capital in bilingual (Finnish-Swedish) Finland, but not in France, where one highly coded language is used by the intelligentsia. Sensitivity to questions of gender and ethnicity is a must for any American scholar and intellectual, but less of a concern for a French intellectual. Likewise, knowledge of the classics may not be an issue when defining cultural competence in the United States, but will be one in France. Further, not only quantities along a single scale but also qualities—forms of contents, to use a linguistic term[33]—must be accounted for.

The kind of contextual analysis I am proposing addresses three biases inherent in the current mode of international circulation of ideas. A first bias appears when social and historical aspects of personal characteristics such as verbal skills or a style of writing are not examined. Conceptual originality or scientific extremism might be taken as a thinker's achievement and not as something internalized and forming part of the habitus of the thinker. The multiple forces that structure agency and subjectivity are left unexplored. A second bias occurs when local restrictions, for instance the lack of knowledge of foreign languages or specialized fields of research, are taken as signs of a superior mind.

Foucault's total amateurism in sociology is a case in point. For an audience lacking competence, competence is found even in signs of incompetence. The characteristics of an intellectual have to be related to the characteristics of his/her audience. A third bias takes place when prestige outside of France is seen as a sign of domestic prestige. For instance, it comes as a surprise to many American "deconstructionists" to find out that Derrida was for a long time a marginal intellectual figure.

In order to develop an adequate comparative approach to symbolic goods, an element which is going to be compared in one context to a similar element in another context has to be mapped in relation to the environment. It is, for instance, highly problematic to compare social classes in the United States and in France[34] without having mapped the relative positions and dynamics of these entities in their relative contexts: a holistic point of view is missing.[35] Likewise, to argue for heterologous practices[36] makes sense only in a context—such as the United States—where ethnic and religious diversity is the rule and politico-administrative decentralization is relatively important. It is less appropriate to do so in a culturally relatively homogeneous European country like France, subjected to centuries of administrative, cultural, and political centralization.

The fragmentation and multipolarity of the American intellectual field seems to be its basic feature. This enables the co-existence within it of many conflicting hierarchies: it cannot possibly be analyzed in the same terms as the French intellectual field has been analyzed in this study. Thus, the background of the social stage, or the structure of the intellectual field is not the same everywhere. To assume that the structure is the same indirectly reproduces the traditional French tendency toward universalism. In its turn, this inhibits the ability to draw a table of human diversity. In some works in cultural sociology, French intellectual cosmopolitism thus meets its match in Anglo-American scientific cosmopolitism. The naive theoreticism[37] to which this leads can be avoided and even made obsolete once the contextual character of both the instruments of research—especially different epistemological traditions and styles—and research concerns are taken as a given of comparative and theoretical work.

Notes

INTRODUCTION

1. Wolf Lepenies, *Between Literature and Science: The Rise of Sociology*, English translation by R. J. Hollingdale (Cambridge: Cambridge University Press, 1988), 7.

2. Ezra Suleiman, *Elites in French Society: The Politics of Survival* (Princeton: Princeton University Press, 1978).

3. See, for instance, Johan Heilbron, *The Rise of Social Theory*, English translation by Sheila Gogol (London: Polity Press, 1995); Diane Rubenstein, *What's Left? The École Normale Supérieure and the Right* (Madison: University of Wisconsin Press, 1990); and Robert J. Smith, *The École Normale Supérieure and the Third Republic* (Albany: SUNY Press, 1982).

4. Tony Judt, *Past Imperfect: French Intellectuals 1944–1956* (Berkeley: University of California Press, 1992), 299. For an English language presentation of the ideas of the most important thinkers, cf. R. Macksey and E. Donato, eds., *The Language of Criticism and the Sciences of Man: The Structuralist Controversy* (London and Baltimore: Johns Hopkins University Press, 1970).

5. Pierre Bourdieu, "Hommage à Michael Pollak," *Actes de la recherche en sciences sociales* 94 (1992): 106.

6. Jean-François Revel, *Pourquoi des philosophes?* (Paris: Julliard, 1957).

7. Alan Sheridan, *Michel Foucault: The Will to Truth* (London and New York: Tavistock Publications, 1980), 2.

8. Cf. Michel Foucault, *Les mots et les choses* (Paris: Gallimard, 1966); Sheridan, *Michel Foucault*, 82.

9. See Pierre Bourdieu, *Homo Academicus*, English translation by Peter Collier (Stanford: Stanford University Press, 1988); Jean-Claude Chevalier and Pierre Encrevé, "La création de revues dans les années 60: matériaux pour une histoire récente de la iinguistique en France," *Langue française* 63 (1984): 101; François Dosse, *Histoire du*

141

structuralisme II: Le chant du cygne, 1967 à nos jours (Paris: La Découverte, 1992); Marcel Hénaff, *Claude Lévi-Strauss* (Paris: Belfond, 1991), 80; and Georges Mounin, *Introduction à la sémiologie* (Paris: Minuit, 1970).

10. Cf., for instance, Peter Burke, *The French Historical Revolution: The Annales School 1929–1989* (Stanford: Stanford University Press, 1990); *Le développement des sciences sociales en France au tournant des années soixante* (Paris: Éditions du CNRS, 1989); Brigitte Mazon, *Aux origines de l'E.H.E.S.S.: Le rôle du mécénat américain* (Paris: Cerf, 1988); and Traian Stoianovich, *French Historical Method: The Annales Paradigm* (Ithaca: Cornell University Press, 1976).

11. There exists a complex set of social conventions relative to intellectual excellence, which is formed by the constant reorganization of various elements. Some of these elements "are strong and stable, while others are weak and transient, such as a lot of peripheral connotative couplings" (Umberto Eco, *A Theory of Semiotics* [Bloomington: Indiana University Press, 1976], 125). The strong ones are tied to formal and informal education, the schooling system and social class (e.g., diverse institutions), the medium strong ones to structural positions of the agent, for instance the affinities between marginal writers and marginal academics in the 1960s, and the weak ones to conjuncture such as signing a petition without engaging into further cooperation. These levels have to be separated from one another in the analysis.

12. Cf. Bourdieu, *Homo Academicus*; Niilo Kauppi, *The Making of an Avant-Garde: Tel Quel*, English translation by Anne R. Epstein (Berlin and New York: Mouton de Gruyter, 1994), xvii–xviii.

13. Raymond Bellour, *Le livre des autres* (Paris: Union Générale d'Éditions, 1978), 334, 354.

14. This might involve knowledge of previous works, respect of academic etiquette, verification, use of statistics and interviews, etc.

15. Cf. Louis Pinto, "Mass Media Mandarins," in *Vanguards of Modernity*, edited by Niilo Kauppi and Pekka Sulkunen (Jyväskylä: Publications of the Research Unit for Contemporary Culture 32, 1992), 98–106.

16. For some of these, cf. James Boon, *From Symbolism to Structuralism: Lévi-Strauss in a Literary Tradition* (New York: Harper & Row, 1972); Régis Debray, *Le pouvoir intellectuel en France* (Paris: Gallimard, 1986); Descombes, *Modern French Philosophy*; François Dosse, *Histoire du structuralisme I: Le champ du signe, 1945–1966* (Paris: La Découverte, 1991) and *Histoire du structuralisme II*; Howard Gardner, *The Quest for Mind: Piaget, Lévi-Strauss and the Structuralist Movement* (New York: Knopf, 1973); David Pace, *Claude Lévi-Strauss: The Bearer of Ashes* (London: Routledge and Kegan Paul, 1983); and Thomas Pavel, *The Feud of Language: A History of Structuralist Thought* (Oxford: Basil Blackwell, 1989).

17. This analysis does not exclude the examination of the political activities of intellectuals like Foucault, although these aspects will not be explicitly analyzed in this work. In other words, being a specialized intellectual does not exclude political militancy.

18. By intellectual field is meant the social positions and discourses occupied by individuals considered as being intellectuals. Definitions of the intellectual abound. What they have in common is that an intellectual is usually a learned individual who takes part in public debate. In France, the history of the intellectual is a long one. It is tied to another social role, that of the writer.

19. The closest to this are Dosse, *Histoire du structuralisme I* and *Histoire du structuralisme II*.

20. Cf. the English version of my Ph.D. thesis: Kauppi, *The Making of an Avant-Garde*.

21. For instance, Alain Accardo, *Initiation à la sociologie de l'illusionisme social* (Bordeaux: Éditions le Mascaret, 1983); Alain Caillé, "Esquisse d'une critique de l'économie générale de la pratique," *Cahiers du L.A.S.A.* 8–9 (1988): 103–214.

22. Especially Pierre Bourdieu, "Disposition esthétique et compétence artistique," *Les Temps modernes* 295 (1971): 1345–78; *Homo Academicus*; and *The Field of Cultural Production. Essays on Art and Literature*, English translation by Randall Johnson et al. (New York: Columbia University Press, 1993).

23. Foucault, *Les mots et les choses.*

24. Norbert Elias, *The Civilizing Process: A History of Manners*, vol. 1, English translation by Edmund Jephcott (Oxford: Basil Blackwell, 1978).

25. Bourdieu, *The Field of Cultural Production.*

26. I separate Bourdieu's works on culture from his other studies. Bourdieu has examined the French state as a sociological entity in *La noblesse d'état: Grandes écoles et esprit de corps* (Paris: Minuit, 1989).

27. Foucault, *Les mots et les choses.*

28. In the French sense of the term, as Sheridan points out, Sheridan, *Michel Foucault*, 82.

29. Cf. Émile Durkheim, *L'évolution pédagogique en France*, tomes I and II (Paris: Alcan, 1938); and Elias, *The Civilizing Process*. By *habitus* is meant a mechanism which enables individuals to adapt themselves to social life and "do the right things" without necessarily having explicitly learned them.

30. For a critique of the "linguistic turn," cf. Roger Chartier, *Forms and Meanings: Texts, Performances, and Audiences from Codex to Computer* (Philadelphia: University of Pennsylvania Press, 1995), 94–95. A recent example of an emphasis on individual actions is John R. Hall's article, "The Capitals of Cultures: A Non–Holistic Approach to Status Situations, Class, Gender, and Ethnicity," in *Cultivating Differences: Symbolic Boundaries and the Making of Inequality*, edited by Michèle Lamont and Marcel Fournier (Chicago: University of Chicago Press, 1992), 257–85.

31. Elias, *The Civilizing Process.*

32. See, for instance, Talcott Parsons, *The Structure of Social Action* (New York: The Free Press, 1968), 762–63.

33. Herbert Spencer, *The Study of Sociology* (Ann Arbor: The University of Michigan Press, 1961), 26–28.

34. Cf. John Lechte, *Julia Kristeva* (London: Routledge, 1990); Philippe Forest, *Philippe Sollers* (Paris: Gallimard, 1992).

35. On the art of "writing well" or of *explication de texte* in the French case, cf. Georges Mounin, *La littérature et ses technocraties* (Paris: Casterman, 1978), 125.

36. Norbert Elias, *The Society of Individuals*, English translation by Edmund Jephcott (Oxford: Basil Blackwell, 1991), 214.

37. By "culture" I mean shared understanding, common ways of doing things and looking at things (Howard S. Becker, "Culture: A Sociological View," *The Yale Review* 72 [Summer 1982]: 518), which change over time and which offer only approximate solutions to cultural problems. Culture is also the object of struggle between social groups striving to define cultural canons in such as way as to favor their own assets.

38. Ruth Benedict, *Patterns of Culture* (Boston and New York: Houghton Mifflin Company, 1934), 2–3.

39. Cf., for instance, Hubert Dreyfus and Paul Rabinow, *Michel Foucault: Beyond Structuralism and Hermeneutics* (Brighton: Harvester, 1983); Hénaff, *Claude Lévi-Strauss*; Barry Smart, *Foucault, Marxism and Critique* (London: Routledge and Kegan Paul, 1983); Robert Wuthnow, James Davison Hunter, Albert Bergesen, and Edith Kurzweil, eds., *Cultural Analysis: The Work of Peter L. Berger, Mary Douglas, Michel Foucault and Jürgen Habermas* (London: Routledge and Kegan Paul, 1984).

40. Cf. David Hollinger, "How Wide is the Circle of the 'We'? American Intellectuals and the Problem of the Ethos since World War II," *American Historical Review* 98, April 1993: 317.

41. Craig Calhoun, "Culture, History, and the Problem of Specificity in Social Theory," in *Postmodernism and Social Theory*, edited by Steve Seidman and David G. Wagner (London: Basil Blackwell, 1992), 244–88; Calhoun, "Habitus, Field and Capital: The Question of Historical Specificity," in *Bourdieu: Critical Perspectives*, edited by Craig Calhoun, Edward LiPuma, and Moishe Postone (Chicago: University of Chicago Press, 1993), 61–88; Steve Seidman, "The End of Sociological Theory: The Postmodern Hope," *Sociological Theory* 9 (1991): 131–46.

42. For example, philosophy, *Annales*-history, anthropology, linguistics, and economics.

43. Cf. Denis Hollier, ed., *A New History of French Literature* (Cambridge, Mass.: Harvard University Press, 1989); Leon S. Roudiez, *French Fiction Revisited* (New York: Columbia University Press, 1991).

PART I

1. Lionel Abel, "Sartre vs. Lévi-Strauss," in *Claude Lévi-Strauss: The Anthropologist as Hero*, edited by E. Nelson Hayes and Tanya Hayes (Cambridge, Mass.: MIT Press, 1970), 235–46; Pierre Bourdieu and Jean-Claude Passeron, "Sociology and Philosophy in France since 1945," *Social Research* 38 (1967): 162–212; Dosse, *Histoire du structuralisme I*, 30–35; Michel Foucault, "Truth and Power," in *French Sociology: Rupture and Renewal Since 1968*, edited by Charles Lemert (New York: Columbia University Press, 1981), 293–307; Judt, *Past Imperfect*, 290.

2. The inspiration for this type of analysis has been provided by Donald Broady's thorough study, *Sociologi och epistemologi: Om Pierre Bourdieu's författarskap och den historiska epistemologin* (Stockholm: HLS Förlag, 1991).

3. Cf. especially Pierre Bourdieu, *Distinction: A Social Critique of Judgement of Taste*, English translation by Richard Nice (Cambridge: Cambridge University Press, 1984), xi–xiv.

1. THE ANCIEN RÉGIME

1. Priscilla P. Clark, *Literary France: The Making of a Culture* (Berkeley: University of California Press, 1987), 1–14; Pace, *Claude Lévi-Strauss*, 3.

2. Russia seems to have been in many respects closer to the French model in the nineteenth century (cf. Vladimir C. Nahirny, *The Russian Intelligentsia: From Torment to Silence* [New Brunswick: Transaction Books, 1983]); and Igor Zolotusskii, "Rossiia na polputi k zapadu," *Iunost* 3 [1992]: 3).

3. Priscilla P. Clark and Terry N. Clark, "Writers, Literature, and Student Movements in France," *Sociology of Education* 42, no. 4 (1969): 293–314; Elias, *The Civilizing Process*, 3–32; Christophe Charle, *Naissance des "intellectuels" 1880–1900* (Paris: Minuit, 1990) and "The Characteristics of Intellectuals in France around 1900 in a Comparative Perspective," in *Vanguards of Modernity*, edited by Niilo Kauppi and Pekka Sulkunen, 26–32 (Jyväskylä: Publications of the Research Unit for Contemporary Culture 32, 1992).

4. Durkheim, *L'évolution pédagogique en France I*.

5. Jean-Claude Chevalier, in Chevalier and Encrevé, "La création des revues dans les années 60," 73.

6. Bourdieu, *Homo Academicus*, 238.

7. Georges Steiner, "Orpheus with His Myths," in *Claude Lévi-Strauss: The Anthropologist as Hero*, edited by E. Nelson Hayes and Tanya Hayes, 171 (Cambridge, Mass.: MIT Press, 1970).

8. Durkheim, *L'évolution pédagogique en France II*, 129.

9. It should be kept in mind, however, that the French intellectual field is highly gendered. Women are, apart from a few exceptions that prove the rule, always dominated.

10. Terry N. Clark, *Prophets and Patrons* (Cambridge, Mass.: Harvard University Press, 1973); and Joseph Ben-David, *Scientific Growth: Essays on the Social Organization and Ethos of Science* (Berkeley: University of California Press, 1991).

11. Didier Eribon has monopolized the major French intellectual stars (Pierre Bourdieu, George Dumézil, Michel Foucault, Claude Lévi-Strauss) by interviewing them in newspapers such as *Le Monde* and *Libération* and weeklies like *Le Nouvel Observateur*, or by writing their biographies, as in Foucault's case. The social demand for intellectual portraits of the superstars has also fuelled the creation of audiovisual intellectual portraits, on stars like Edmond Jabès, Lévi-Strauss, Bourdieu, and Derrida.

12. Lévi-Strauss, *Conversations with Claude Lévi-Strauss*, 178.

13. For illustrations of this, see the discussions with Charbonnier: Georges Charbonnier, *Entretiens avec Claude Lévi-Strauss* (Paris: Julliard, 1961).

14. Cf. Hénaff, *Claude Lévi-Strauss*, 25.

15. Pace, *Claude Lévi-Strauss*, 8.

16. See Eco, *A Theory of Semiotics*, 190–205, for a sophisticated discussion of the problem of iconicity.

17. Cf. Robert Darnton, *The Great Cat Massacre and Other Episodes in French Cultural History* (New York: Norton, 1984); Clark and Clark, "Writers, Literature and the Student Movements in France"; Charle, *Naissance des "intellectuels"*; Anna Boschetti, *The Intellectual Enterprise: Sartre and Les Temps modernes*, English translation by Richard C. McCleary (Evanston: Northwestern University Press, 1988); Kauppi, *The Making of an Avant-Garde*; Louis Pinto, *La philosophie entre lycée et avant-garde: Les métamorphoses de la philosophie dans la France d'aujourd'hui* (Paris: L'Harmattan, 1987) and "Mass Media Mandarins," 98–106.

18. Alexander I. Herzen, *My Past and Thoughts*, English translation by Constance Garnett (Berkeley: University of California Press, 1982), 234.

19. These concepts were often borrowed from other fields, like physical chemistry in the case of Greimasian semiology, or the evolving social sciences. The objects of research had been appropriated and shaped by previous avant-gardes, or they were part of the national cultural heritage.

20. I believe that the current dominant French sociology of culture represented by Pierre Bourdieu and his students demonstrates clearly this specific intellectual habitus by combining traditional literary and philosophical culture (references in Greek and Latin to philosophers such as Leibniz and Spinoza; Proustian construction of sentences, complexity in style and levels of analysis; use of French literary classics), radical political discourse (Republicanism, critique of social domination); and sociological and anthropological methods and objects of research (statistics, interviews, class structure, reproduction of social structure). In this way, the work meets the requirements of a part of the intellectual public.

21. Chevalier and Encrevé, "La création de revues dans les années 60," 81; Bernard Laks, "Le champ de la sociolinguistique française de 1968 à 1983, production et fonctionnement," *Langue française* 63, (September 1984): 103–27.

22. A comparable rapid expansion of the young segments of the intellectual public, which had favored extensive changes in the intellectual field had occurred previously at the end of the nineteenth century.

23. Especially sixty posts at the Sixth Section of the École Pratique des Hautes Etudes in the first half of the 1960s, cf. *Les idées en France 1945–1988: Une chronologie* (Paris: Gallimard, 1989).

24. Julia Kristeva provides a prime example of this, becoming a full professor at the age of 32.

25. Jean-Louis Fabiani, *Les philosophes de la République* (Paris: Minuit, 1988), 171–72; Pinto, *La philosophie entre lycée et avant-garde*, 67–109.

26. Alain Robbe–Grillet, "L'exercice problématique de la littérature," in *Les enjeux philosophiques des années* 50, edited by Christian Descamps (Paris: Centre Georges Pompidou, 1989), 25.

27. This aspect has been unduly minimized by outside observers. In order to perceive the dynamics of the French intellectual field one must at least trace a simplistic outline of the general direction of changes. With the expansion of the public and production, the "third public" in fact enabled the creation of a symbolically and economically profitable submarket of avant-garde goods in the 1960s. Consequently, the social value of avant-garde changed radically. Institutionalization also includes literary institutionalization, and more generally the institutionalization of the avant-garde. Outside observers have also minimized the impact of the many new economic and symbolic awards available to the new generation. This larger structural and morphological change explains the unforeseen intellectual and economic success of some intellectuals such as Barthes, Derrida, and Foucault, and reviews such as *Critique* and *Tel Quel*.

28. Positions in university committees for instance, cf. Didier Eribon, *Michel Foucault*, English translation by Betsy Wing (Cambridge, Mass.: Harvard University Press, 1991).

29. Appearing in paperback form, Yvonne Johannot, *Quand le livre devient poche* (Grenoble: Presses Universitaires de Grenoble, 1978).

30. Roland Barthes, "Réponses," *Tel Quel* 47 (1971): 99.

31. Cf. Burke, *The French Historical Revolution*, and Ronald Schleifer, "Introduction," in A. J. Greimas, *Structural Semantics: An Attempt at a Method*, English translation by Daniele McDowell, Ronald Schleifer, and Alan Velie (Lincoln and London: University of Nebraska Press, 1983), xi–lvi.

32. Honoré de Balzac, "Avant-propos à la Comédie Humaine," in *Scènes de la vie privée*, tome 1 (Paris: Furne, 1842), 7–42, and Émile Zola, *Carnets d'enquête: Une ethnographie inédite de la France* (Paris: Plon, 1986).

33. Lévi-Strauss, *Conversations with Claude Lévi-Strauss*, 59.

34. Clifford Geertz, *The Interpretation of Cultures* (New York: Basic Books, 1973), 347.

35. Dosse, *Histoire du structuralisme I*, 47.

36. In fact, in Althusser's case the unmasking of illusions in his autobiography amounted to a social suicide.

37. Pierre Bourdieu, *Outline of a Theory of Practice*, English translation by Richard Nice (Cambridge: Cambridge University Press, 1977); Marc Bloch, "Language, Anthropology and Cognitive Science," *Man* 26, no. 2 (1991): 185.

38. Charles Lemert, "Introduction," in *French Sociology: Rupture and Renewal Since 1968*, edited by Charles Lemert (New York: Columbia University Press, 1981), 14–15; Christophe Charle, *Naissance des "intellectuels"*.
An overt concentration on internal institutionalization of the university when assessing the state of intellectual modernity leads some outside observers to transfer—probably unconsciously—methods working in some contexts into other contexts without a preliminary analysis of the contextual aspects of their models. Scientific creation cannot be reduced to the level of institutionalization of the university. This may cause the role of the third public to be interpreted in a strictly negative way: such a third public simply prevents professionalization (Ben-David, *Scientific Growth*, 369). Its positive role in the dynamics of an academic culture or more largely an intellectual culture is not assessed. The relationship between the two seems to be the recurrent blind spot. Questions such as why some English mandarins and intellectuals "especially among university dons and students, cannot afford to be just brilliant intellectuals or writers, as they can be in France" (Ben-David, *Scientific Growth*, 59), are left unsolved.

39. Johan Heilbron, "The Tripartite Division of French Social Science: A Long-Term Perspective," in *Discourses on Society. The Shaping of the Social Science Disciplines*, edited by Peter Wagner, Björn Wittrock, and Richard Whitley (Dordrecht: Kluwer, 1990), 73–92.

40. Robbe–Grillet, "L'exercice problématique de la littérature," 32.

41. Pinto, "Mass Media Mandarins," 98–106.

42. Cf., for instance, Bourdieu, *Homo Academicus*; Descombes, *Modern French Philosophy*, 5–7; Fritz Ringer, *Fields of Knowledge: French Academic Culture in Comparative Perspective* (Cambridge: Cambridge University Press, 1992); Rubenstein, *What's Left?*

43. Charles Lemert, "Literary Politics and the Champ of French Sociology," *Theory and Society* 10 (1981): 645–69; David Maybury-Lewis, "Science or Bricolage," in *Claude Lévi-Strauss: The Anthropologist as Hero*, edited by E. Nelson Hayes and Tanya Hayes (Cambridge, Mass.: MIT Press, 1970), 150–63.

44. Clark and Clark, "Writers, Literature, and Students Movements in France," 298.

45. Robbe-Grillet, "L'exercice problématique de la littérature," 26.

46. Cf. Alfred von Martin, *Sociology of the Renaissance* (New York: Harper Torchbooks, 1963), 71.

47. Michel Foucault, *The Birth of the Clinic: An Archeology of Medical Perception*, English translation by A. M. Sheridan (London: Tavistock, 1976), ix.

48. Cf. for an earlier example of this type of transcoding Reino Virtanen, "Proust's Metaphors from the Natural and Exact Sciences," *Publications of the Modern Language Association of America (PMLA)* (1954): 1038–59.

2. THE NOUVEAU RÉGIME

1. Anna Boschetti, *The Intellectual Enterprise*; Michel Foucault, "Truth and Power," 293–307.

2. Descombes, *Modern French Philosophy*, 3.

3. Lévi-Strauss, *Conversations with Claude Lévi-Strauss*, 76.

4. Jean-Luc Godard, "Luttes sur deux fronts: Conversation avec Jean-Luc Godard," *Cahiers du cinéma* 194, October (1967): 21.

5. Godard, "Luttes sur deux fronts," 21.

6. For this term, see J. M. Lotman, L. I. Ginsburg, and B. A. Uspenskij, *The Semiotics of Russian Cultural History*, English translation (Ithaca, N.Y.: Cornell University Press, 1985), 94.

7. To use Lévi-Strauss's coinage, Lévi-Strauss, *Conversations with Claude Lévi-Strauss*, 91.

8. Often the problem with the approaches of foreign observers, which have the advantage of not being tied to local etiquette and rules of convenience, is that they do not analyze in a relational perspective either the ideas or the institutions. It is not enough to examine the work of an individual, be it even Lévi-Strauss (Pace, *Claude Lévi-Strauss*) or Foucault (Sheridan, *Michel Foucault*). Ideas have to be examined in relation to a *modus operandi* of intellectual work. In order to understand the specific meaning of a work, the state of the whole social structure at a precise moment in time must be grasped for effective evaluation of the subtle complicities and oppositions between individuals and institutions.

9. These restrictions were synonymous with the criteria of reception of certain parts of the public and of inherited literary culture.

10. There are two obstacles to a sophisticated social scientific analysis of intellectual creation: first, a strict sociology of science does not take into account wider cultural dynamics; second, a "theoretical" reading hides the relations between intellectual practices and social structure. Usually, "theoretical" readings of "structuralism" or "poststructuralism" lead to nothing more than an intellectual parade—to purely formal presentations of already known, recycled facts. For the thousandth time, Saussure, Foucault, Derrida, and Lévi-Strauss (the antecedents) are made to march in the first row (occasionally one can "discover" somebody until then relatively unknown); in the second row come the minor prophets; and in the third row contemporary commentators, including the author of the work him- or herself.

11. *Normalien/ne* and *agrégé(e)* in philosophy forming elements of a heritage shared by individuals having these properties.

12. Jean-Marie Domenach, *Enquête sur les idées contemporaines* (Paris: Seuil, 1981), 111.

13. The effects of literary culture include the difficulty in publishing social scientific works in the cultural press once their novelty has faded. Cf. also *Les pratiques culturelles des français* (Paris: La Documentation Française, 1989).

14. "Advertisement for Scherzo Publishers," *Libération*, December 13 (1990): 49.

15. Cf. Pace, *Claude Lévi-Strauss*, 109–17.

16. Paul DiMaggio, "Cultural Boundaries and Structural Change: The Extension of the High Culture Model to Theater, Opera, and the Dance, 1900–1940," in *Cultivating Differences: Symbolic Boundaries and the Making of Differences*, edited by Michèle Lamont and Marcel Fournier (Chicago: University of Chicago Press, 1992), 21–57.

17. Max Weber, *Economy and Society*, English translation by Ephraim Fischoff et al. (Berkeley: University of California Press, 1978), 1144.

18. Cf. for instance Edward Shils, "Charisma, Order, and Status," *American Sociological Review* 30 (1965): 199–213.

19. For a more nuanced analysis of this, see Marcel Mauss, *A General Theory of Magic*, English translation by Robert Brain (London: Routledge and Kegan Paul, 1972).

20. By strategy is meant the implementation of actions which are not necessarily conscious but rather adapted to certain structural conditions, combining habitus and social structure.

PART II

1. Bourdieu, *La noblesse d'état*; Heilbron, "The Tripartite Division of French Social Science," 73–92; Suleiman, *Elites in French Society*.

2. For instance, Bloch, "Language, Anthropology and Cognitive Science," 183–98.

3. Fabiani, *Les philosophes de la République*; Louis Pinto, "Politiques de philosophes 1960–1976," *La Pensée* 197 (1978): 52–71.

4. Norbert Elias, *The Symbol Theory* (London: Sage, 1991), 19; Serge Moscovici, *The Invention of Society: Psychological Explanations of for Social Phenomena*, English translation by W. D. Halls (Cambridge: Polity Press, 1993).

3. DURKHEIM, MAUSS, LÉVI-STRAUSS, BOURDIEU

1. Or genetic structuralism, Pierre Ansart, *Les sociologies contemporaines* (Paris: Seuil, 1990), 29–46.

2. For a reconstruction of Bourdieu's intellectual trajectory, cf., for instance, Donald Broady, *Sociologi och epistemologi*.

3. After 1975 the Sixth Section of the École Pratique des Hautes Études became the École des Hautes Études en Sciences Sociales. See Mazon, *Aux origines de l'E.H.E.S.S.*

4. Raymond Aron, *Mémoires: 50 ans de réflexion politique* (Paris: Julliard, 1983), 349.

5. The term *structural constructivism* was not yet in use when the work was published. *The Craft of Sociology: Epistemological Preliminaries*, English translation by Richard Nice (Berlin and New York: Walter de Gruyter, 1991).

6. See Broady, *Sociologi och epistemologi*, 309–92.

7. Cf., for instance, Marcel Mauss, *Sociologie et anthropologie* (Paris: Presses Universitaires de France, 1985), 391.

8. Claude Lévi-Strauss, *Le regard éloigné* (Paris: Plon, 1983).

9. Pierre Bourdieu, "Intellectual Field and Creative Project," *Social Science Information* 8 (1968): 89–119.

10. A principle propagated also by François Simiand, "Historical Method and Social Sciences," *Review* 9, no .2 (1985): 163–213.

11. Émile Durkheim, *The Rules of Sociological Method*, English translation by Sarah A. Solovay and John H. Mueller (Chicago: The Free Press of Glencoe, 1938), 11–12.

12. Bourdieu et al., *The Craft of Sociology*, 18.

13. Paul Ricoeur, "Structure et herméneutique," *Esprit*, November 1963, 596.

14. Lévi-Strauss, *Structural Anthropology*, 203.

15. Plato, *Timaeus*, English translation by H. D. P. Lee (Hammondsworth: Penguin Classics, 1965), 49–50.

16. Cf. also Simiand, "Historical Methods and Social Sciences," 170.

17. Durkheim, *The Rules of Sociological Method*, 141–44.

18. Durkheim, *The Rules of Sociological Method*; Norbert Elias, *What is Sociology?*, English translation by Stephen Mennell and Grace Morrissey (New York: Columbia University Press, 1978).

19. Gaston Bachelard, *Épistémologie: Textes choisis* (Paris: Presses Universitaires de France, 1971), 12–13; *La formation de l'esprit scientifique: Contribution à une psychanalyse de la connaissance objective* (Paris: Vrin, 1983), 13–22.

20. Bourdieu, *Homo Academicus*, xiii.

21. Elias, *What is Sociology?*, 111.

22. Durkheim, *The Rules of Sociological Method*, 31.

23. Émile Durkheim, "Préface," *Année Sociologique* 1896–1897 (1898): v.

24. Raymond Aron, *Main Currents in Sociological Thought II: Durkheim/Pareto/Weber*, English translation by Richard Howard and Helen Weam (New York: Basic Books, 1967), 202.

25. Bourdieu, *Homo Academicus*, 17.

26. Bourdieu, *Outline of a Theory of Practice*.

27. Durkheim, "Préface," i–vii.

28. For an analysis of its success, see Victor Karady, "Durkheim, les sciences sociales et l'université: bilan d'un demi–échec," *Revue française de sociologie* 28, no. 2 (1976): 267–311.

29. For a presentation of the idea, Émile Durkheim, *The Elementary Forms of Religious Life*, English translation by Joseph Ward Swain (London: George Allen and Unwin, 1935), 16.

30. Cf. also Moscovici, *The Invention of Society*.

31. Bourdieu et al., *The Craft of Sociology*, 19.

32. Durkheim, *The Rules of Sociological Method*, 32.

33. Mounin, *Introduction à la sémiologie*.

34. Lévi-Strauss, *Structural Anthropology*, 33.

35. Pierre Bourdieu, "Genèse et structure du champ religieux," *Revue française de sociologie* 12, no. 3 (1971): 296.

36. Ibid., 300.

37. Ibid., 334.

38. This principle is originally found in Ferdinand de Saussure, *Cours de linguistique générale* (Paris: Payot, 1960).

39. Mauss, *A General Theory of Magic*, 18.

40. Claude Lévi-Strauss, "Introduction à l'oeuvre de Marcel Mauss," in Marcel Mauss, *Sociologie et anthropologie* (Paris: Presses Universitaires de France, 1985), xxviii.

41. Mauss, *Sociologie et anthropologie*, 303.

42. This might involve examining relations between disciplines, the strategies applied by individuals, and so on.

43. Bourdieu et al., *The Craft of Sociology*, 33–56.

44. Pierre Fougeyrollas, *L'obscurantisme contemporain*. Lacan, Lévi-Strauss, Althusser (Paris: Spag-Papyrus, 1983), 76.

45. Bourdieu, *Homo Academicus*, 28.

46. Boschetti, *The Intellectual Enterprise*; Kauppi, *The Making of an Avant-Garde*.

47. Charle, *Naissance des "intellectuels"*; Fabiani, *Les philosophes de la République*; Pinto, *La philosophie entre lycée et avant-garde*.

48. Rémy Ponton, "Naissance du roman psychologique," *Actes de la recherche en sciences sociales* 4 (1975): 66–85.

49. Louis Pinto, "Épistémologies nationales des sciences sociales en France et en Allemagne," 6 February (Paris: Institut de Recherche sur les Sociétés Contemporaines [IRESCO], 1990).

50. Michel Pinçon and Monique Charlot–Rendu, *Les beaux–quartiers* (Paris: Seuil, 1989).

51. Monique de Saint Martin, *L'espace de la noblesse* (Paris: Métaillié, 1994).

52. Bourdieu, *Homo Academicus*.

53. Pierre Bourdieu, *La noblesse d'état*; *Les règles de l'art: Genèse et structure du champ littéraire* (Paris: Seuil, 1992); and *The Field of Cultural Production*.

4. THE USES OF THE "ECONOMY" IN STRUCTURAL CONSTRUCTIVISM

1. The *economic* in the traditional sense of the term will be used with quotation marks. In Bourdieu's sociology, the same word—economy—is used but the methods and objects differ from that of the concept in the traditional sense. Economic terms and schemas are redefined in order to be integrated into a sociological framework, cf. Bourdieu, "Réponse aux économistes," *Économies et sociétés* 28 (1984): 23–32, and Hubert Brochier, "La valeur heuristique du paradigme économique," *Économies et sociétés* 28 (1984): 3–21.

2. The emphasis on a specific form of science throughout Bourdieu's work has to be calibrated within French sociological tradition and historical epistemology (Bachelard, Canguilhem, Duhem), and their specific contradictions and problems. Bourdieu's emphasis on the independence of sociology from psychology, political economy and especially philosophy, his holistic approach and the importance attached to collective beliefs are to be understood in relation to this specific heritage (cf. Heilbron, "The Tripartite Division of French Social Science," 73–75).

3. Bourdieu, *Outline of a Theory of Practice*, 173.

4. Caillé, "Esquisse d'une critique de l'économie générale de la pratique," 103–214; Annie L. Cot and Bruno Laurier, "Métaphore économique et magie sociale chez Pierre Bourdieu," in *L'Empire du sociologue* (Paris: La Découverte, 1984), 70–86; Luc Ferry and Alain Renaut, *La pensée 68: Essai sur l'antihumanisme contemporain* (Paris: Gallimard, 1985), 199–235; Axel Honneth, "Dir zerrissene Welt der symbolischen Formen: Zum kultursoziologischen Werk Pierre Bourdieus," *Kölner Zeitschrift für Soziologie und Sozialpsychologie* 36 (1984): 147–64; Michèle Lamont, *Money, Morals, and Manners: The Culture of the French and American Upper Middle-Class* (Chicago: University of Chicago Press, 1992), 181–88; Michèle Lamont and Annette Lareau, "Cultural Capital: Allusions, Gaps and Glissandos in Recent Theoretical Developments," *Sociological Theory* 6 (1988): 153–68; André Mary, "Métaphores et paradigmes dans le bricolage de la notion d'habitus," *Cahiers du L.A.S.A.* 8–9 (1988): 9–102; Jacques Rancière, "L'éthique de la sociologie," in *L'Empire du sociologue* (Paris: La Découverte, 1984), 13–36; Alain Raynaud, "Le sociologue contre le droit," *Esprit*, March 1980, 82–93.

5. Broady, *Sociologi och epistemologi*; Pekka Sulkunen, "Society Made Visible: On the Cultural Sociology of Pierre Bourdieu," *Acta Sociologica* 25, no. 2 (1985): 110; Vera Zolberg, "Taste as a Social Weapon," *Contemporary Sociology* 15, no. 4 (1986): 511–15.

6. The relationship of Bourdieu's sociology to other sciences—such as economics, psychology (especially Piaget's dialectics of assimilation, or more recently cognitive science), art history (Panofsky's structural studies), statistics (Benzécri's analysis of

correspondence especially)—and their schemas and terms have to be read historically (for a similar approach, Broady, *Sociologi och epistemologi*; Rogers Brubaker, "Rethinking Classical Theory: The Sociological Vision of Pierre Bourdieu," *Theory and Society* 14 [1985]: 745–75). Bourdieu's work seems to create specific problems and ambiguities mostly once the reader starts decoding Bourdieu's work as if it was a theoretical work, by classifying it as Marxist, Weberian, Durkheimian, utilitarian, objectivist, subjectivist, idealist, materialist, and so on. This kind of reading seriously injures Bourdieu's work in the sense that it is detached from the social context of production and in this way prevents a sociological understanding of sociology. The relationship of Bourdieu's sociology with parts of the French intellectual public and the state of the field of sociological production are not addressed. At another level, these readings approach Bourdieu's work from an analytical point of view ("either . . . or") and not from a dialectical point of view ("and . . . and"). In my view, it would be very fruitful to compare, from the point of view of theoretical principles, Bourdieu's approach to that of Piagetian constructive psychology. In France, the most severe criticisms have been formulated, not surprisingly, mostly by "liberal" and ex–Althusserian philosophers (Ferry and Renaut, *La pensée 68*, 199–235; Rancière, "L'éthique de la sociologie," 13–36; Raynaud, "Le sociologue contre le droit," 82–93), and "liberal" sociologists (Raymond Boudon, *À quoi sert la notion de structure?* [Paris: Gallimard, 1968]; François Bourricaud, "Contre le sociologisme: une critique et des propositions," *Revue française de sociologie* 26 [1975]: 583–603).

7. Pierre Bourdieu, *Le sens pratique* (Paris: Minuit, 1980), 85.

8. The concept of "social market" enables emphasis of both the differences between "field" and "market" and the similarities between the concepts.

9. For instance, André Mary, "Métaphores et paradigmes dans le bricolage de la notion d'habitus," 60.

10. Knowing how to talk about food and wine is part of cultural capital in France.

11. Incorporated capital might manifest itself as good manners or good taste, objectified capital as manuals of good behavior, and institutionalized capital as specialized schools which are intended to train individuals to acquire good manners.

12. Inheritance is in Bourdieu's view a precondition for the effective accumulation of cultural capital.

13. Bourdieu and Passeron, *The Inheritors: French Students and their Relation to Culture*, English translation by Richard Nice (Chicago and London: University of Chicago Press, 1979); Passeron, "L'inflation des diplômes," 551–84. It is against this background that an iconoclastic posture is adopted. This iconoclasm is one of the motives behind the use of such terms as *interest* when interests seem to be missing (Bourdieu et al., *The Craft of Sociology*, 251) or of a term like *market* when analyzing cultural creation. In order to succeed, an intellectual has to shock, but *comme il faut*, properly. In Bourdieu's approach detachment from preconstructed notions has to be repeated over again. This critique is thus not a ritual that could be effectuated at the beginning of the

research ("critique of previous research," for instance) and which would abruptly liberate the researcher and open access to "science."

14. Temporality is at the core of *homo economicus*. In order to save, one has to have a conception of the future which is abstract and impersonal. Working does not begin for *homo economicus* when provisions have been used. Time being a scarce resource, the simplest way to analyze different lifestyles in relation to capital structures is to examine the uses and "misuses" of time.

15. For a critique of this view, Noëlle Bisseret, *Les inégaux ou la sélection universitaire* (Paris: Presses Universitaires de France, 1974), 61–73, 94–99.

16. The dichotomy between cultural and economic capital should be questioned, as Lamont (*Money, Morality, and Manners*) has done. But instead of postulating a third dimension, "morality," the dichotomy could be generalized formally and the contents of each type of capital and of their relations redefined. For instance, instead of cultural capital in the French sense of the term, in the Nordic countries a mixture of organizational capital—tied to political organizations and labor unions (until now the Social Democratic Party)—and educational capital, with economic capital, is decisive in the material and symbolic reproduction of these societies. From a field theoretical point of view the following questions should be clarified: which social groups have "morality" as their main type of capital, how does this capital differ from economic and cultural capital, and how is the amount of "morality" determined?

17. Durkheim, *L'évolution pédagogique en France I*, 37.

18. Bourdieu, *Distinction*, 237–39.

19. For detailed analysis, Broady, *Sociologi och epistemologi*, 167–308.

20. There are considerable differences in the forms of contents, to use Hjelmslev's term, of the terminology in different languages. These are often hidden behind nominal equivalence (domination = *domination*, culture = *culture*, capital = *capital*). Terms such as field (*champ*) and capital (*capital*) have a deeper scope in French than in English, the Germanic languages, or Finnish, a non–Indo–European language. *Capital* is very widely used in French in relation to different areas of social activity, as is the term *champ*. It does not have the almost uniquely economic connotation it seems to have in many other languages. This semantic elasticity can be considered one of the main linguistic conditions for the terminological innovations in Bourdieu's sociology. The French term *culture* can be understood as being close to the German term *Bildung*. However, to have culture does not require having a university degree, or an *Abitur* as in Germany (Ringer, *Fields of Knowledge*, 94–108) or as in the Nordic countries, where the role of academe is more central to intellectual life than in France. *Culture* connotates something rather more like "well-read": i.e., familiar with certain texts. Lemert ("Literary Politics and the Champ of French Sociology," 645–69) has also discussed the term *champ*, and Broady has analyzed extensively the key terms and their historical development (Broady, *Sociologi och epistemologi*, 167–308).

21. These have to do with antinomies like tactics versus strategy, long–term versus short–term strategy, conscious versus unconscious strategy, etc., Jean-Claude Passeron, "L'inflation des diplômes: Remarques sur l'usage de quelques concepts analogiques en sociologie," *Revue française de sociologie* 23 (1982): 570.

22. For the first presentation, cf. Bourdieu, "Champ intellectuel et projet créateur," *Les Temps modernes* 246 (1966): 865–906; for the most developed one, cf. Bourdieu, *Le sens pratique*, 333–440; for critiques cf. François Bourricaud, "Contre le sociologisme: une critique et des propositions," 583–603 and Paul DiMaggio, "Review Essay: On Pierre Bourdieu," *American Journal of Sociology* 84, no. 6 (1979): 1460–74.

23. Bourdieu, *Sociologie de l'Algérie* (Paris: Presses Universitaires de France, 1958), 68.

24. Sulkunen, "Society Made Visible," 110.

25. Pierre Bourdieu and Loïc Wacquant, *An Invitation to Reflexive Sociology* (Chicago: University of Chicago Press, 1992), 161. In this sense, Cassirer's neo–Kantism and Bachelard's scientific epistemology are central, not Anglo–Saxon epistemology of the social sciences, which is at the bottom of the hierarchy of intellectual values ("positivism"). Bourdieu is are also very close to the views presented by Norbert Elias and to Merleau–Ponty's "philosophy of ambiguity."

26. Stanley Hoffman, "Monsieur Taste," *New York Review of Books* 33, no. 6 (186): 45–48; Lamont, *Money, Morality, and Manners*, 181–88.

27. Bourdieu, "What Makes a Social Class? On the Theoretical and Practical Existence of Groups," *Berkeley Journal of Sociology* 32 (1987): 1–17.

28. Apart from the usual philosophical critiques of atomism, utilitarianism, and non-reflexive individualism, see Bourdieu's comments in *Outline of a Theory of Practice*, 183–86; and *Distinction*, 3–6.

29. This "causality of the probable" leads to many problems, which have to be analyzed in more detail. It is not always clear what is the precise relationship in specific cases between the sense of placement and the practical logic (or spontaneous statistics) of the agents on the one hand and the statistical regularities constructed by the researcher on the other hand.

30. Bourdieu, *Sociologie de l'Algérie*, 105–6.

31. Bourdieu, *Distinction*, 180.

32. Bourdieu's view of symbolic consumption is very Simmelian; cf. Georg Simmel, "Fashion," *American Journal of Sociology* 62, no. 6 (1957): 541–58. What Bourdieu has introduced, among other things, is a linguistic definition of structure, a differential entity, following Saussure and Lévi-Strauss, which poses numerous tensions in relation to the sociological or statistical definition of structure, regularities in social interaction. If two modalities of structuration (cf. Paul DiMaggio, "Review Essay: On Pierre Bourdieu,"

1468; Mary, "Métaphores et paradigmes dans le bricolage de la notion d'habitus," 91–92) can be isolated, an element of overlap has to supposed—in order for the analysis to combine these—which enables, for instance, the statistically improbable to be transformed by the subject into the "not possible" or the "forbidden" following a dualistic practical logic. In this sense, it could be argued that Lévi-Strauss's abstract and universal "laws of equivalence" are replaced by "partial homologies" or "practical equivalences." Theoretically, this is the case. Concretely, structural principles prevail. In Bourdieu's work, symbolic differentiation takes place mostly vertically and the innovators are always at the top of the hierarchy ("trickle down"). Although adequate in many cases, especially in the case of traditional French culture, this does not take into account some other cases in modern Western societies, such as horizontal movements of "trickle across" (e.g., imitation by social groups in the "dominant class") or upward movements. The latter might include the adoption of jeans by the upper middle class, or the transformation by working-class groups of razor blades from utilitarian objects into aesthetic objects and the appropriation of this aesthetic function by fashion designers.

33. A possible fruitful line of inquiry into this research logic would be to compare French historical epistemology and Bourdieu's practical logic to Charles Peirce's ideas on abduction as opposed to both induction and deduction (cf. Eco, *A Theory of Semiotics*, 131–33).

34. If this is one of the advantages of Bourdieu's approach, it is not always clear if— in an analysis—a general statement is a formal or substantial generalization, or if it is a generalization at all (Brubaker, "Rethinking Classical Theory," n. 60). In my view, this ambiguity is tied to the rationalism of his epistemology, and to Bourdieu's ambition to establish sociology as philosophy's successor as the leading human and social science.

35. Bourdieu, *La noblesse d'état*, 516.

36. Cf., for instance, Bourdieu et al., *The Craft of Sociology*, 251–52.

37. It is especially difficult to evaluate the quality of the practices when studying a social phenomena. One easily either gives too much credit to the agents or too little. They might be more rational and conscious of their actions on paper than in reality because the status of their retrospective rationalizations is not properly evaluated. The limits of the applicability of homologies in cases of dispositional lags is crucial. Obviously, for the human capital approach, which imposes on the objects of research the ideals of the subject of research, this does not constitute a problem (cf., for instance, Theodore W. Schultz, "Investment in Human Capital," *The American Economic Review* 51 [1961]: 1–17).

38. *Métier* (translated as "craft") refers to practical mastery, manual work, skill, and experience. A point which is often emphasized by Bourdieu to his students is that acquiring the sociological craft—because of its relatively uncodified nature—takes a long time and short-cuts do not exist. The uses of the term "craft" also serve as a critique of theoreticism.

39. His students are concerned with the same problems: changes in the relevant features of a field, social properties of the agents, how the agents apply certain strategies

relative to their positions in order to accumulate specific capital, and so on (cf. for instance Charle, *Naissance des "intellectuels"*; Fabiani, *Les philosophes de la République*; Pinto, *La philosophie entre lycée et avant-garde*; Ponton, "Naissance du roman psychologique," 66–85). The works vary in the specific interests and problem settings, the availability of diverse material, the complex restrictions which are imposed by the sociological and intellectual community (Bourdieu's *Homo Academicus* is an excellent example of these) (Bennett M. Berger, "Review Essay: Taste and Domination," *American Journal of Sociology* 91, no. 6 [1986]: 1451), the time and experience invested and the availability of research assistants, and so on. Stylistic "choices" also fulfill specific, culturally biased criteria of excellence (intellectual complexity, sensitivity to details, flexible use of concepts and other instruments, for instance) and in this sense they are not just formal, as opposed to substantial factors of intellectual productions. Basically, the heuristic devices and the general approach used are the same, constituting the vital lead of this research. An interesting element in this could be the influence models of analysis of the social world transmitted by French writers and social critics of the nineteenth century and the beginning of the twentieth century—especially Balzac, Flaubert, and Proust—have had on Bourdieu's sociological approach (cf. Bourdieu et al., *The Craft of Sociology*, 251; Brubaker, "Rethinking Classical Theory," 768; Heilbron, "The Tripartite Division of French Social Science," 73–92; Henri Toboul, "P. Bourdieu et les horloges de Leibniz," *Cahiers du L.A.S.A.* 8–9 [1988]: 274n. 46).

40. Bourdieu, "Structuralism and the Theory of Sociological Knowledge," *Social Research* 35, no. 4 (1968): 686.

41. Bourdieu, "Champ intellectuel et projet créateur," 865–906; "Disposition esthétique et compétence artistique," 1345–78.

42. The difference between analogy and homology has to do mostly with the extent to which a structure is implied in the analysis. Homology requires two distributions of elements which have a similar structure, whereas analogy is looser and implies change. Analogy can refer to actions, for instance.

43. Pierre Bourdieu, *Sociologie de l'Algérie*, 94; Broady, *Sociologi och epistemologi*, 237.

44. Cf. Michael Pollak, *Max Weber en France: l'itinéraire d'une oeuvre* (Paris: Cahiers de l'histoire du temps présent 3, 1986); Monique Hirschhorn, *Max Weber et la sociologie française* (Paris: L'Harmattan, 1988): 126–41; Weber, *Economy and Society*, 439–42.

45. For Husserl, see François Héran, "La seconde nature de l'habitus: Tradition philosophique et sens commun dans le langage sociologique," *Revue française de sociologie* 28 (1987): 385–416. For Merleau–Ponty, see Broady, *Sociologi och epistemologi*, 257–59.

46. When translated and introduced into other academic cultures, a specific work might not be put in its "right place" both temporally in relation to the author's work as a

whole and spatially in relation to other works in the same area at a precise point in time and for this reason will lead to misleading interpretations. For instance, Bourdieu's and his colleages' work *Le métier de sociologue* was published in 1968 in a very specific context (Fabiani, "La sociologie et le principe de réalité," 790–801) four years before *Esquisse d'une théorie de la pratique*. However, the latter work was translated into English fourteen years before the former (*Outline of a Theory of Practice*, 1977; *The Craft of Sociology* 1991). This inversion might hide certain developments, present previously in other forms in Bourdieu's work, such as the incorporation in *Outline of a Theory of Practice* of a more sophisticated reflexive and empirical analysis. Another bias is that ideas will be imported and appropriated by scholars as part of specific scientific strategies which, as their condition of success, demand that the complexity of the issues and the whole body of critical reading present in the production context be reduced or even eliminated (cf. Samuel Weber, *Institution and Interpretation* [Minneapolis: University of Minnesota Press, 1987], 41; Kevin Murray, "Introduction," in *The Judgment of Paris: Recent French Theory in a Local Context*, edited by Kevin D. S. Murray [Sydney: Allen and Unwin, 1992], xxviii). In this way, misunderstandings will be generated. The symbolic and economic importance of the Anglo-Saxon market might also explain Bourdieu's ambition of becoming the "philosophical bad conscience" of "Anglo–Saxon sociology," seen by Bourdieu as being the dominant pole in world sociology.

47. Cf. also Judt, *Past Imperfect*, 253.

48. Brubaker, "Rethinking Classical Theory," 749.

49. It is however unclear in what precise way the field of the economy or the field of the social would be just like any other, more specialized field. They are rather generic fields. Generic fields should be, theoretically and practically, separated from more specialized fields.

50. Caillé, "Esquisse d'une critique de l'économie générale de la pratique," 126–38.

51. Ferry and Renaut, *La pensée 68*, 199–235; Honneth, "Der zerrissene Welt der symbolischen Formen," 149.

52. Cf., for instance, Caillé, "Esquisse d'une critique de l'économie générale de la pratique," 124, 127.

53. Broady, *Sociologi och epistemologi*, 201.

54. Bourdieu, "Reproduction interdite: La dimension symbolique de la domination économique," *Études rurales* 113–14 (1989): 35n. 22; Roos, "Pelin säännöt," 11.

55. Bourdieu, *Distinction*, 234.

56. Bourdieu, "La transmission de l'héritage culturel," in *Le partage des bénéfices*, edited by Darras (Paris: Minuit, 1966), 423.

57. Bourdieu, "Reproduction interdite," 26.

58. I believe that this point of view puts into a meaningful perspective the lexicological strategies and terminological innovations adopted from economic discourse (such as *économie de la grandeur*) by an ex-associate of Bourdieu's, Luc Boltanski (cf. Boltanski and Thévenot, *De la justification: les économies de la grandeur* [Paris: Gallimard, 1991]).

59. Jean-Pierre Terrail, "Les vertus de la nécéssité sujet/objet en sociologie," *Cahiers du L.A.S.A.* 8–9 (1988): 218–19.

60. Cf. Bourdieu, *Distinction*, 94. Thus dozens of variations can be found, which basically fulfill the same purpose of objectification in relation to areas which traditionally have been cast into the "irrational": *commerce de l'honneur, économie des biens symboliques, économie générale des pratiques, marché des biens symboliques, marché linguistique, économie des échanges linguistiques* . . .

61. The constant problem is thus to determine when a field exists, when a social space has gained, even momentarily, so much autonomy that it can be said to exist in its own right. This is an enormous problem for structural constructivism.

62. Albert O. Hirschman, "Against Parsimony: Three Easy Ways of Complicating Some Categories of Economic Discourse," *American Economic Association (AEA) Papers and Proceedings*, May 1984, 89–96.

63. For an example of this, cf. Lamont, *Money, Morals, and Manners*, 181.

64. Alain Viala, *Naissance de l'écrivain: Sociologie de la littérature à l'âge classique* (Paris: Minuit 1985); "Formations de langues légitimes en Europe," *École des Hautes Études en Sciences Sociales* (E.H.E.S.S.), 15 May 1990.

65. Bourdieu, *Distinction*, 94.

66. Bourdieu et al., *The Craft of Sociology*, 147–48.

67. This phase would include operations such as the critique of preconstructed objects, the use of analogical reasoning and homologies by the transfer of schemas from other research areas, and the construction of pertinent features of the field such as the division between the writer and the academic, for instance.

68. Bourdieu, *Distinction*, 24. The contradictions to which multipositionality (occupying many positions in different fields) can lead are not explicitly studied, nor are the relations between a field and a subfield. As the approach is in many ways topological, the only way to analyze this multipositionality is to examine an individual's position at the intersection of different fields—that is, combining different social resources. But temporal patterns relative to the formation of a specific habitus are missing. Also, situations and social interaction are not studied (cf. Nicos Mouzelis, *Sociological Theory: What Went Wrong? Diagnosis and Remedies* [London: Routledge, 1995]). This lack prevents a more sophisticated analysis of subjectivity.

69. In the sense of egoist as the opposite of altruist. Cf. Amartya K. Sen, "Rational Fools: A Critique of the Behavioral Foundations of Economic Theory," in *Beyond Self-Interest*, edited by Jane Mansbridge (Chicago: University of Chicago Press, 1990), 29.

70. Cf., for instance, Mary, "Métaphores et paradigmes dans le bricolage de la notion d'habitus," 66.

71. For instance, when other professions start earning more, or when there are important changes in the social dispositions of the new individuals entering the field and in those of the public, or when monetary revenues start being considered as the main social measure of success.

72. Christophe Charle, "Le beau mariage d'Émile Durkheim," *Actes de la recherche en sciences sociales* 55 (1984): 45–49.

73. Bourdieu, *Le sens pratique*, 192.

74. Symbolic capital is tied to meanings, such as educational titles, family name, and so on.

75. The degree of institutionalization of capital will depend on the role of the state as a guarantor of the values of the titles.

76. From another perspective, cf. Richard Swedberg, "'The Battle of Methods': Toward a Paradigm Shift?" in *Socio-Economics: Toward a New Synthesis*, edited by Amitai Etzioni and Paul R. Lawrence (Armonk, N.Y.: M. E. Sharpe, 1991), 27.

77. This heterogeneity is reflected in the combination of details and general statements, of ethnology and macro-sociology, circular and linear construction, and so on.

78. Marc Ragon, "Les gardes du corps," *Libération*, 27 April 1989, 12.

79. *L'Événement du Jeudi*, 2 February 1989, 66.

5. SEMIOLOGY

1. Louis-Jean Calvet, *Roland Barthes* (Paris: Flammarion, 1990), 167. *Écrivant* signifies a writer devoid of creativity and originality, in opposition to the *écrivain*, the "real" writer.

2. For professionals of the universal studying specific cases is not gratifying psychologically and socially.

3. Steve Seidman, "The End of Sociological Theory: The Postmodern Hope," 192.

4. Calhoun, "Culture, History, and the Problem of Specificity in Social Theory"; Lemert, "Literary Politics and the Champ of French Sociology," 645–69.

5. Heilbron, "The Tripartite Division of French Social Science," 73.

6. James Jacob Lizska, "Peirce in France: An Essay on the Two Founders of Modern Semiotics," *Semiotica* 93 (1993): 139–53.

7. Charle, *Naissance des "intellectuels"*, 231–34; Lepenies, *Between Literature and Science*; Ringer, *Fields of Knowledge*.

8. Ben-David, *Scientific Growth*, 59; Clark, *Prophets and Patrons*, 237.

9. Peter Wagner and Björn Wittrock, "Analyzing Social Science: On the Possibility of the Social Sciences," in *Discourses on Society: The Shaping of the Social Science Discipline*, edited by Peter Wagner, Björn Wittrock, and Richard Whitley (Dordrecht: Kluwer, 1990), 5–7.

10. Bellour, *Le livre des autres*.

11. Jean-Claude Coquet, "La sémiologie en France," in *Le champ sémiologique*, edited by André Helbo (Brussels: Éditions Complexe, 1979), 13.

12. Calvet, *Roland Barthes*, 161.

13. A comparable expansion of the younger segment of the intellectual public had also occurred at the end of the nineteenth century. This growth had favored extensive changes in the intellectual field, such as the partial institutionalization of the social sciences and of social inventions, for instance, of the group "the intellectuals."

14. Dosse, *Histoire du structuralisme I*, 85.

15. T. F. Broden III, "The Development of A. J. Greimas," Ph.D. diss., Indiana University, Bloomington, 1986, 61.

16. Chevalier and Encrevé, "La création de revues dans les années 60," 99.

17. A. J. Greimas, "La linguistique statique et la linguistique structurale," *Le Français moderne* 31 (1963): 68.

18. Mazon, *Aux origines de l'E.H.E.S.S.*; Stoianovich, *French Historical Method*.

19. This subject has been widely studied in France. See, for instance, Denis Hollier and R. Howard Bloch, eds., *The College of Sociology*, English translation by Betsy Wing (Minneapolis: University of Minnesota Press, 1988); and Elizabeth Roudinesco, *Jacques Lacan and Co.*, English translation by Jeffrey Mehlman (Chicago: University of Chicago Press, 1990).

20. Chevalier and Encrevé, "La création de revues dans les années 60," 100.

21. See for instance Bourdieu, *Homo Academicus*, 105–12. This term should be used carefully, especially in order to avoid polemic. The term is not an "invention" of the researcher, who would in this way bring into the object of research, "semiology," certain value judgments from the outside. Marginality is a term produced by this specific entity, the French university system, and it is an essential element in the reproduction of its dual model.

22. Charle, *Naissance des "intellectuels"*, 227–34; Heilbron, "The Tripartite Division of French Social Science," 73–92.

23. Chevalier and Encrevé, "La création de revues dans les années 60," 90.

24. Coquet, "La sémiologie en France," 12; Dosse, *Histoire du structuralisme I*, 247.

25. Louis Pinto, *"Tel Quel*: Au sujet des intellectuels de parodie," *Actes de la recherche en sciences sociales* 66 (1991): 66–77. For a more nuanced view, cf. Kauppi, *The Making of an Avant-Garde*, 344–52.

26. These included Roland Barthes and A. J. Greimas, to name the most famous ones in the case of semiology.

27. Cf., for instance, Barthes, "Réponses," 89–107.

28. Ibid., 90.

29. This intellectual code of etiquette, "good manners," is one of the most important epistemological obstacles in the study of semiology, or for that matter any subject relative to the intellectual field in France. As many of the pioneers of semiology in France are still living, there exist only a few strategies for "locals" who want to approach the object. To avoid waiting thirty years for a historical analysis of the topic, one has to be very abstract, use euphemisms, or preferably do both at the same time. Criticism is always indirect. This restriction is mostly due to the power of the informal social conventions, which are related to the structural features of the field. For this reason a bolder approach, which would lead to typologies for instance, has been totally lacking, even in social-scientific approaches.

30. This resulted from the transcoding of texts, schemas, and terms from one part of intellectual activity to another.

31. Cf. Dosse, *Histoire du structuralisme II* for a discussion of this.

32. A. J. Greimas, "On Meaning," *New Literary History* 203 (1989): 541.

33. Especially Julia Kristeva, *Séméiotiké: Recherches pour une sémanalyse* (Paris: Seuil, 1969).

34. These subareas included linguistics, computer science, information theory, and logic, for instance. The formations in question could be anthropological, literary, linguistic, or philosophical. The relative symbolic heterogeneity is expressed by Greimas in these terms, "I can say that as a linguist I was more inspired by Dumézil and Lévi-Strauss than by other linguists, with the exceptions of Saussure and Hjelmslev of course" (Greimas, "On Meaning," 541).

35. These services could include directions of academic works and publication of book reviews, for instance.

36. This space has to be refined and more precise divisions included so that the properties of other representatives of the new disciplines, like Pierre Guiraud, Claude Brémond, and Georges Mounin, can be taken into account.

37. Barthes and Greimas were old friends. They met for the first time in Alexandria, Egypt in 1950.

38. Greimas, "On Meaning," 542.

39. Barthes, "Réponses," 97.

40. Miller would later become Jacques Lacan's son-in-law.

41. Julia Kristeva, *The Samurai*, English translation by Barbara Bray (New York: Columbia University Press, 1992), 14–16.

42. These included French translations and interpretations of Heidegger and Husserl, for instance. Barthes was from the beginning concerned mainly about literature. He was constantly worried about the literary effects his writing would have on the audience. He wanted to be a *écrivain* and not an *écrivant*, that is, a scientific writer (Calvet, *Roland Barthes*, 167).

43. Marc Buffat, "Le simulacre: Notes pour une diachronie," *Tel Quel* 47 (1971): 108–14.

44. Calvet, *Roland Barthes*, 224–25; Mounin, *Introduction à la sémiologie*, 189–97.

45. Philippe Sollers, cited in Calvet, *Roland Barthes*, 198.

46. Lévi-Strauss, *Conversations with Claude Lévi-Strauss*, 107.

47. Chevalier and Encrevé, "La création de revues dans les années 60," 69; Dosse, *Histoire du structuralisme I*, 93.

48. Frederic Jameson, "Foreword," in A. J. Greimas, *On Meaning: Selected Writings in Semiotic Theory*, English translation by Paul J. Perron and Frank H. Collins (Minneapolis: University of Minnesota Press, 1987), iv.

49. Randall Collins, "Cumulation and Anticumulation in Sociology," *American Sociological Review* 55 (1990): 462.

50. This was the case of Lévi-Straussian anthropology. "I found I was doing structuralism as the linguists did" (Lévi-Strauss, *Conversations with Claude Lévi-Strauss*, 68).

51. Influencing Greimasian semiology and later semiotics, and Bourdieu's sociology.

52. Bloch, "Language, Anthropology and Cognitive Science," 183–98.

53. Greimas, "On Meaning," 541.

54. Schleifer, "Introduction," xii.

55. Greimas, "On Meaning," 539.

56. This could include equally well Freud, Marx, Canguilhem, or Lacan and also, to a certain extent, "empirical" problems.

57. Claudio Segre, "The Style of Greimas and its Transformations," *New Literary History* 203 (1989): 685.

58. Coquet, "La sémiologie en France," 21.

59. These included centralization, high density, and a high level of interaction.

60. Greimas, "On Meaning," 541.

61. Barthes, "Réponses," 94.

62. Ibid., 98.

63. Lévi-Strauss, *Conversations with Claude Lévi-Strauss*, 62.

64. Greimas, "On Meaning," 541–42.

65. *Les idées en France*, 176.

66. Lévi-Strauss, *Conversations with Claude Lévi-Strauss*, 63.

67. Ibid., 74.

68. This initial rapid development led to "the imperialism of literary semiotics" (Coquet, "La sémiologie en France," 113).

69. Coquet, "La sémiologie en France," 11; A. J. Greimas, "Sémiotique," in *La Grande Enclycopédie Larousse* (Paris: Larousse, 1976), 10987.

70. Jacques Fontanille, "Personal Discussion with the Author," Imatra, 19 July 1991.

6. ON SCIENTIFIC STYLE

1. Edouard Delruelle, *Claude Lévi-Strauss et la philosophie* (Brussels: Éditions Universitaires, 1989), 9–18.

2. Hénaff, *Claude Lévi-Strauss*, 8.

3. Althusser, *L'avenir dure longtemps* . . . , 168. For a fine analysis of French novelistic styles, cf. Stephen Ullmann, *Style in the French Novel* (Cambridge: Cambridge University Press, 1957). For Bourdieu's relationship with philosophy, cf. *Critique* 578–79 (1995).

4. Colin Gordon, quoted in Clare O'Farrell, *Foucault: Historian or Philosopher?* (London: Macmillan, 1993), 135.

5. For outright rejections of some types of modern French philosophy, cf., for instance, Alfred Ayer, "Wittgenstein selon Sir Alfred Ayer," *Le Magazine littéraire* 237 (1987): 108–13; and Malcolm Bradbury, *Mensonge* (London: André Deutsch, 1987). For a critique of Lévi-Strauss from a distinctly foreign point of view, cf., for instance, David Maybury-Lewis, "Science or Bricolage," 150–63.

6. Revel, *Pourquoi des philosophes?*, 10.

7. Cf. also Aron's comment, *Mémoires*, 580n. 1.

8. Althusser, *L'avenir dure longtemps* . . . , 158.

9. Maybury-Lewis, "Science or Bricolage," 151.

10. Paul Bové, "Foreword. The Foucault Phenomenon: The Problematics of Style," in Gilles Deleuze, *Foucault*, English translation by Sean Hand (Minneapolis: University of Minnesota Press, 1988), viii.

11. Aron, *Mémoires*, 584.

12. Maybury-Lewis, "Science or Bricolage," 160–61.

13. Revel, *Pourquoi des philosophes?*, 37.

14. Durkheim, *L'évolution pédagogique en France I*, 193–94.

15. Mounin, *La littérature et ses technocraties*, 153.

16. Jean-Louis Fabiani, "La sociologie et le principe de réalité," *Critique* 545 (1992): 790–801.

17. Althusser, *L'avenir dure longtemps* . . . , 169; Collins, *Sociology in Midcentury*, 173.

18. Revel, *Pourquoi des philosophes?*, 37.

19. Judt, *Past Imperfect*, 252.

20. Althusser, *L'avenir dure longtemps* . . . , 159.

21. Ibid., 157–58.

22. The trap of schools of thought is especially cruel in an intellectual field such as the French one, where division is to such a degree that there are no alternatives to submission to its logic. An individual belongs to this or that group, choice being compulsory.

23. For this reason, *romans à clef* (Philippe Sollers, *Women*, English translation by Barbara Bray [New York: Columbia University Press, 1990]; Kristeva, *The Samurai*) are so popular, as they satisfy the requirements of this logic of the oblique. Attacks must be indirect and put into appropriate forms. It is therefore very rare to read anything as straightforward as Raymond Aron's memoirs, in which Aron describes the political differences between himself and Bourdieu (cf. Aron, *Mémoires*, 350, 474, 478), or Althusser's memoirs (Althusser, *L'avenir dure longtemps* . . .), or Revel's work (*Pourquoi des philosophes?*) on French philosophical culture.

24. O'Farrell, *Foucault*, 46–47.

25. This discourse relied on similarities between the natural and the social sciences, the separation of object and subject, and the use of experimental method.

26. See Broady, *Sociologi och epistemologi*, for an analysis of Bourdieu's sociology and this epistemological tradition.

27. Aron, *Mémoires*, 584.

28. In Foucault's work these led to an exploration of the limits of Western rationality, in Bourdieu's studies to an analysis of Kantian aesthetics.

29. Murray, "Introduction," xxviii.

30. This would be considered enough, as is clear in this passage of Mauss's essay on social morphology. This text also shows Mauss's naive scientism, legitimized in opposition to a ridiculed, necessarily equally naive impressionism, exemplified by Anglo-Saxon anthropology and scholars like Edward Westermarck:

> Furthermore, it is an error to believe that the validity of a scientific proposition is narrowly dependent on the number of cases in which it can be verified. When a link has been established in one, even unique case in methodical and minute manner, reality is known in a different manner than when numerous, but disparate facts and curious examples confusedly borrowed from the most heterogeneous societies, races and civilizations, serve as illustrations to demonstrate a link. Stuart Mill has said somewhere that a well made experiment is enough to demonstrate a law. It certainly is much more demonstrative than numerous badly made experiments. Now, this methodical rule applies to sociology as it does to the other sciences of nature. (Mauss, *Sociologie et anthropologie*, 391)

31. The social bond between protagonists and their followers were such that silence was guaranteed, except in exceptional cases such as Althusser's. The most zealous protagonists of the scientific spirit had to stay the most zealous ones, as this was the condition for their symbolic domination over others. I think that what is needed for the analysis of these sciences is a sociology of belief or an ethnology of academic culture, not a sociology of science which reduces science to the level of organizational complexity (for an example of this, see Ben-David, *Scientific Growth*).

32. Cf. Pierre Bourdieu, *Les règles de l'art*.

33. Cf., for instance, Zola, *Carnets d'enquête*.

34. Its motto could be "think of the particular but present it in the form of the universal." For instance, Bourdieu's introduction to his work *Les règles de l'art* (1992) could well be a literary or philosophical introduction if only his authorship was not revealed and certain sociological passages were edited out. What do the use of terms such as "market of symbolic goods" or "capital structure" convey to the local readership? For the majority of the audience, that is nonsociologists, they mean that the study has

scientific pretensions. However, this part of the audience is unable and probably unwilling to examine the exact status of this scientificity. For sociologists, these terms say that even the study of literature can be examined legitimately by a sociologist, a *savant*, if it is done in the name of the quest for truth previously monopolized by the *philosophe* or man or woman of letters. For a sociologist, Bourdieu's work legitimizes examination of the most culturally valued topics.

35. Cf. Kristeva, *Séméiotiké*.

36. Judt, *Past Imperfect*, 252.

37. Marc Adriaens, "Ideology and Literary Production: Kristeva's Poetics," in *Semiotics and Dialectics: Ideology in the Text*, edited by Peter V. Zima (Amsterdam: Johns Benjamins, 1981), 179–220; Mounin, *Introduction à la sémiologie*, and *La littérature et ses technocraties*, 181.

38. Adriaens, "Ideology and Literary Production," 179–220.

39. For a convincing critique of Kristeva's uses of modal logic, cf. Pierre Lusson and Jacques Roubaud, "Sur la sémiologie des paragrammes de Julia Kristeva," *Change* 45 (1970): 65–61.

40. For Lévi-Strauss, the use of structural linguistics was an intellectual stimulation. It was also a means to legitimize the scientific pretentions of structural anthropolgy. Structural linguistic enabled Lévi-Strauss to develop his own theory. For Bourdieu, economics served the same purposes of stimulation and justification, as we have seen.

41. Descombes, *Modern French Philosophy*, 7.

42. Mounin, *Introduction à la sémiologie*, 181.

43. For all this, see ibid.

44. Cf., for instance, Greimas, "Sémiotique," 10987–90.

45. Semanalysis was a sort of analytical semiotics, supposed to be more sophisticated and more scientific than semiology.

46. This idea was borrowed from Bakhtin and redefined to suit her own purposes.

47. This self-censorship led to the dismissal and ridiculing of intellectuals like Sartre, Aron, and humanist Marxists such as Garaudy.

48. Durkheim, *L'évolution pédagogique en France I*, 36.

49. Alvin W. Gouldner, *The Coming Crisis of Western Sociology* (New York: Basic Books, 1970), 173.

50. The rule to get to the real value is to take at least one superlative off.

51. Bourdieu, *Homo Academicus*, 276.

52. Previous users of this technique include Miguel de Cervantes, Diego Velasquez, and Magritte.

53. Or, which means the same in this context, theoretical.

7. SYSTEM OF SUCCESSION AND SYSTEM OF CORONATION

1. Lindon, "Entretien avec Pierre Assouline," 29.

2. *Esprit*, 7–8 (July–August 1958): 25–26.

3. Jean Pouillon, "Sur *L'Emploi du temps*," *Les Temps modernes*, April 1957.

4. Roland Barthes, *Critical Essays*, English translation by Richard Howard (Evanston: Northwestern University Press, 1972), 23.

5. Cf. especially Roland Barthes, *Essais critiques* (Paris: Seuil, 1964), 252–57; *Critique et vérité* (Paris: Seuil, 1966), 31n. 39.

6. Some of these can be found in Barthes, *Essais critiques*; Olivier de Magny, "Panorama d'une nouvelle littérature romanesque," *Esprit* 7–8 (1958): 3–17; and Pouillon, "Sur *L'Emploi du temps*."

7. *Esprit* 7–8 (1958): 25–26.

8. De Magny, "Panorama d'une nouvelle littérature romanesque," 16.

9. *Esprit* 7–8 (1958): 25–26; De Magny, "Panorama d'une nouvelle littérature romanesque," 3.

10. Philippe Sollers, *Vision à New York* (Paris: Denoël, 1981), 58, 65.

11. For instance, should one define the new literary school as only the writers published by *Les éditions de Minuit?*

12. Jean Paulhan and Francis Ponge, *Correspondance 1923–1968*, tome 2, 1940–1968 (Paris: Gallimard, 1986), 626.

13. Barthes, *Critical Essays* (cf. note 4) English version, 54.

14. This includes the temporal orders and rhythms relative to publications of novels and book reviews, and of literary consecration, for instance.

15. This should not, however, be interpreted as meaning that this was the result of straightforward calculations and conscious activity on the part of the jury.

16. "Obscene, scatological," Paulhan and Ponge, *Correspondance*, 210.

17. Bernard Pivot, "La déshalliérisation de *Tel Quel*," *Le Figaro littéraire*, 16 March 1963, 6.

18. Jérôme Lindon, "Interview with the Author," Paris, 28 March 1989.

19. Pierre-Henri Simon, "Littérature de laboratoire: *L'Observatoire de Cannes* de Jean Ricardou," *Le Monde*, 13 Septembre 1961, 9.

20. Jean Thibaudeau, "La leçon de l'école," *Critique*, October 1961, 835–42.

21. Michel Foucault, "Distance, aspect, origine," in Tel Quel: *Théorie d'ensemble* (Paris: Seuil, 1968), 13–26.

22. For more favorable interpretations, cf. Philippe Forest, *Philippe Sollers*, and Malcolm Charles Pollard, *The Novels of Philippe Sollers: Narrative and the Visual* (Amsterdam, Atlanta: Rodopi, 1994).

23. Barthes, *Critical Essays*, 56.

24. Foucault, "Distance, aspect, origine," 13.

25. As literary and intellectual history is always written *a posteriori*, there are constant symbolic struggles to mold this history into specific forms, which would satisfy local interests. The latest is Sollers's efforts to foster a positive public image of himself as a legitimate writer, by separating his adventure with *Tel Quel* from his career as a writer (cf. Forest, *Philippe Sollers*; "L'éternel réflexe de réduction," *L'Infini* 39 (1992): 56–73; Christiane Lemire and Olivier Renault, "La littérature hors prix," *L'Infini* 39 (1992): 74–85; Josyane Savigneau, "La tranquille victoire de Philippe Sollers, *Le Monde*, 8 January 1993, 27, 32). Another, even more recent development has been the efforts of Sollers and his friends to interpret in the most favorable way possible *Tel Quel*'s history (Catherine Clément, "La saga de *Tel Quel*," *Le Magazine littéraire* 332 [1995]: 91–92; Philippe Forest, *Histoire de* Tel Quel *1960–1982* [Paris: Gallimard, 1995]; "De *Tel Quel* à *L'Infini*," *L'Infini*, 49–50 [1995]; Josyane Savigneau, "'*Tel Quel*,' une histoire à l'infini," *Le Monde*, 7 April 1995, I). These various attempts have been challenged by a group of social scientists (Pierre Bourdieu, "Sollers tel quel," *Liber*, 21–22 March 1995, 40; Kauppi, *The Making of an Avant-Garde*, 344–51; Pinto, "*Tel Quel*," 66–77). After the publication of Forest's history of *Tel Quel* and *L'Infini*'s special issue on *Tel Quel*, *Le Monde des livres* devoted two pages to *Tel Quel* (cf. Philippe–Jean Catinchi, "L'Avant-garde ne se rend pas," *Le Monde*, 7 April 1995, x; Nicholas Weill, "Et maintenant . . . ," *Le Monde*, 7 April 1995, xi). The only former Telquelian to courageously question Sollers's and his advocates' "official history of *Tel Quel*" is Thibaudeau (cf. Jean Thibaudeau, *Mes années Tel Quel* [Paris: Écriture, 1994]).

26. Foucault, "Distance, aspect, origine," 14–15.

27. André Stil, "Telsquels," *L'Humanité*, 5 June 1964; Jacques Brenner, *Histoire de la littérature française de 1940 à aujourd'hui* (Paris: Fayard, 1978), 459; Dominique Jamet, "Vivons–nous la fin du roman?," *Le Figaro littéraire*, 14 April 1966; Pinto, "*Tel Quel*," 66–77; Jean Ristat, "Un pape sans évangile," *Les Lettres françaises*, 16 December 1965.

28. Cf. François Nourissier, "Le recrutement littéraire," *France-Observateur*, 17 April 1960, 17.

29. Bernard Pivot, "Quand Sollers qualifie Robbe-Grillet de romancier de moins en moins nouveau," *Le Figaro littéraire*, 16 December 1965, 2; Kauppi, *The Making of an Avant-Garde*, 67–70.

8. THE CASE OF TEL QUEL

1. These Italian intellectuals included names like Umberto Eco, Pier–Paolo Pasolini, and Edoardo Sanguinetti. The most well–known members of the review *Tel Quel* (1960–82) were the linguist, psychoanalyst, and writer Julia Kristeva and the writer/ publishers Denis Roche and Philippe Sollers. However, as an avant-garde, the review's intellectual prestige is to a large extent due to its collaborators, among others Barthes, Derrida, Foucault, Genette, and Todorov.

2. For this concept, see Luc Boltanski, "L'espace positionnel: Multiplicité des positions institutionnelles et habitus de classe," *Revue française de sociologie* 14 (1973): 3–26.

3. Jean-Paul Aron, *Les modernes* (Paris: Gallimard, 1984), 135.

4. Pierre Bourdieu and Jean-Claude Passeron, *The Inheritors*, 102–3. For instance, the number of students in literature rose from 35,156 in the year 1950–51 to 85,063 in the year 1962–63.

5. Peter Bürger, *Theory of the Avant-Garde*, English translation by Michael Shaw (Minneapolis: University of Minnesota Press, 1986).

6. Today, the material means of production of symbolic goods have evolved further as a consequence of technological developments, notably computer and editing software, leading to the existence of one-person firms.

7. Notably the philosopher François Wahl, the *éminence grise* of Le Seuil's new products.

8. At the time, Michel Butor's *La modification* and Françoise Sagan's *Bonjour tristesse* were the best examples of literary success.

9. Bourdieu, *Homo Academicus*, xxv.

10. Cf. Bourdieu, "Champ intellectuel et projet créateur," 865–906; Weber, *Economy and Society*.

11. Most of the prophets held at this time permanent jobs instead of being free intellectuals, while the academics were the priests. Generally speaking, a review's power structure also depends on its position in relation to other reviews. Is it in an ascending or descending trajectory? Is it more traditional than "rebellious?" If it is more traditional, its

power structure is probably more stable; however, it can still be monopolistic in term of its leaders' characteristics and its publisher's investments.

12. This pole is largely excluded from the reproduction of the academic body.

13. See, for example, the collection of theoretical essays by Philippe Sollers, *Writing and the Experience of Limits*, English translation by Philip Barnard and David Hayman (New York: Columbia University Press, 1983).

14. Pace, *Claude Lévi-Strauss*, 8. Delirium was followed by *désenchantement*. In the 1970s Maoism became, for some time, the substitute for Communism and scientism; cf. Ieme van der Poel, *Une révolution de la pensée: maoïsme et féminisme à travers* Tel Quel, Les Temps modernes *et* Esprit (Amsterdam, Atlanta: Rodopi, 1992), 102–22.

15. See Johannot, *Quand le livre devient poche*. The impact of paperback book industry on avant-garde publication was twofold. First, the works themselves are republished in paperback versions, and second the publication of avant-garde works are counterbalanced financially by paperback publications.

16. Constructed by the objectivations of other intellectuals, by the author's explanations, and by the introductions and notes of paperback editions.

17. In this case avant-garde meant more than just "new." It was a phrase which evoked an entire avant-gardist tradition including Futurism, Formalism, Surrealism, and Dadaism, for instance, and its canonic thinkers or reliable values, authors like Joyce, Mallarmé, Lautréamont, and de Sade. This contradiction between belonging to a tradition and refusing tradition was, at the same time, the main characteristic of *Tel Quel*'s position ("the conformism of the avant-garde").

18. For instance, Chevalier and Encrevé, "La création de revues dans les années 60"; Dosse, *Histoire du structuralisme II*.

19. Philippe Sollers, "Écriture et révolution," in Tel Quel: *Théorie d'ensemble* (Paris: Seuil, 1968), 70.

20. For instance, the revision from a Maoist or Marxist–Leninist perspective of the history of the review, the reconstruction of the "initial" meaning of a work, or the construction of a literary *oeuvre* (Kauppi, *The Making of an Avant-Garde*, 320–24).

21. This might have to do with the creation of the social sciences and the professionalization process of intellectual labor.

22. Essentially for this reason accessibility—low price of purchasing and no need for special knowledge for purchase—was of crucial importance in the creation of new intellectual categories; in fact, in this case, the governing power mechanics consisted of the exploitation of a specific uncertainty, largely due to the existential uncertainty of students and marginal intellectuals. This democratization process meant that the base of reception of the "new" and dangerous was enlarged.

23. The École Normale Supérieure at rue d'Ulm was considered as being the dominant school in the Écoles Normales Supérieures-hierarchy.

24. Works that were published include, for example, Louis Althusser's *Pour Marx* in 1965, in 1966 Jacques Lacan's *Écrits*, Michel Foucault's *Les mots et les choses*, and Lucien Sebag's *Structuralisme et marxisme*.

25. This was due for example to low levels of foreign language proficiency and the scarcity of foreign university teachers.

26. Pinto, "Politiques de philosophes," 60. In accordance with these hierarchies, Anglo-Saxon empirism and thinkers like David Hume and John Locke were not valued and constituted a missing dimension in nearly all the avant-garde works of the 1960s, including those of the most empirically minded, like Bourdieu. This same hierarchy can explain the lack of interest in American semiotics and philosophical pragmatism, which thus did not fit the system of reference of the majority of the audience.

27. Cf. Jean-Joseph Goux, *Freud, Marx: Économie et symbolique* (Paris: Seuil, 1973).

28. For details, cf. Kauppi, *The Making of an Avant-Garde*, 247–51.

29. Julia Kristeva, "À propos de l'idéologie scientiste," *Promesse* 27 (1969): 78–80. For a general view of *Tel Quel*'s theoretical activity, see Tel Quel: *Théorie d'ensemble* (Paris: Seuil, 1968).

30. Kristeva, "À propos de l'idéologie scientiste," 78–80.

31. At the time the Communist cultural press was very influential and included the newspaper *L'Humanité* and journals like *La Nouvelle critique*, *Les Lettres françaises*, and *La Pensée*.

32. Writing (*écriture*) had a dual meaning: the act of writing and the "textuality" of the text.

33. The clearest example of this idealism is Pierre Rottenberg's text "Lecture de codes," in Tel Quel: *Théorie d'ensemble* (Paris: Seuil, 1968), 169.

34. Or even, following the tendency for a global and at the same time abstract criticism typical for a French writer and self-made theorist, "The theory treats 'literature' (and the whole of the culture within which it is located) as closed" (Sollers, *Writing and the Experience of Limits*, 9).

35. Philippe Sollers, "Support/Surfaces (bloc)/Conflits," *Tel Quel* 36 (1969).

36. See, for example, *Citation Index in the Arts and Humanities* (Philadelphia: Institute for Scientific Information, 1988); Alan Meggill, "Reception of Foucault by Historians," *Journal of the History of Ideas* 68 (1987): 117–41.

37. Such as the concepts of "structure," "logocentrism," "plurality," etc., all of which were in tune with the prevalent conceptual romanticism.

38. The accepted version of this blurring is called interdisciplinarity, which would come into vogue in the 1970s.

39. Cf. Jean-Philippe Mathy, *Extrême–Occident: French Intellectuals and America* (Chicago: University of Chicago Press, 1993).

40. Such instruments must, of course, be used with care.

41. These could include major cities, language groups, or "para–national social formations," to use Raymond Williams's term (Raymond Williams, *Culture* [London: Fontana, 1989]).

42. Dosse, Histoire du structuralisme II, 201.

EPILOGUE

1. Cf. also Saint Martin, *L'espace de la noblesse.*

2. Dosse, *Histoire du structuralisme I,* 105.

3. In this perspective, Debray's "age of media" offers an overly simplistic and polemical vision of these changes.

4. *Lire,* April 1981, 38–39.

5. Ibid.

6. *L'Événement du Jeudi,* 2–8 February 1989, 66.

7. Ibid.

8. *Lire,* April 1981, 38–39.

9. *L'Événement du Jeudi,* 2–8 February 1989, 66.

10. Among others, Debray, *Le pouvoir intellectuel en France;* Dosse, *Histoire du structuralisme I et II.*

11. It is assumed that the structures of capital and of the field are more or less homologous. For instance, cultural celebrities have to be distributed in relation to the volume and structure of their capital and subcapital. It would also be possible to quantitatively verify the amount of mobility between these three parts of the field, that is between the literary, the media, and the university poles. An important aspect would also be the distribution of economic revenues between these groups (salaries and other revenues, for instance, from book sales), one of the motives for seeking wide recognition being money.

12. This is an extremely vast topic, which would require comparative analysis of social conventions regulating capital conversion.

13. This has been analyzed by Elias, *The Civilizing Process*.

14. Charle, *Naissance des "intellectuels"*; Pascal Ory and Jean-François Sirinelli, *Les intellectuels en France, de l'affaire Dreyfus à nos jours* (Paris: Armand Colin, 1986); Christophe Prochasson, *Les intellectuels, le socialisme et la guerre* (Paris: Seuil, 1993); Jean-François Sirinelli, *Génération intellectuelle: khagneux et normaliens dans l'entre-deux-guerres* (Paris: Fayard, 1988).

15. As presented by Bourdieu in *Homo Academicus*, for instance.

16. Sartre's case is a good example; cf. Boschetti, *The Intellectual Enterprise*.

17. The effects of a tripolar structure can be verified by examining the profiles of scholars circulating and crossing the boundaries between the various poles. But instead of creating the impression, as French observers who are themselves players in the French intellectual game do, that only one's enemies have used cultural celebrity to further their academic careers, it would be more correct to say that all intellectuals had to adapt themselves to various degrees to the new criteria. The problem with local informants is that they, by turning themselves into exceptions, often do not see the local character of their own judgments and actions.

18. Other intellectuals of the same generation, Barthes and Bourdieu, were also nominated to the Collège de France, and Lévi-Strauss was appointed to the Collège de France in 1959 and to the Académie française in 1973.

19. Foucault entered the École Normale Supérieure, passed his *agrégation* and defended an old-style doctorate in 1961.

20. This information is from Clare O'Farrell's bibliography (O'Farrell, *Foucault*). Only Barthes's visibility in the cultural press was superior to Foucault's during the 1970s. Scholars such as Bourdieu were far from unknown to the larger intellectual public. Bourdieu published texts in *Esprit* (1961) and especially in Sartre's *Les Temps modernes* (twice in 1962, once in 1963 and 1966). However, it was *The Inheritors* (1964), written with Jean-Claude Passeron, that made Bourdieu's reputation. Bourdieu and Passeron quickly became idols of the leftist student movement. Like Foucault in the 1960s, Bourdieu also invested in reviews with wide readerships.

21. He collaborated with *Tel Quel* and showed an interest in authors like Raymond Roussel, the Surrealists, Bataille, Blanchot, and Hölderlin (cf. Eribon, *Michel Foucault*; Kauppi, *The Making of an Avant-Garde*, 110–11; Sheridan, *Michel Foucault*, 46–47).

22. Bourdieu, *Homo Academicus*; Laks, "Le champ de la sociolinguistique française de 1968 à 1983," 103–27; Jean-Claude Passeron, "Histoire et sociologie: identité sociale et identité logique," in *Histoire et sociologie aujourd'hui* (Paris: Éditions du CNRS, 1985), 195–208.

23. Bourdieu, *Homo Academicus*, 276.

24. Bellour, *Le livre des autres*, 66–77.

25. For instance, notes, bibliographies, references to authorities in the area, cf. Bellour, *Le livre des autres*, 97, 334.

26. An urgent task for the social and human sciences would be to create, using modern audiovisual technology, multimedia works on social- and human-scientific topics, thus bridging the gap between book culture and audiovisual culture.

27. The trajectories of intellectuals such as Julia Kristeva should be modelled in a similar fashion. One could construct a more complex model of social ascension during this period of time. Indeed, until now commentators have presented either a structural or historical picture of French intellectual life. For an example of the first, cf. Bourdieu, *Homo Academicus*. For the second, see, for instance, Dosse, *Histoire du structuralisme I et II*.

28. For instance, in the social sciences as a whole, cf. *Le développement des sciences sociales en France*.

29. Pinto, *La philosophie entre lycée et avant-garde*, 19–23.

30. *Lire*, April 1981, 38–39; *L'Événement du Jeudi*, 2–8 February 1989, 66.

31. In literature, these established values consisted of the traditional psychological novel and Sartrian commitment, and in the university, of the classical humanities.

32. These hybrid roles were represented, for instance, by the journalist/editor Pierre Nora and the historian/journalist/editor François Furet.

33. See, for one of the first exponents of this idea, Marc Bloch, "Pour une histoire comparée des sociétés européennes," *Revue de synthèse historique* 46 (1925): 15–50.

34. Lamont, *Money, Morals, and Manners*.

35. Cf. Beate Krais, "Review of Lamont 1992," *European Sociological Review* 9, no. 3 (1993): 388.

36. Hall, "The Capitals of Culture," 257–85.

37. This includes expressions of surprise that cultural theories developed in the French context do not address the same questions of ethnicity, for instance, or do not refer to the same "known" authors and works on gender.

References

Abel, Lionel. "Sartre vs. Lévi-Strauss." In *Claude Lévi-Strauss: The Anthropologist as Hero*, edited by E. Nelson Hayes, and Tanya Hayes, 235–46. Cambridge, Mass.: MIT Press, 1970.

Accardo, Alain. *Initiation à la sociologie de l'illusionisme social.* Bordeaux: Éditions le Mascaret, 1983.

Adriaens, Marc. "Ideology and Literary Production: Kristeva's Poetics." In *Semiotics and Dialectics: Ideology in the Text*, edited by Peter V. Zima, 179–220. Amsterdam: Johns Benjamins, 1981.

Althusser, Louis. *L'avenir dure longtemps suivi de Les faits.* Paris: Stock/IMEC, 1992.

Ansart, Pierre. *Les sociologies contemporaines.* Paris: Le Seuil, 1990.

Aron, Jean-Paul. *Les modernes.* Paris: Gallimard, 1984.

Aron, Raymond. *Main Currents in Sociological Thought II: Durkheim/Pareto/Weber.* English translation by Richard Howard and Helen Weam. New York and London: Basic Books, 1967.

————. *Mémoires: 50 ans de réflexion politique.* Paris: Julliard, 1983.

Ayer, Alfred. "Wittgenstein selon Sir Alfred Ayer." *Le Magazine littéraire* 237 (1987): 108–13.

Bachelard, Gaston. *Épistémologie: Textes choisis.* Paris: Presses Universitaires de France, 1971.

————. *La formation de l'esprit scientifique: Contribution à une psychanalyse de la connaissance objective.* Paris: Vrin, 1983.

Balzac, Honoré de. "Avant-propos à la Comédie humaine." In *Scènes de la vie privée.* Tome 1, 7–42. Paris: Furne, 1842.

————. *Scènes de la vie privée.* Tome 1. Paris: Furne, 1842.

179

Barthes, Roland. *Essais critiques*. Paris: Seuil, 1964.

———. *Critique et vérité*. Paris: Seuil, 1966.

———. "Réponses." *Tel Quel* 47 (1971): 89–107.

———. *Critical Essays*. English translation by Richard Howard. Evanston: Northwestern University Press, 1972.

Becker, Howard S. "Culture: A Sociological View." *The Yale Review* 72, Summer (1982): 513–27.

Bellour, Raymond. *Le livre des autres*. Paris: Union Générale d'Éditions, 1978.

Ben-David, Joseph. *Scientific Growth: Essays on the Social Organization and Ethos of Science*. Berkeley: University of California Press, 1991.

Benedict, Ruth. *Patterns of Culture*. Boston and New York: Houghton Mifflin Company, 1934.

Berger, Bennett M. "Review Essay: Taste and Domination." *American Journal of Sociology* 91 (1986): 1445–53.

Bisseret, Noëlle. *Les inégaux ou la sélection universitaire*. Paris: Presses Universitaires de France, 1974.

Bloch, Marc. "Pour une histoire comparée des sociétés européennes." *Revue de synthèse historique* 46 (1925): 15–50.

Bloch, Marc. "Language, Anthropology and Cognitive Science." *Man* 26, no. 2 (1991): 183–98.

Boltanski, Luc. "L'espace positionnel: Multiplicité des positions institutionnelles et habitus de classe." *Revue française de sociologie* 14 (1973): 3–26.

Boltanski, Luc, and Laurent Thévenot. *De la justification: les économies de la grandeur*. Paris: Gallimard, 1991.

Boon, James. *From Symbolism to Structuralism: Lévi-Strauss in a Literary Tradition*. New York: Harper & Row, 1972.

Boschetti, Anna. *The Intellectual Enterprise: Sartre and* Les Temps modernes. English translation by Richard C. McCleary. Evanston: Northwestern University Press, 1988.

Boudon, Raymond. *À quoi sert la notion de structure?* Paris: Gallimard, 1968.

Bourdieu, Pierre. *Sociologie de l'Algérie*. Paris: Presses Universitaires de France, 1958.

———. "Champ intellectuel et projet créateur." *Les Temps modernes* 246 (1966): 865–906.

———. "La transmission de l'héritage culturel." In *Le partage des bénéfices: Expansion et inégalités en France*, edited by Darras, 383–420. Paris: Minuit, 1966.

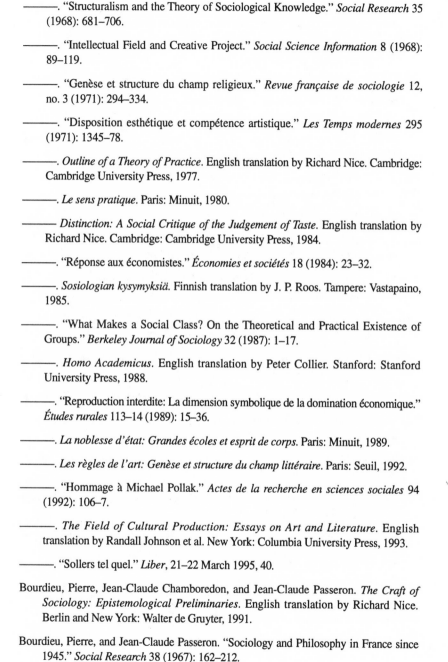

―――. "Structuralism and the Theory of Sociological Knowledge." *Social Research* 35 (1968): 681–706.

―――. "Intellectual Field and Creative Project." *Social Science Information* 8 (1968): 89–119.

―――. "Genèse et structure du champ religieux." *Revue française de sociologie* 12, no. 3 (1971): 294–334.

―――. "Disposition esthétique et compétence artistique." *Les Temps modernes* 295 (1971): 1345–78.

―――. *Outline of a Theory of Practice.* English translation by Richard Nice. Cambridge: Cambridge University Press, 1977.

―――. *Le sens pratique.* Paris: Minuit, 1980.

―――― *Distinction: A Social Critique of the Judgement of Taste.* English translation by Richard Nice. Cambridge: Cambridge University Press, 1984.

―――. "Réponse aux économistes." *Économies et sociétés* 18 (1984): 23–32.

―――. *Sosiologian kysymyksiä.* Finnish translation by J. P. Roos. Tampere: Vastapaino, 1985.

―――. "What Makes a Social Class? On the Theoretical and Practical Existence of Groups." *Berkeley Journal of Sociology* 32 (1987): 1–17.

―――. *Homo Academicus.* English translation by Peter Collier. Stanford: Stanford University Press, 1988.

―――. "Reproduction interdite: La dimension symbolique de la domination économique." *Études rurales* 113–14 (1989): 15–36.

―――. *La noblesse d'état: Grandes écoles et esprit de corps.* Paris: Minuit, 1989.

―――. *Les règles de l'art: Genèse et structure du champ littéraire.* Paris: Seuil, 1992.

―――. "Hommage à Michael Pollak." *Actes de la recherche en sciences sociales* 94 (1992): 106–7.

―――. *The Field of Cultural Production: Essays on Art and Literature.* English translation by Randall Johnson et al. New York: Columbia University Press, 1993.

―――. "Sollers tel quel." *Liber,* 21–22 March 1995, 40.

Bourdieu, Pierre, Jean-Claude Chamboredon, and Jean-Claude Passeron. *The Craft of Sociology: Epistemological Preliminaries.* English translation by Richard Nice. Berlin and New York: Walter de Gruyter, 1991.

Bourdieu, Pierre, and Jean-Claude Passeron. "Sociology and Philosophy in France since 1945." *Social Research* 38 (1967): 162–212.

————. *The Inheritors: French Students and Their Relation to Culture*. English translation by Richard Nice. Chicago and London: The University of Chicago Press, 1979.

Bourdieu, Pierre, and Loïc J. D. Wacquant. *An Invitation to Reflexive Sociology*. Chicago: University of Chicago Press, 1992.

Bourricaud, François. "Contre le sociologisme: une critique et des propositions." *Revue française de sociologie* 16 (1975): 583–603.

Bové, Paul. "Foreword: The Foucault Phenomenon: The Problematics of Style." In Gilles Deleuze, *Foucault*. English translation by Sean Hand, vii–xl. Minneapolis: University of Minnesota Press, 1988.

Bradbury, Malcolm. *Mensonge*. London: André Deutsch, 1987.

Brenner, Jacques. *Histoire de la littérature française de 1940 à aujourd'hui*. Paris: Fayard, 1978.

Broady, Donald. *Sociologi och epistemologi: Om Pierre Bourdieu's författarskap och den historiska epistemologin*. Stockholm: HLS Förlag, 1991.

Brochier, Hubert. "La valeur heuristique du paradigme économique." *Économies et sociétés* 18 (1984): 3–21.

Broden, T. F. III. "The Development of A. J. Greimas: Lexicology, Structural Semantics, Semiotics." Ph.D. dissertation, Indiana University, Bloomington, 1986.

Brubaker, Rogers. "Rethinking Classical Theory. The Sociological Vision of Pierre Bourdieu." *Theory and Society* 14 (1985): 745–75.

Buffat, Marc. "Le simulacre: Notes pour une diachronie." *Tel Quel* 47 (1971): 108–14.

Burke, Peter. *The French Historical Revolution: The Annales School 1929–1989*. Stanford: Stanford University Press, 1990.

Bürger, Peter. *Theory of the Avant-Garde*. English translation by Michael Shaw. Minneapolis: University of Minnesota Press, 1986.

Caillé, Alain. "Esquisse d'une critique de l'économie générale de la pratique." *Cahiers du L.A.S.A.* 8–9 (1988): 103–214.

Calhoun, Craig. "Culture, History, and the Problem of Specificity in Social Theory." In *Postmodernism and Social Theory*, edited by Steve Seidman and David G. Wagner, 244–88. London: Basil Blackwell, 1992.

————. "Habitus, Field and Capital: The Question of Historical Specificity." In *Bourdieu: Critical Perspectives*, edited by Craig Calhoun, Edward LiPuma, and Moishe Postane, 61–88. Chicago: University of Chicago Press, 1993.

Calhoun, Craig, Edward LiPuma, and Moishe Postane, eds. *Bourdieu: Critical Perspectives*. Chicago: University of Chicago Press, 1993.

Calvet, Louis-Jean. *Roland Barthes*. Paris: Flammarion, 1990.

Catinchi, Philippe-Jean. "L'avant-garde ne se rend pas." *Le Monde*, 7 April 1995, x.

Charbonnier, Georges. *Entretiens avec Claude Lévi-Strauss*. Paris: Julliard, 1961.

Charle, Christophe. "Le beau mariage d'Émile Durkheim." *Actes de la recherche en sciences sociales* 55 (1984): 45–49.

———. *Naissance des "intellectuels" 1880–1900*. Paris: Minuit, 1990.

———. "The Characteristics of Intellectuals in France around 1900 in a Comparative Perspective." In *Vanguards of Modernity*, edited by Niilo Kauppi and Pekka Sulkunen, 19–32. Jyväskylä: Publications of the Research Unit for Contemporary Culture 32, 1992.

Chartier, Roger. *Forms and Meanings: Texts, Performances, and Audiences from Codex to Computer*. Philadelphia: University of Pennsylvania Press, 1995.

Chevalier, Jean-Claude, and Pierre Encrevé. "La création de revues dans les années 60: matériaux pour une histoire récente de la linguistique en France." *Langue française* 63 (1984): 57–102.

Citation Index in the Arts and Humanities. Philadelphia: Institute for Scientific Information, 1987.

Clark, Priscilla P. *Literary France: The Making of a Culture*. Berkeley: University of California Press, 1987.

Clark, Priscilla P., and Terry N. Clark. "Writers, Literature, and Students Movements in France." *Sociology of Education* 42, no. 4 (1969): 293–314.

Clark, Terry N. *Prophets and Patrons: The French University and the Emergence of the Social Sciences*. Cambridge, Mass.: Harvard University Press, 1973.

Clément, Catherine. "La saga de *Tel Quel*." *Le Magazine littéraire* 332 (1995): 91–92.

Collins, Randall. *Sociology in Midcentury*. New York: Academic Press, 1981.

———. "Cumulation and Anticumulation in Sociology." *American Sociological Review* 55 (1990): 462–63.

Coquet, Jean-Claude. "La sémiologie en France." In *Le champ sémiologique*, edited by André Helbo, 11–29. Brussels: Éditions Complexe, 1979.

Cot, Annie L., and Bruno Lautier. "Métaphore économique et magie sociale chez Pierre Bourdieu." In *L'empire du sociologue*, 70–86. Paris: La Découverte, 1984.

Critique. Special issue on Pierre Bourdieu. No. 578–79, 1995.

Darnton, Robert. *The Great Cat Massacre and Other Episodes in French Cultural History*. New York: Norton, 1984.

Darras, ed. *Le partage des bénéfices: Expansion et inégalité en France*. Paris: Minuit, 1966.

Debray, Régis. *Le pouvoir intellectuel en France*. 2d ed. Paris: Gallimard, 1986.

Deleuze, Gilles. *Foucault*. English translation by Sean Hand. Minneapolis: University of Minnesota Press, 1988.

Delruelle, Edouard. *Claude Lévi-Strauss et la philosophie*. Brussels: Éditions Universitaires, 1989.

Descamps, Christian, ed. *Les enjeux philosophiques des années 50*. Paris: Centre Georges Pompidou, 1989.

Descombes, Vincent. *Modern French Philosophy*. English translation by L. Scott-Fox and J. M. Harding. Cambridge: Cambridge University Press, 1980.

Le développement des sciences sociales en France au tournant des années soixante. Paris: Éditions du Centre National de la Recherche Scientifique, 1989.

DiMaggio, Paul. "Review Essay: On Pierre Bourdieu." *American Journal of Sociology* 84 (1979): 1460–74.

———. "Cultural Boundaries and Structural Change: The Extension of the High Culture Model to Theater, Opera, and the Dance, 1900–1940." In *Cultivating Differences: Symbolic Boundaries and the Making of Differences*, edited by Michèle Lamont and Marcel Fournier, 21–57. Chicago: University of Chicago Press, 1992.

Domenach, Jean-Marie. *Enquête sur les idées contemporaines*. Paris: Seuil, 1981.

Dosse, François. *Histoire du structuralisme. I: Le champ du signe, 1945–1966*. Paris: La Découverte, 1991.

———. *Histoire du structuralisme. II: Le chant du cygne, 1967 à nos jours*. Paris: La Découverte, 1992.

Dreyfus, Hubert, and Paul Rabinow. *Michel Foucault: Beyond Structuralism and Hermeneutics*. Brighton: Harvester, 1983.

Durkheim, Émile. "Préface." *Année sociologique* 1896–1897 (1898): i–vii.

———. *The Elementary Forms of Religious Life*. English translation by Joseph Ward Swain. London: George Allen and Unwin, 1935.

———. *The Rules of Sociological Method*. English translation by Sarah A. Solovay and John H. Mueller. Chicago: The Free Press of Glencoe, 1938.

———. *L'évolution pédagogique en France*. Tomes I and II. Paris: Alcan, 1938.

Eco, Umberto. *A Theory of Semiotics*. Bloomington: Indiana University Press, 1976.

Elias, Norbert. *The Civilizing Process: A History of Manners.* Vol. 1. English translation by Edmund Jephcott. Oxford: Basil Blackwell, 1978.

———. *What is Sociology?* English translation by Stephen Mennell and Grace Morrissey. New York: Columbia University Press, 1978.

———. *The Society of Individuals.* English translation by Edmund Jephcott. Oxford: Basil Blackwell, 1991.

———. *The Symbol Theory.* London: Sage, 1991.

L'Empire du sociologue. Paris: La Découverte, 1984.

Eribon, Didier. *Michel Foucault.* English translation by Betsy Wing. Cambridge, Mass.: Harvard University Press, 1991.

Esprit 7–8 (July–August 1958): 25–26.

Etzioni, Amitai, and Paul R. Lawrence, eds. *Socio-Economics: Toward a New Synthesis.* Armonk, N.Y.: M. E. Sharpe, 1991.

L'Événement du Jeudi. 2–8 February 1989, 66.

Fabiani, Jean-Louis. *Les philosophes de la République.* Paris: Éd. de Minuit, 1988.

———. "La sociologie et le principe de réalité." *Critique* 545 (1992): 790–801.

Ferry, Luc, and Alain Renaut. *La pensée 68: Essai sur l'anti-humanisme contemporain.* Paris: Gallimard, 1985.

Fontanille, Jacques. "Personal Discussion with the Author." Imatra: International Semiotics Institute. 19 July 1991.

Forest, Philippe. *Philippe Sollers.* Paris: Gallimard, 1992.

———. "L'éternel reflèxe de réduction." *L'Infini* 39 (1992): 56–73.

———. *Histoire de* "Tel Quel" *(1960–1982).* Paris: Le Seuil, 1995.

Foucault, Michel. *Les mots et les choses.* Paris: Gallimard, 1966.

———. "Distance, aspect, origine." In *Tel Quel. Théorie d'ensemble*, 13–26. Paris: Le Seuil, 1968.

———. *The Birth of the Clinic: An Archeology of Medical Perception.* English translation by A. M. Sheridan. London: Tavistock Publications, 1976.

———. "Truth and Power." In *French Sociology: Rupture and Renewal Since 1968*, edited by Charles Lemert, 293–307. New York: Columbia University Press, 1981.

Fougeyrollas, Pierre. *L'obscurantisme contemporain: Lacan, Lévi-Strauss, Althusser.* Paris: Spag-Papyrus, 1983.

Gardner, Howard. *The Quest for Mind: Piaget, Lévi-Strauss and the Structuralist Movement.* New York: Knopf, 1973.

Geertz, Clifford. *The Interpretation of Cultures.* New York: Basic Books, 1973.

Godard, Jean-Luc. "Luttes sur deux fronts: Conversation avec Jean-Luc Godard." *Cahiers du cinéma* 194 (1967): 13–28, 66–70.

Gouldner, Alvin W. *The Coming Crisis of Western Sociology.* New York: Basic Books, 1970.

Goux, Jean-Joseph. *Freud, Marx: Économie et symbolique.* Paris: Le Seuil, 1973.

Greimas, Algirdas Julien. "La linguistique statique et la linguistique structurale." *Le Français moderne* 30–31 (1962–63): 241–53, 55–68.

———. "Sémiotique." In *La Grande Encyclopédie Larousse*, 10987–90. Paris: Larousse, 1976.

———. *Structural Semantics: An Attempt at a Method.* English translation by Daniele McDowell, Ronald Schleifer, and Alan Velie. Lincoln: University of Nebraska Press, 1983.

———. *On Meaning: Selected Writings in Semiotic Theory.* English translation by Paul J. Perron and Frank H. Collins. Minneapolis: University of Minnesota Press, 1987.

———. "On Meaning." *New Literary History* 203 (1989): 539–50.

Hall, John R. "The Capitals of Cultures: A Non-Holistic Approach to Status Situations, Class, Gender, and Ethnicity." In *Cultivating Differences: Symbolic Boundaries and the Making of Inequality*, edited by Michèle Lamont and Marcel Fournier, 257–85. Chicago: University of Chicago Press, 1992.

Hamon, Hervé, and Pierre Rotman. *Les intellocrates.* Paris: Ramsay, 1979.

Hayes, E. Nelson, and Tanya Hayes eds. *Claude Lévi-Strauss: The Anthropologist as Hero.* Cambridge, Mass.: MIT Press, 1970.

Heilbron, Johan. "The Tripartite Division of French Social Science: A Long-Term Perspective." In *Discourses on Society: The Shaping of the Social Science Disciplines*, edited by Peter Wagner, Björn Wittrock, and Richard Whitley, 73–92. Dordrecht: Kluwer, 1990.

———. *The Rise of Social Theory.* English translation by Sheila Gogol. Minneapolis: University of Minnesota Press, 1995.

Hénaff, Marcel. *Claude Lévi-Strauss.* Paris: Belfond, 1991.

Héran, François. "La seconde nature de l'habitus: Tradition philosophique et sens commun dans le langage sociologique." *Revue française de sociologie* 28 (1987): 385–416.

Herzen, Alexander I. *My Past and Thoughts.* English translation by Constance Garnett. Berkeley: University of California Press, 1982.

Hirschhorn, Monique. *Max Weber et la sociologie française.* Paris: L'Harmattan, 1988.

Hirschman, Albert O. "Against Parsimony: Three Easy Ways of Complicating Some Categories of Economic Discourse." *American Economic Association Papers and Proceedings* (1984), 89–96.

Hoffman, Stanley. "Monsieur Taste." *New York Review of Books* 33 (1986): 45–48.

Hollier, Denis, ed. *The College of Sociology.* English translation by Betsy Wing. Minneapolis: University of Minnesota Press, 1988.

Hollier, Denis, and R. Howard Bloch, eds. *A New History of French Literature.* Cambridge, Mass.: Harvard University Press, 1989.

Hollinger, David A. "How Wide the Circle of the 'We'? American Intellectuals and the Problem of the Ethos since World War II." *American Historical Review* 98, April 1993, 317–37.

Honneth, Axel. "Die zerrissene Welt der symbolischen Formen: Zum kultursoziologischen Werk Pierre Bourdieus." *Kölner Zeitschrift für Soziologie und Sozialpsychologie* 36 (1984): 147–64.

Les idées en France, 1945–1988: Une chronologie. Paris: Gallimard, 1989.

L'Infini. "*Tel Quel* à *l'Infini*." No. 49–50, 1995.

Jamet, Dominique. "Vivons-nous la mort du roman?" *Le Figaro littéraire,* 14 April 1966.

Jameson, Frederic. "Foreword." In A. J. Greimas, *On Meaning: Selected Writings in Semiotic Theory.* English translation by Paul J. Perron and Frank H. Collins, iv–x. Minneapolis: University of Minnesota Press, 1987.

Johannot, Yvonne. *Quand le livre devient poche.* Grenoble: Presses Universitaires de Grenoble, 1978.

Judt, Tony. *Past Imperfect: French Intellectuals 1944–1956.* Berkeley: University of California Press, 1992.

Karady, Victor. "Durkheim, les sciences sociales et l'université: bilan d'un semi-échec." *Revue française de sociologie* 18 (1976): 267–311.

Kauppi, Niilo. *The Making of an Avant-Garde: Tel Quel.* English translation by Anne R. Epstein. Berlin and New York: Mouton de Gruyter, 1994.

Kauppi, Niilo, and Pekka Sulkunen, eds. *Vanguards of Modernity: Society, Intellectuals, and the University.* Jyväskylä: Publications of the Research Unit for Contemporary Culture 32, 1992.

Krais, Beate. "Review of Lamont 1992." *European Sociological Review* 9 (1993): 336–38.

Kristeva, Julia. "La sémiologie: science critique et/ou critique de la sciences." In Tel Quel: *Théorie d'ensemble*, 83–96. Paris: Le Seuil, 1968.

———. *Séméiotiké: Recherches pour une sémanalyse*. Paris: Le Seuil, 1969.

———. "À propos de l'idéologie scientiste." *Promesse* 27 (1969): 78–80.

———. *The Samurai*. English translation by Barbara Bray. New York: Columbia University Press, 1992.

Laks, Bernard. "Le champ de la sociolinguistique française de 1968 à 1983, production et fonctionnement." *Langue française* 63 (1984): 103–28.

Lamont, Michèle. *Money, Morals, and Manners: The Culture of the French and American Upper Middle Class*. Chicago: University of Chicago Press, 1992.

Lamont, Michèle, and Annette Lareau. "Cultural Capital: Allusions, Gaps and Glissandos in Recent Theoretical Developments." *Sociological Theory* 6 (1988): 153–68.

Lamont, Michèle, and Marcel Fournier, eds. *Cultivating Differences: Symbolic Boundaries and the Making of Differences*. Chicago: University of Chicago Press, 1992.

Lechte, John. *Julia Kristeva*. London: Routledge, 1990.

Lemert, Charles. "Literary Politics and the Champ of French Sociology." *Theory and Society* 10 (1981): 645–69.

———. "Introduction." In *French Sociology: Rupture and Renewal Since 1968*, edited by Charles Lemert, 3–32. New York: Columbia University Press, 1981.

———, ed. *French Sociology: Rupture and Renewal Since 1968*. New York: Columbia University Press, 1981.

Lemire, Christiane, and Olivier Renault. "La littérature hors prix." *L'Infini* 39 (1992): 74–85.

Lepenies, Wolf. *Between Literature and Science: The Rise of Sociology*. English translation by R. J. Hollingdale. Cambridge: Cambridge University Press, 1988.

Lévi-Strauss, Claude. *Structural Anthropology*. English translation by Claire Jacobson and Brooke Grundfest Schoepf. New York: Basic Books, 1963.

———. *Le regard éloigné*. Paris: Plon, 1983.

———. "Introduction à l'oeuvre de Marcel Mauss." In Marcel Mauss. *Sociologie et anthropologie*, ix–lii. Paris: Presses Universitaires de France, 1985.

———. *Conversations with Claude Lévi-Strauss*. With Didier Eribon. English translation by Paula Wissing. Chicago and London: University of Chicago Press, 1991.

Libération. "Advertisement for Scherzo Publishers." 13 December 1990, 49.

Lindon, Jérôme. "Entretien avec Pierre Assouline." *Lire*. February 1988, 17–24.

———. "Personal Interview with the Author." Paris. 28 March 1989.

Lire. April 1981, 38–39.

Lizska, James Jakob. "Peirce in France: An Essay on the Two Founders of Modern Semiotics." *Semiotica* 93 (1993): 139–53.

Lotman, J. M., L. I. Ginsburg, and B. A. Uspenskij. *The Semiotics of Russian Cultural History*. English translation. Ithaca and London: Cornell University Press, 1985.

Lusson, Pierre, and Jacques Roubaud. "Sur la sémiologie des paragrammes de Julia Kristeva." *Change* 45 (1970): 56–61.

Macksey, R., and E. Donato, eds. *The Language of Criticism and the Sciences of Man: The Structuralist Controversy*. Baltimore: Johns Hopkins University Press, 1970.

Magny, Olivier de. "Panorama d'une nouvelle littérature romanesque." *Esprit* 7–8 (1958): 3–17.

Mansbridge, Jane, ed. *Beyond Self-Interest*. Chicago: University of Chicago Press, 1990.

Martin, Alfred von. *Sociology of the Renaissance*. New York: Harper Torchbooks, 1963.

Mary, André. "Métaphores et paradigmes dans le bricolage de la notion d'habitus." *Cahiers du L.A.S.A.* 8–9 (1988): 9–102.

Mathy, Jean-Philippe. *Extrême-Occident: French Intellectuals and America*. Chicago: University of Chicago Press, 1993.

Mauss, Marcel. *A General Theory of Magic*. English translation by Robert Brain. London and Boston: Routledge and Kegan Paul, 1972.

———. *Sociology and Psychology: Essays*. English translation by Ben Brewster. London and Boston: Routledge and Kegan Paul, 1972.

———. *Sociologie et anthropologie*. 2d ed. Paris: Presses Universitaires de France, 1985.

Maybury-Lewis, David. "Science or Bricolage." In *Claude Lévi-Strauss: The Anthropologist as Hero*, edited by E. Nelson Hayes, and Tanya Hayes, 150–63. Cambridge, Mass.: MIT Press, 1970.

Mazon, Brigitte. *Aux origines de l'E.H.E.S.S.: Le rôle du mécénat américain*. Paris: Cerf, 1988.

Meggill, Allan. "Reception of Foucault by Historians." *Journal of the History of Ideas* 48 (1987): 117–41.

Moscovici, Serge. *The Invention of Society: Psychological Explanations for Social Phenomena.* English translation by W. D. Halls. Cambridge: Polity Press, 1993.

Mounin, Georges. *Introduction à la sémiologie.* Paris: Minuit, 1970.

———. *La littérature et ses technocraties.* Paris: Casterman, 1978.

Mouzelis, Nicos. *Sociological Theory: What Went Wrong? Diagnosis and Remedies.* London: Routledge, 1995.

Murray, Kevin. "Introduction." In *The Judgment of Paris: Recent French Theory in a Local Context*, edited by Kevin D. S. Murray, xi–xxviii. Sydney: Allen and Unwin, 1992.

———, ed. *The Judgment of Paris: Recent French Theory in a Local Context.* Sydney: Allen and Unwin, 1992.

Nahirny, Vladimir C. *The Russian Intelligentsia: From Torment to Silence.* New Brunswick: Transaction Books, 1983.

Nourissier, François. "Le recrutement littéraire." *France-Observateur*, 7 April 1960, 17.

O'Farrell, Clare. *Foucault: Historian or Philosopher?* 2d ed. London: Macmillan, 1993.

Ory, Pascal, and Jean-François Sirinelli. *Les intellectuels en France, de l'affaire Dreyfus à nos jours.* Paris: Armand Colin, 1986.

Pace, David. *Claude Lévi-Strauss: The Bearer of Ashes.* London: Routledge and Kegan Paul, 1983.

Parsons, Talcott. *The Structure of Social Action.* New York: The Free Press, 1968.

Passeron, Jean-Claude. "L'inflation des diplômes: Remarques sur l'usage de quelques concepts analogiques en sociologie." *Revue française de sociologie* 23 (1982): 551–84.

———. "Histoire et sociologie: identité sociale et identité logique d'une discipline." In *Historiens et sociologues aujourd'hui*, Journées d'études annuelles de la Société Française de Sociologie, 195–208. Paris: Éditions du CNRS, 1986.

Paulhan, Jean, and Francis Ponge. *Correspondance 1923–1968.* Tome 2, 1940–1968. Paris: Gallimard, 1986.

Pavel, Thomas. *The Feud of Language: A History of Structuralist Thought.* 2d ed. Oxford: Basil Blackwell, 1989.

Pinçon, Michel, and Monique Charlot-Rendu. *Les beaux-quartiers.* Paris: Le Seuil, 1989.

Pinto, Louis. "Politiques de philosophes 1960–1976." *La Pensée* 197 (1978): 52–71.

———. *La philosophie entre lycée et avant-garde: Les métamorphoses de la philosophie dans la France d'aujourd'hui.* Paris: L'Harmattan, 1987.

———. "Épistémologies nationales des sciences sociales en France et en Allemagne." Paper delivered at Institut de Recherche sur les Sociétés Contemporaines (IRESCO), Paris. 6 February 1990.

———. "*Tel Quel*: au sujet des intellectuels de parodie." *Actes de la recherche en sciences sociales* 66 (1991): 66–77.

———. "Mass Media Mandarins." In *Vanguards of Modernity*, edited by Niilo Kauppi and Pekka Sulkunen, 98–106. Jyväskylä: Publications of the Research Unit for Contemporary Culture 32, 1992.

Pivot, Bernard. "La déshalliérisation de *Tel Quel.*" *Le Figaro littéraire*, 16 March 1963, 6.

———. "Quand Sollers qualifie Robbe-Grillet de romancier de moins en moins nouveau." *Le Figaro littéraire*, 16 December 1965, 2.

Plato. *Timaeus*. English translation by H. D. P. Lee. Harmondsworth: Penguin Classics, 1965.

Pollak, Michael. *Max Weber en France: l'itinéraire d'une oeuvre*. Paris: Cahiers de l'histoire du temps présent 3, 1986.

Pollard, Malcolm Charles. *The Novels of Philippe Sollers: Narrative and the Visual*. Amsterdam, Atlanta: Rodopi, 1994.

Ponton, Rémy. "Naissance du roman psychologique." *Actes de la recherche en sciences sociales* 4 (1975): 66–85.

Pouillon, Jean. "Sur *L'Emploi du temps.*" *Les Temps modernes*, April 1957.

Les pratiques culturelles des français. Paris: La Documentation Française, 1989.

Prochasson, Christophe. *Les intellectuels, le socialisme et la guerre*. Paris: Le Seuil, 1993.

Ragon, Marc. "Les gardes du Corps." *Libération*, 27 April 1989, 2.

Rancière, Jacques. "L'éthique de la sociologie." In *L'empire du sociologue*, 13–36. Paris: La Découverte, 1984.

Raynaud, Alain. "Le sociologue contre le droit." *Esprit*, March 1980, 82–93.

Revel, Jean-François. *Pourquoi des philosophes?* Paris: Julliard, 1957.

Ricoeur, Paul. "Structure et herméneutique." *Esprit*, November 1963, 596–627.

Ringer, Fritz. *Fields of Knowledge: French Academic Culture in Comparative Perspective, 1890–1920*. Cambridge: Cambridge University Press, 1992.

Ristat, Jean. "Un pape sans évangile." *Les Lettres françaises*, 16 December 1965.

Robbe-Grillet, Alain. "L'exercice problématique de la littérature." In *Les enjeux philosophiques des années 50*, edited by Christian Descamps, 25–32. Paris: Centre Georges Pompidou, 1989.

Roos, J. P. "Pelin säännöt: intellektuellit, luokat ja kieli." In Pierre Bourdieu, *Sosiologian kysymyksiä*, 7–25. Tampere: Vastapaino, 1985.

Rottenberg, Pierre. "Lecture de codes." In Tel Quel: *Théorie d'ensemble*, 159–71. Paris: Le Seuil, 1968.

Roudiez, Leon S. *French Fiction Revisited*. New York: Columbia University Press, 1991.

Roudinesco, Elisabeth. *Jacques Lacan and Co*. English translation by Jeffrey Mehlman. Chicago: University of Chicago Press, 1990.

Rubenstein, Diane. *What's Left? The École Normale Supérieure and the Right*. Madison: University of Wisconsin Press, 1990.

Saint Martin, Monique de. *L'espace de la noblesse*. Paris: Métaillié, 1994.

Saussure, Ferdinand de. *Cours de linguistique générale*. Paris: Payot, 1960.

Savigneau, Josyane. "La tranquille victoire de Philippe Sollers." *Le Monde*, 8 January 1993, 27, 32.

———. "'Tel Quel,' une histoire à l'infini." *Le Monde*, 7 April 1995, i.

Schleifer, Ronald. "Introduction." In A. J. Greimas, *Structural Semantics: An Attempt at a Method*. English translation by Daniele McDowell, Ronald Schleifer, and Alan Velie, xi–lvi. Lincoln: University of Nebraska Press, 1983.

Schultz, Theodore W. "Investment in Human Capital." *The American Economic Review* 51 (1961): 1–17.

Segre, Claudio. "The Styles of Greimas and their Transformations." *New Literary History* 203 (1989): 679–92.

Seidman, Steve. "The End of Sociological Theory: The Postmodern Hope." *Sociological Theory* 9 (1991): 131–46.

Seidman, Steve, and David G. Wagner, eds. *Postmodernism and Social Theory*. London: Basil Blackwell, 1992.

Sen, Amartya K. "Rational Fools: A Critique of the Behavioral Foundations of Economic Theory." In *Beyond Self-Interest*, edited by Jane Mansbridge, 25–43. Chicago: University of Chicago Press, 1990.

Sheridan, Alan. *Michel Foucault: The Will to Truth*. London and New York: Tavistock Publication, 1980.

Shils, Edward. "Charisma, Order, and Status." *American Sociological Review* 30 (1965): 199–213.

Simiand, François. "Historical Method and Social Sciences." *Review* 9, no. 2 (1985): 163–213.

Simmel, Georg. "Fashion." *American Journal of Sociology* 62 (1957): 541–58.

Simon, Pierre-Henri. "Littérature de laboratoire: *L'Observatoire de Cannes* de Jean Ricardou." *Le Monde*, 13 September 1961, 9.

Sirinelli, Jean-François. *Génération intellectuelle: khagneux et normaliens dans l'entre-deux-guerres*. Paris: Fayard, 1988.

Smart, Barry. *Foucault, Marxism and Critique*. London: Routledge and Kegan Paul, 1983.

Smith, Robert J. *The École Normale Supérieure and the Third Republic*. Albany: SUNY Press, 1982.

Sollers, Philippe. "Écriture et révolution." In *Tel Quel. Théorie d'ensemble*, 13–18. Paris: Le Seuil, 1968.

———. *Vision à New York*. Paris: Denoël, 1981.

———. *Writing and the Experience of Limits*. English translation by Philip Barnard and David Hayman. New York: Columbia University Press, 1983.

———. *Women*. English translation by Barbara Bray. New York: Columbia University Press, 1990.

Spencer, Herbert. *The Study of Sociology*. Ann Arbor: The University of Michigan Press, 1961.

Staël-Holstein, Madame de. *De la littérature considérée dans ses rapports avec les institutions sociales*. 2 vols. Paris: Libraire Maradan, 1800.

Steiner, Georges. "Orpheus with His Myths." In *Claude Lévi-Strauss: The Anthropologist as Hero*, edited by E. Nelson Hayes and Tanya Hayes, 170–83. Cambridge, Mass.: MIT Press, 1970.

Stil, André. "Telsquels." *L'Humanité*, 5 June 1964.

Stoianovich, Traian. *French Historical Method: The Annales Paradigm*. Ithaca: Cornell University Press, 1976.

Suleiman, Ezra N. *Elites in French Society: The Politics of Survival*. Princeton: Princeton University Press, 1978.

Sulkunen, Pekka. "Society Made Visible: On the Cultural Sociology of Pierre Bourdieu." *Acta Sociologica* 25 (1982): 103–15.

Swedberg, Richard. "'The Battle of Methods': Toward a Paradigm Shift?" In *Socio-Economics: Toward a New Synthesis*, edited by Amitai Etzioni and Paul R. Lawrence, 13–33. Armonk, N.Y.: M. E. Sharpe, 1991.

Tel Quel. Théorie d'ensemble. Paris: Le Seuil, 1968.

Terrail, Jean-Pierre. "Les vertus de la nécéssité sujet/objet en sociologie." *Cahiers du L.A.S.A.* 8–9 (1988): 215–56.

Thibaudeau, Jean. "La leçon de l'École." *Critique*, October 1961, 835–42.

―――. *Mes années Tel Quel*. Paris: Écriture, 1994.

Toboul, Henri. "P. Bourdieu et les horloges de Leibniz." *Cahiers du L.A.S.A.* 8–9 (1988): 257–76.

Ullmann, Stephen. *Style in the French Novel*. Cambridge: Cambridge University Press, 1957.

Van der Poel, Ieme. *Une révolution de la pensée: maoïsme et féminisme à travers Tel Quel, Les Temps Modernes et Esprit*. Amsterdam and Atlanta: Rodolpi, 1992.

Viala, Alain. *Naissance de l'écrivain: Sociologie de la littérature à l'âge classique*. Paris: Éd. de Minuit, 1985.

―――. "Formation de langues légitimes en Europe." Paper delivered at EHESS, Paris, 15 May 1990.

Virtanen, Reino. "Proust's Metaphors from the Natural and the Exact Sciences." *PMLA* 69 (1954): 1038–59.

Wagner, Peter, and Björn Wittrock. "Analyzing Social Science: On the Possibility of the Social Sciences." In *Discourses on Society: The Shaping of the Social Science Discipline*, edited by Peter Wagner, Björn Wittrock, and Richard Whitley, 3–22. Dordrecht: Kluwer, 1990.

Wagner, Peter, Björn Wittrock, and Richard Whitley, eds. *Discourses on Society: The Shaping of the Social Science Discipline*. Dordrecht: Kluwer, 1990.

Weber, Max. *Economy and Society*. English translation by Ephraim Fischoff et al. Berkeley: University of California Press, 1978.

Weber, Samuel. *Institution and Interpretation*. Minneapolis: University of Minnesota Press, 1987.

Weill, Nicholas. "Et maintenant . . ." *Le Monde*, 7 April 1995, xi.

Williams, Raymond. *Culture*. 2d ed. London: Fontana Press, 1989.

Wuthnow, Robert, James Davison Hunter, Albert Bergesen, and Edith Kurzweil, eds. *Cultural Analysis: The Work of Peter L. Berger, Mary Douglas, Michel Foucault and Jürgen Habermas*. London: Routledge and Kegan Paul, 1984.

Zola, Émile. *Carnets d'enquête: Une ethnographie inédite de la France*. Paris: Plon, 1986.

Zolberg, Vera. "Taste as a Social Weapon." *Contemporary Sociology* 15 (1986): 511–15.

Zolotusskii, Igor. "Rossiia na polputi k zapadu." *Iunost* 3 (1992): 2–5.

Index

academic disciplines
  and deontology, 78, 82
  formation of, 17, 18, 71–82, 119, 120
  comparison of, 70–71, 150n. 8, 177n. 37
  see also philosophy; semiology and
    semiotics; structural constructivism
Académie française, 51, 99, 105, 176n. 18
Actes de la recherche en sciences sociales,
    50
Adriaens, Marc, 91
agency, 139
  see also habitus
agrégation, 40, 68, 72, 114, 136, 150n. 11,
    176n. 19
  see also educational ideals
Althusser, Louis, 20, 35, 43, 46, 80, 84–86,
    117, 119, 120, 122, 123, 148n. 36,
    167n. 23, 168n. 31, 174n. 24
  see also Marxism, structural
Amy Gilbert, 109
analogy, 61, 159n. 42, 161n. 67
  see also homology; structural
    constructivism, principles of
Annales school, 19, 72, 81, 144n. 42
Anthropologie structurale, 79
Apostrophes, 128
Aragon, Louis, 104
archeology, 18, 92, 120
  see also neologisms; new sciences
Armand Colin
  see publishers, Armand Colin

Aron, Thomas, 77
Aron, Raymond, 39, 42, 44, 85, 167n. 23,
    169n. 47
Arouet, François-Marie (pseud. Voltaire)
  see Voltaire
Arrivé, Michel, 78
Artaud, Antonin, 118
audience
  changes in, 15, 17, 19, 131–38,
    163n. 13, 172n. 4
  intellectual, 15, 20, 67, 78, 79, 114, 131,
    147n. 27, 168n. 34
  specialized, 78, 118, 168n. 34
  see also students
audiovisual culture, 28, 128, 146n. 11,
    177n. 26
  see also cultural celebrity; mass media
avant-garde
  academic, 18, 35–82, 133–38
  contradictions of, 18, 173nn. 17, 22
  literary, 18, 109–11, 130, 132–33, 135
  meaning of, 116–18, 127, 147n. 27,
    173n. 15
  and writers, 1–4, 99–125, 133, 138
  see also cultural models; publishing
    houses

Bachelard, Gaston, 42, 43, 49, 60, 87,
    154n. 2, 157n. 25
Bakhtin, Mikhail, 75, 169n. 46

195